EPHOD AND ARK

A STUDY IN THE RECORDS AND RELIGION OF THE ANCIENT HEBREWS

BY

WILLIAM R. ARNOLD

HITCHCOCK PROFESSOR OF HEBREW IN ANDOVER THEOLOGICAL SEMINARY

WIPF & STOCK · Eugene, Oregon

רדף כי השג תשיג והצל תציל

I Samuel 30, 8

Wipf and Stock Publishers
199 W 8th Ave, Suite 3
Eugene, OR 97401

Ephod and Ark
A Study in the Records and Religion of the Ancient Hebrews
By Arnold, William R.
ISBN 13: 978-1-55635-766-4
ISBN 10: 1-55635-766-4
Publication date 12/10/2007
Previously published by Harvard University Press, 1917

CONTENTS

	PAGE
EPHOD AND ARK	5
EXCURSUS I: THE DIVINE NAME YAHWE ṢEBAOTH	142
EXCURSUS II: ON A TROUBLESOME PASSAGE IN THE ELEPHANTINE TEMPLE PAPYRUS	149
INDEX OF SCRIPTURE PASSAGES	161
CHART: ארון IN THE OLD TESTAMENT — At the End of the Volume	

EPHOD AND ARK

I

THE present state of knowledge and critical opinion regarding both the "ephod" and the "ark" of our Old Testament is extremely unsatisfactory.

The so-called "ark of the Covenant" is still wrapped in mystery. What was it? Where did it come from? Where did it go to? The later Deuteronomistic diaskeuasts [1] and the Priestly source of the Pentateuch [2] do indeed pretend to tell us what it was and where it came from; but critics very properly reject their statements as unhistorical. Yet while the Priestly "tabernacle" has long since been consigned to the limbo of imaginary institutions which never in fact existed, the ark refuses to be dealt with so summarily. For the most ancient historical records in the Old Testament bear unimpeachable witness to the existence of such an object at the very beginning of the Israelitish monarchy.[3] On the other hand, when once the post-exilic statements have been discarded, the greatest divergence of opinion prevails as to what the object so designated actually was, whether in respect to its form or its function, — to say nothing of the remoter questions of its origin and ultimate fate.

The word ארון is plain Hebrew for *box*. It is used of the coffin in which the remains of Joseph were carried from Egypt to Canaan,[4] and of the collection-box which stood in the temple at Jerusalem to

---

[1] Deut. 10, 1–5; 1 Kings 8, 9 21. The diaskeuastic character of 1 Kings 8, 9 21 is obtrusive. The same is true of the references to the ark in Deut. 10, 1–5: verse 1b is obviously interpolated between 1a and 2; 3aa (and with it doubtless the last two words of verse 2) before 3aβ; and verse 5 before verse 10. These passages, it is needless to say, are in no way supported by Deut. 31, 26.

[2] Ex. 25, 10 ff; 37, 1 ff; cf. 31, 18.

[3] 1 Sam. 4–7; 2 Sam. 6; 11, 11; 15, 24 ff; 1 Kings 2, 26.

[4] Gen. 50, 26; cf. Ex. 13, 19.

receive the money contributions of the people for the repairs of the sacred edifice.[1]

But if the ark which the Israelites carried into battle against the Philistines, and David later removed to his sanctuary at Jerusalem, was a box, what did it contain? For of course a box, *qua* box, must contain something.[2] However closely another utensil — whether a stool, a chair, or a couch — might resemble a box in shape and appearance, it would scarcely be called a "box" in ancient times, any more than we should speak of such an object as a "receptacle."[3] Some are accordingly of the opinion that the ark contained a meteorite or other sacred stone, transported in pre-historic times from the desert or perhaps from Sinai-Horeb. Others think it may have contained an idol or image of Yahwe. Still others suggest one or two aniconic stones employed for purposes of divination, which may have furnished the cue for the later fiction of two tables of stone inscribed with the commandments declarative of the divine will. One writer seriously proposes the brazen serpent made by Moses.[4] The only point upon which critics are very generally agreed is that the ark did not contain the Decalogue engraved on two tables of stone, as represented by P and the Deuteronomists.

Just now, however, it is the fashion to deny that the ark was a box at all, except perhaps as to its shape. It was a throne, carried about on military expeditions or deposited in the principal sanctuary, with possibly a purely imaginary Yahwe conceived as seated upon it. So Dibelius, who has written the most elaborate mono-

---

[1] 2 Kings 12, 10 f; 2 Chron. 24, 8 10 f. In recent times ארון הקדש has been used in the synagogue to designate the press or shrine in which the rolls of Holy Scripture are deposited. This usage was unknown to the early centuries of our era; v. *Jewish Encyclopedia*, II, pp. 108 f.

[2] The view that the ark was a mere box, which contained nothing, is actually put forward by Kittel, *Geschichte des Volkes Israel*², I, p. 542; cf. also Schwally, *Semitische Kriegsaltertümer*, I, p. 10.

[3] This is the common sense view of the matter, in spite of all the cases of secondary meaning (which might be multiplied a hundredfold) adduced by Meinhold (*Studien und Kritiken*, LXXIV, 1901, pp. 593 ff) to justify the opinion that the ark was a chair called a "box."

[4] Kennett, *Encyclopaedia of Religion and Ethics*, I, p. 792.

graph on the ark.[1] But for an extreme example of the sort of thing now being printed upon this subject, we must cite Hugo Gressmann. In that farrago of twentieth-century *midrash* covering five hundred pages and entitled *Mose und seine Zeit*,[2] which is already quoted as authority for facts by some Old Testament students, Gressmann represents the ark as the original throne (that is, box-shaped stool) of Yahwe and his most sacred symbol, which, at the urgent entreaty of Moses, Jethro the Midianite obligingly brought from the mother sanctuary of Sinai to Kadesh and bestowed upon the Israelites. Invisibly seated upon this vacant stool, Yahwe thereafter rode before his new-found people, their guide in the journeyings through the wilderness and their palladium in the day of battle.[3] This is the actual history of the ark. The Israelitish tradition concerning it went much further. One form of that tradition related how the sacred stool had been wrenched from Yahwe's own hands by Moses in a mighty tussle on the top of Mount Sinai (*tuentibus hircis*, we may suppose). And with this indispensable object in his possession, Moses forced the helpless Yahwe to accompany the Children of Israel.[4] But the learned author knows that this is not the only form of the tradition which was not handed down. So much for the ark.

As regards the ephod, our plight is even worse. Here we suffer not merely from ignorance, which tempts to unbridled exploits of the imagination, but from more or less definite data which are mutually contradictory.

The ephod was — perhaps among other things, but certainly — an *apron* or *loincloth*[5] assumed by laymen as well as by priests when engaged in solemn religious exercises. The boy Samuel wore an

---

[1] *Die Lade Jahves*. Göttingen, 1906. [3] *L. c.*, pp. 440, 449; cf. pp. 235 ff, 353 f.
[2] Göttingen, 1913. [4] *Ibid.*, pp. 230 f.
[5] Etymologically אפוד (analogous in form to אזור, *girdle*) probably signifies "that which is worn *in front*"; cf. Arabic *'afada* and *wafada*. Lagarde made the mistake of deriving from a usage which is itself secondary a meaning still further removed from the primary sense of the root. For the rest, the prevalent assumption that Hebrew אפד is denominative — which rests mainly upon the fact that the verb occurs only in P — is extremely precarious.

ephod when doing duty at the sanctuary of Shiloh[1]; David wore an ephod, and apparently not much else, when leaping and dancing before the ark as he conveyed it in triumph to Jerusalem.[2] David was not a priest, and had no conceivable use for an "oracle pouch," or "oracle belt," or anything else connected with oracles[3]; and whatever duties the boy Samuel may have performed at Shiloh, the author of the story certainly has no intention of implying that Eli immediately surrendered to that stripling his most sacred and important function.

In the Priestly institutions of later times, the word אפוד is used in a somewhat specialized, but closely related sense, to designate a ceremonial vestment worn by the High Priest over both his tunic (כתנת) and his robe (מעיל).[4] Repeated readings of the identical description of the High Priest's ephod contained in the statutory directions of Ex. 28 and in the account of its manufacture in Ex. 39, yield only a vague idea of its appearance; but it is sufficiently clear that the writer thinks of it as a piece of sumptuous drapery, of no great extent, fastened about the waist by means of a belt or sash, and suspended from the shoulders by straps. These last, however, were apparently less for the support of the ephod than for the sake of the breast-piece (חשן) and other insignia which were attached to them. And here again the point should be especially emphasized that the ephod itself had no connection with the oracular function of the High Priest; that function attached to the חשן, not to the ephod. The Urim and Thummim were to be put אל the חשן[5] —

[1] 1 Sam. 2, 18. [2] 2 Sam. 6, 14.

[3] Against Foote, *Journal of Biblical Literature*, XXI, 1902, pp. 1 ff; Elhorst, *Zeitschrift für die alttestamentliche Wissenschaft*, XXX, 1910, pp. 259 ff; and, less distinctly, Sellin, *Orientalische Studien Theodor Nöldeke zum siebzigsten Geburtstag gewidmet*, pp. 669 ff, who compromises on the view that the ephod was a linen loincloth worn exclusively by priests in their sacred ministrations, which however, when employed in divination, was gradually differentiated into a gorgeous apron supplemented with a receptacle for the sacred lots.

[4] Ex. 29, 5; Lev. 8, 7; cf. Sirach 45, 8–10.

[5] Ex. 28, 30; Lev. 8, 8. In the Letter of Aristeas, § 97, the High Priest bears on his breast τὸ λεγόμενον λόγιον, while the ephod is merely a magnificent ζώνη; cf. Josephus, *Antiquities*, iii, 216 f.

whatever that may mean. In point of fact, however, we have the evidence of Josephus [1] as well as of rabbinical tradition [2] that divination by means of the חשן with Urim and Thummim never got beyond the pages of the Pentateuch.

A third application of the word אפוד in our Old Testament texts has no relation to either of the foregoing. It stands for a *solid body, carried*, not *worn*, and *only by priests*, who cherish it as the *specific instrument of divination*. In the sanctuary at Nob, the sword of Goliath (itself wrapped in a cloak) lay behind such an "ephod"; [3] evidently the latter was an object in the round, standing free. Gideon, we are told, manufactured an "ephod" out of *seventeen hundred shekels of gold* which the people contributed for the purpose.[4]

All sorts of attempts have been made to explain away the traits which render this use of the word irreconcilable with the other two.— The ceremonial apron was sometimes so heavily decorated with gold embroidery that it "stood of itself." — "Ephod" was used also of an idol attired in an ephod. — Conversely, the ephod was primarily the idol, then the idol's garment, and finally the ministrant's loin-cloth. — It was neither an idol nor a loincloth, but always a bag for the sacred lots; and Gideon devoted to it at most a very small portion of the seventeen hundred shekels placed at his disposal. — The ephod was essentially an *instrument of divination*, which might be either a costly idol or a sacerdotal vestment. — And so forth. To

---

[1] *Antiquities*, iii, 218. The absence of any mention of אורים and תמים in Sirach 45, 10 f (H) should also be noted. On the other hand, their omission in Aristeas § 97, which pretends to describe only what was seen by the visiting Alexandrians, should not be pressed.

[2] Mishna, *Soṭa* ix. 12, משמתו נביאים הראשונים בטלו אורים ותומים; cf. b. *Yoma* 21b. According to b. *Soṭa* 48b and j. *Qiddushin* 65b, to say עד עמד כהן לאורים ולתמים (Ezra 2, 63 = Neh. 7, 65), in the time of the Second Temple, was as if one should say, "until the dead come to life," or "until the Messiah appears" — that is, "till doomsday."

[3] 1 Sam. 21, 10.

[4] Judges 8, 23–27. Verse 26b enumerates objects taken from the Midianites which Gideon did not require of the people for his "ephod"; he asked only for their נזמי זהב, and these yielded 1700 shekels of gold. The statement of Foote (*l. c.*, p. 14) that אותו of verse 27 "refers as much to the purple raiment as to the gold ornaments" is erroneous, even if 26b is retained as authentic. Cf. Moore's commentary, *ad loc*.

discuss these and similar suggestions in detail would be both tedious and unprofitable. Some are manifestly absurd; all are far-fetched. Special condemnation must, however, be passed upon so insidiously uncritical a statement as that of Benzinger, who sails over the difficulty of explaining Gideon's "ephod" as "ein Lendenschurz, reich mit Gold durchwoben" with the concession that "die Zahl von 28 kg Gold freilich gewaltig übertrieben ist."[1] The question for the archaeologist is not how much Gideon's "ephod" really weighed, nor whether Gideon really manufactured an "ephod" of any sort, nor indeed whether such a person as Gideon ever in fact existed; but whether the author of our story and his prospective readers could picture to themselves an "ephod" weighing seventeen hundred shekels (about sixty-five pounds). If they could, the object in question was no kind of a garment. Ancient authors are rarely silly.

II

There is in fact but one sensible solution of the enigma of the solid "ephod" — a solution which has the double merit of meeting satisfactorily all the difficulties of the case, and at the same time clearing up several other knotty problems in Hebrew history and literature: *The reading* אפוד, *wherever in the Old Testament it stands for a solid object, has been deliberately substituted by Jewish scribes for a more troublesome word.*[2]

What was that troublesome word? The readiest conjecture, following the prevalent opinion that "ephod" stands for an idol of some kind, is פסל, the generic word for *idol*, though primarily a *graven image*. But a glance at Judges 18, where פסל and מסכה have (consequent upon the insertion of 17, 2-4) been systematically added to אפוד ותרפים (as the text now reads), and continue to stand there side by side with the latter, makes it impossible to suppose that אפוד represents an attempt to eliminate an objectionable פסל.

---

[1] *Hebräische Archäologie*², p. 347.

[2] This solution of the difficulty has been suggested as regards the two most obstinate passages, Judges 8, 27 and 1 Sam. 21, 10, by Moore, *Encyclopaedia Biblica*, col. 1308 f; cf. col. 1307, note 2.

And even assuming — what is less likely — that the alteration to אפוד in Judges 17 f took place before the interpolation of פסל and מסכה, it is just as hard to imagine that אפוד was substituted for an original פסל only to be regularly supplemented later by the same word. A like argument applies of course to the word מסכה, the specific term for an *idol cast in metal*, which Judges 8, 27 would seem to favor. Moreover, it may be confidently affirmed that no scribe with whom תרפים could pass muster in that context would have found an image of any kind embarrassing.

The fact is, however, that every sort of image is positively ruled out by the language of 1 Sam. 2, 28, where Yahwe declares that the family of Eli had been chosen לשאת אפוד לפני, *to carry an "ephod" before me*.[1] For, manifestly, a physical representation of Yahwe could not itself be said to be carried "before him"; and it is quite impossible to assume that an image of some other divinity or numen was carried before Yahwe or employed so conspicuously in his service. Clearly אפוד has not displaced any word signifying an image.

But the same passage, 1 Sam. 2, 28, renders untenable the hypothesis that the word displaced was אלהים, as suggested by Moore for Judges 8, 27 and 1 Sam. 21, 10; לשאת אלהים לפני, in the mouth of Yahwe, being likewise quite impossible. Moreover, though אלהים might be used by metonymy to indicate physical objects consecrated to, or representative of, deity, and to emphasize incidentally their paramount significance — as when Laban says to Jacob, of the family teraphim purloined by Rachel, למה גנבת את אלהי, *Why hast thou stolen my divinities?* and Jacob answers, עם אשר תמצא אלהיך לא יחיה, *With whomsoever thou findest thy divinities, let him not live*[2]; or when Micah protests to the Danites, regarding his captured "ephod" and teraphim, את אלהי אשר עשיתי לקחתם וגו׳, *Ye have taken my divinities which I made, and how say ye unto me, What aileth thee?*[3] or again when the Philistines, on learning that the ark of Yahwe has been

---

[1] αἴρειν εφουδ of GB is palpably truncated. לשאת אפוד in this context, unlike נשא אפוד of 1 Sam. 14, 3 and 22, 18, demands a complement.

[2] Gen. 31, 30 32.   [3] Judges 18, 24.

brought down to the Israelitish army, say to themselves, בא אלהים אל המחנה, *Deity has arrived in the camp* [1]; or, finally, when the priest accompanying Saul's army says to the king, נקרבה הלם אל האלהים, *Let us draw nigh here to the deity*, with obvious reference to the portable instrument of divination [2] — I say, in spite of this well-attested usage,[3] we cannot for a moment suppose that David said to Abiathar הגישה האלהים, *Bring me the deity!* where the present text has הגישה האפוד.[4] Though the physical object indicated be the same, the tropical designation אלהים, permissible after נקרבה אל, would be the height of irreverence after הגישה. This distinction, I am confident, will appear not at all refined to those familiar with the connotation and associations of the Hebrew word. And lastly, אלהים cannot be the word displaced, because as a matter of fact, like פסל and מסבה, it has been suffered to remain standing in the very texts which contain the spurious אפוד, not merely in such a phrase as בית אלהים,[5] but even when it serves to designate vaguely and indirectly the very object which אפוד has been employed to conceal.[6]

III

Fortunately, we are not left to speculation or conjecture regarding the object which has been displaced by אפוד. There is one passage in the Old Testament where this systematic alteration was carried

---

[1] 1 Sam. 4, 7. The emendations of the commentaries are entirely unnecessary. There was nothing "absolute" (Driver, *Notes on the Hebrew Text of the Books of Samuel*[2], p. 46; and Budde, *Sacred Books of the Old Testament, ad loc.*) about אלהים in the mouth of any inhabitant of Canaan. Against Wellhausen's reading (*Der Text der Bücher Samuelis*, p. 55), and the Septuagint text upon which it is based, it is enough to point out that an unhampered Hebrew author would hardly have prepetrated the cacophony of בא אלהים אליהם אל המחנה. In verse 7a אמרו means *they thought*, which is followed in 7b by ויאמרו, *and they said*. Verse 8, however, is interpolated entire, במדבר being an authentic and characteristic editorial solecism.

[2] 1 Sam. 14, 36; cf. verse 37 and chap. 22, 13 15; Judges 18, 5.

[3] This reverent, tropical usage should not be confused with the contemptuous allusions to "gods of silver and gold" of Old Testament polemics, which are best disregarded in discussing the ideas and language of ancient Israel.

[4] 1 Sam. 23, 9; 30, 7.

[5] Judges 17, 5.

[6] Judges 18, 5 24; 1 Sam. 22, 13 15 (note 21, 10).

out in one family of Hebrew manuscripts and was omitted in another. The Alexandrian Greek has preserved the text of the first; the Masoretic Hebrew represents that of the second.

In 1 Sam. 14, 18 the text of G^B reads: καὶ εἶπεν Σαοὺλ τῷ 'Αχειά, προσάγαγε τὸ ἐφούδ· ὅτι αὐτὸς ἦρεν τὸ ἐφοὺδ ἐν τῇ ἡμέρᾳ ἐκείνῃ ἐνώπιον 'Ισραήλ.[1] The Hebrew original of this was unquestionably the following: ויאמר שאול לאחיה הגישה האפוד כי הוא נשא האפוד ביום ההוא לפני ישראל.[2] Except for the meaningless stop-gap אפוד, this text is perfectly intelligible and entirely satisfies the context: Saul called for the instrument of divination — whatever it was — which Ahijah the priest manipulated for the Israelitish army on the day in question.

On the other hand, the Masoretic text of the same verse has: ויאמר שאול לאחיה הגישא ארון האלהים כי היה ארון האלהים ביום ההוא ובני ישראל. This seems at first sight distinctly inferior to the Greek tradition. It cannot, as it stands, be the authentic text; for the second half of the verse does not construe. The two last words admit of no interpretation other than *and the children of Israel*,[3] which can be connected neither with what precedes, nor yet with ויהי, *and it came to pass*, which follows at the beginning of the next verse. And even if the last two words be discarded, what remains of verse 18b is equally

---

[1] The only variant worth mentioning is the reading ἦν ἡ κ(ε)ιβωτὸς τοῦ θεοῦ instead of αὐτὸς ἦρεν τὸ ἐφούδ, found in Cod. Alex., H. & P. 44, 106, 120, 134, and the Complutensian and Aldine editions. This, since the reading of B and congeners could not be derived from it, must be the result of an eclectic correction on the basis of the Hebrew.

[2] It is wrong to assume an original הוא היה נשא for αὐτὸς ἦρεν (as Driver, *l.c.*, p. 110, and Budde, *Kurzer Hand-Commentar zum Alten Testament*, p. 94), since the unpointed text might be read הוא נָשָׂא, though נֹשֵׂא was of course the construction intended. Besides, הוא היה נשא would be *he used to carry*, rather than *he was carrying*, which is the sense required before ביום ההוא, *on that day*.

[3] "Dathius: 'Literam Vau pro multiplici ejus significatione putem explicare posse per *cum* sive *apud*.' Credat Judaeus Apella! Certum mihi est legendum esse בבני"
—Maurer, *Commentarius grammaticus criticus in Vetus Testamentum*, Leipsic, 1835, p. 163. Targum of Jonathan, Peshîṭta, Symmachus, and Jerome rendered ובני as if it were בני עם. In support of the same interpretation David Qimḥi adduced ויוסף היה במצרים of Ex. 1, 5, as intending יוסף שהיה במצרים. עם יוסף This was in fact the best he could do.

impossible; since כי היה ארון האלהים ביום ההוא, *for the sacred ark was on that day*, demands a predicate. Nor will the mere alteration of לפני to ובני, after the Greek, furnish the requisite predicate; for היה לפני means *to wait upon*, and requires a personal subject. The plain fact is that the Masoretic text is so palpably and obtrusively defective, while at the same time every word it contains is so simple and familiar, that it is impossible to suppose its present state to have been brought about in any other way than by deliberate mutilation.[1] But why was the original text deliberately mutilated? What did it contain that rendered nonsense preferable to its simple testimony?[2] Surely not the text of G. For time and again the Book of Samuel offers us statements of exactly the same purport. The text of G is entirely in harmony with 1 Sam. 2, 28; 21, 10; 22, 18; 23, 6 9; 30, 7, as well as with verse 3 of this same chapter.

It should be noted that it is verse 3a, and not 18b, as maintained by Wellhausen (*l. c.*, p. 89) and others, that is interpolated. Verse 3a interrupts the flow of the narrative from verse 2 to 3b, and is, moreover, unmistakably tacked on to the שש מאות איש of 2b (which originally, with G, lacked העם אשר). For כהן יהוה בשלה of course refers to Eli, and נשא אפוד (cf. 1 Sam. 22, 18) cannot be a predicate in this context, but only appositive. For the predicate, "trug das Ephod" (Nowack, *Handkommentar zum Alten Testament*, p. 61), נשא האפוד would be required. In spite of its length, therefore, 3a is not a sentence, but an item; and there can be no question of a "parenthesis" (Wellhausen, p. 86). But even a parenthesis must aim to make the story more intelligible or more complete; and the pedigree of Ahijah serves neither purpose. For it is undeniably his pedigree that constitutes the burden of 3a, not the fact that he was army chaplain. This latter fact was gleaned from verse 18, where the clause "for he was carrying the sacred ark before the Israelites that day" is a very pertinent parenthesis, and indicates as clearly as possible that Ahijah is being

---

[1] Cf. Budde, *l. c.*, p. 94: "Der Vers ist gründlich verdorben, vielleicht nicht ganz durch Zufall. . . . Die Entstehung des Verses lehrt überdies am besten, dass man sich der Bedenklichkeit des Gegenstandes [which he thinks was the ephod] bewusst war." He forgets that, for a member of the Jewish church, the High Priest's ephod was authoritatively and quite satisfactorily defined in the Book of Exodus, and had existed from the days of Moses. A pre-exilic emendation, on the other hand, could not have spared the Septuagint.

[2] Students of the Masoretic text need not be reminded that there are numerous passages in the Old Testament where the scribes have preferred nonsense to an utterance which was objectionable on dogmatic or religious grounds. One such instance is discussed in the note on 2 Sam. 6, 21 below.

mentioned by the narrator at that point for the first time. The object of the diaskeuast was to connect Ahijah with the priestly family of Nob (1 Sam. 22, 9. 20) — Ahijah and Ahimelech, being contemporaries, are brothers; and to attach both Ahijah and the priests of Nob to the priestly family of Shiloh (1 Sam. 4, 19–22) — all the historic priests of the period scions of one single stock repudiated bodily by Yahwe in favor of the Zadokites (1 Sam. 2, 27–36; 1 Kings 2, 27; both passages diaskeuastic). That the pedigree is fabricated and has in mind the closing verses of our story of Eli, is evident from the otherwise irrelevant mention of Ichabod; "Ahijah the son of Ahitub, the son of Phinehas, the son of Eli" would be the natural formula. To throw out "the brother of Ichabod" as a gloss, as some scholars do, is to throw away the key to the critical evaluation of the whole passage. The words "the priest of Yahwe at Shiloh" point in the same direction. The connection of Zadok himself with Ahitub in 2 Sam. 8, 17, on the other hand, is the result of purely mechanical error, arising doubtless from the insertion of Abiathar's ancestry (בן אחימלך בן אחיטוב) above and below the line in a crowded manuscript; although the resulting corruption gave rise in turn to the geneaology of 1 Chron, 5, 34; 6, 37 f; cf. 18, 16. For the rest, the worthy genealogist of 1 Sam. 14, 3a would have been better advised to make Ahitub a brother of Hophni and Phinehas or of Eli himself; for if he was a brother of Eli's grandson Ichabod, then according to 1 Sam. 7, 2 (which, to be sure, must also not be taken too seriously, and may be from the same hand) that ill-starred person was not twenty-one years old when his own grandnephew Abiathar had been officiating as priest of David for at least nine years. The old identification of Ahijah with Ahimelech, persisted in by most modern scholars, is quite gratuitous.

This much, however, regarding verse 18 is clear, no matter what the motive for the mutilation of the original: we cannot hesitate to restore to the Hebrew, on the basis of the Greek, those readings which are necessary to the proper syntactical construction of the verse; for on those points there is no room for difference of opinion. We may confidently read כי הוא נשא for כי היה, and לפני ישראל for ובני ישראל. But having made these obvious and insignificant corrections, we face the real problem, whose current solution is by no means so clearly indicated as has been assumed. We are confronted with two antagonistic texts: one that of G; the other identical with G save that in both clauses it reads ארון האלהים where the latter has האפוד. And of course only one of these readings can be what the author himself wrote down.

If now we adopt the Greek reading, everything remains obscure and unaccountable. In the first place, we cannot possibly account for the presence of ארון האלהים in the Masoretic text. No slip of the pen or careless reading can have produced ארון האלהים from an original האפוד; while it is simply inconceivable that a Jewish scribe should have gone out of his way to corrupt a harmless text, and incidentally bedevil the whole orthodox theory of the religious institutions of Israel, by consciously substituting the one for the other. For, a late Jewish scribe it must have been, *ex hypothesi*; since, if the ancestor of the Greek escaped it, the alteration will have been made in the canonical Book of Samuel. And secondly, if we adopt the Greek reading, we have left on our hands a passage which, with its impossible "ephod," is utterly baffling and unintelligible. For although the present Hebrew text of this passage does not construe and the Greek does, that cannot blind us to the fact that, taken as a whole, both are alike defective, and have in reality withstood all efforts at satisfactory interpretation. אפוד, as far as we know, was the name of a garment, and a garment the object here in question cannot be. If, on the other hand, we adopt the Hebrew reading, we have a text which luminously explains both the purposed mutilation of the Hebrew and the palpable mystification of the Greek, and at the same time answers objectively and conclusively the question we have been asking as to the object systematically replaced by אפוד in the historical books of the Old Testament.

Between these alternatives we cannot hesitate to choose. The original text of 1 Sam. 14, 18 was: ויאמר שאול לאחיה הגישה ארון האלהים כי הוא נשא ארון האלהים ביום ההוא לפני ישראל,[1] *And Saul said to Ahijah, Bring hither the sacred ark; for he carried the sacred ark before Israel that day.* The present Masoretic text resulted from one attempt to dull the edge of this obnoxious passage. The Septuagint text resulted from another such attempt. The latter employed the more artful device which was resorted to elsewhere in the Old Testament in the sources of both our Greek and Hebrew texts, namely, the substitution of a harmless and none too transparent אפוד for an embarrassing ארון. *The word we have been seeking in order to unlock*

---

[1] So Köhler, in Eichhorn's *Repertorium für biblische und morgenländische Litteratur*, II, 1778, p. 256.

the secret of the solid "ephod" of our Old Testament is accordingly ארון.¹ And the specific instrument of priestly divination among the ancient Hebrews was the ark.

I venture to call attention once more to the fact that I am not conjecturing that ארון has been displaced by אפוד. It is the objective testimony of the extant manuscripts and editions of the Old Testament that the "ephod" has displaced the ark as the instrument of divination in 1 Sam. 14, 18 and elsewhere, or else the ark has displaced the "ephod" in 1 Sam. 14, 18. I am merely choosing between the two alternatives presented that which satisfactorily explains a series of otherwise inexplicable phenomena.² That it does satisfactorily explain the phenomena, and that the explanation does not, as might be apprehended, raise insuperable difficulties of its own, I hope to show in the following pages.

IV

The Hebrew reading of 1 Sam. 14, 18, as we have been obliged to maintain it, was obnoxious to the Jewish scribes; for it was repugnant to the explicit teaching of the Pentateuch regarding the most sacred object in the cult of Yahwe. It is, however, equally irreconcilable with the opinion which prevails among critics in regard to the ark at the present time. For this reason, and in spite of the principles of sound textual criticism which protect it, that reading is all but universally rejected by modern scholars. And from Thenius, who blazed the path to the systematic exploitation of the Septuagint in 1842, to the present day, it has been rejected in favor

[1] Moore has suggested the possibility that ארון was the original reading in 1 Sam. 21, 10; Encyclopaedia Biblica, col. 1307, note 2.

[2] One of the deplorable effects of the present welter of speculation and conjecture in the Old Testament field, is that many scholars no longer recognize a scientific procedure when they meet it, and treat all conclusions indiscriminately as opinions to be taken or left according to momentary convenience or individual temperament. So a recent writer, for the rest a scholar of considerable attainments, defends the Jewish doctrine — it has long since been shown to be nothing else — of the presence of the Decalogue in the ark in the days of Moses, while rejecting the tradition that the writing was the work of Yahwe's own hand. The Jews themselves, it should be observed, were more consistent, and ultimately more scientific. They never pretended that no miracle was involved.

of the "ephod" of the Greek text and the parallel passages in the Hebrew by every critical commentator on the Book of Samuel without exception.[1] That the impelling reasons for this unanimous rejection are of an *a priori* character, and have little to do with the ordinarily recognized principles of textual criticism, will appear most clearly if the standard commentaries are allowed to speak for themselves.

Earlier commentators do not venture to alter the received Hebrew text, although Drusius cites the Septuagint as according with the plausible interpretation of David Qimḥi (*Annotata ad libros historicos Veteris Testamenti, sive criticorum sacrorum Tomus II*, London, 1660, col. 2312); and Dathe affirms that the Septuagint offers a more satisfactory text, which he refrains from adopting only because the Hebrew is supported by all the other ancient versions (*Libri historici Vet. Test. latine versi et criticis illustrati*, Halle, 1784, p. 239). Vatablus, like Drusius, followed the mediaeval Jewish authorities in explaining ארון האלהים of verse 18a as a sort of metonymy for the Ephod with Urim and Thummim, which were kept "juxta arcam Dei" (*l. c., Annotata*, etc., col. 2305). So Rashi remarks on הגישה ארון האלהים: "Urim and Thummim"; in verse 18b the word שָׁם must be understood after ארון האלהים, presumably leaving ובני ישראל to be understood as a second subject to ויאמר, the Israelites sharing Saul's injunction to Ahijah (so Abravanel). Similarly, as regards 18a, Levi ben Gershon. And David Qimḥi: האפוד והאורים והתמים שהיו עם ארון האלהים לשאול בהם על יהונתן. See the Rabbinical Bibles, *ad loc.* With their common sense, and their belief in the age, authority, and observance of the Mosaic Law, it was impossible for the Jewish exegetes to do otherwise than relate this verse, as best they might, to the High Priest's oracular apparatus. And with such passages as 1 Sam. 23, 6 9; 30, 7, besides 14, 3, before them, it was the most natural thing in the world for Ibn Ezra (on Ex. 28, 6) and Qimḥi to include the Ephod as part of that apparatus. Nor would it be strange if Ibn Ezra had actually paraphrased Saul's utterance with הגישה האפוד; though it must be doubted whether the authentic text of his shorter commentary really did so, as the longer commentary certainly does not. To argue, on such grounds as these, with Aptowitzer ("Das Schriftwort in der rabbinischen Literatur," *Sitzungsberichte der Wiener Academie der Wissenschaften*, 1906, p. 51), that Hebrew manuscripts of the twelfth century still read הגישה האפוד in 1 Sam. 14, 18a, is rank nonsense. — Abravanel likewise interprets Saul's command as referring to the Urim and Thummim; but he

---

[1] I do not class with critical comment such an opinion as that of Ehrlich, *Randglossen zur hebräischen Bibel*, III (1910), p. 213: "[Verse 18] Wiederum ein stark entstellter Text, ohne die Möglichkeit, das Ursprüngliche zu ermitteln. Von der Lade kann an dieser Stelle ursprünglich nicht die Rede gewesen sein." If the last statement is true, criticism has not the shadow of a reason for rejecting the Greek reading.

boldly takes the position that the ארון האלהים here mentioned was not the Ark of the Covenant, which contained the tables of the Law and which, he admits, was at Kirjath-jearim, but a certain movable box used as a receptacle for the Ephod with the Urim and Thummim; and expresses the same opinion regarding the ארון spoken of by Uriah the Hittite in 2 Sam. 11, 11 (*Don Isaaci Abarbanelis Ebraeorum doctissimi commentarius in Prophetas Priores*, Leipsic, 1686, fol. 86ab, 105d). This view, which has since been very generally adopted by Jewish writers, Clericus pronounces pure invention (merum commentum): the only object ever called ארון האלהים was " insignis illa arca quae in sanctissimo Adyto adservanda erat "; this had been brought from Kirjath-jearim to Gibeah, either for safe-keeping or to aid the Israelites in their distress by ensuring God's immediate presence (*Veteris Testamenti libri historici*, Amsterdam, 1708, p. 218). On the other hand, Sebastian Schmidt had no difficulty with the category of place: the ark was already at Gibeah of Benjamin, which was only another name for the Gibeah belonging to Kirjath-jearim; and Saul is merely commanding Ahijah to fetch it from the sanctuary on the hill to the camp, where it was required to ensure God's presence at the consultation of the oracles (*In Librum Priorem Samuelis commentarius*, Strassburg, 1687, pp. 443 f). J. H. Michaelis understood by הגישה " Go and bring hither from Kirjath-jearim " (*Biblia hebraica cum annotationibus*, Halle, 1720, ad loc.). J. D. Michaelis thought the ark was wanted, not for consultation of the oracles, but to assist the Israelites with its presence in the impending battle (*Deutsche Uebersetzung des Alten Testaments mit Anmerkungen für Ungelehrte*, V. 2, Göttingen, 1777, p. 36); similarly Maurer (*Commentarius grammaticus criticus in Vetus Testamentum*, Leipsic, 1835, p. 163).

Thenius: "Abgesehen davon, dass von einer Translocirung der Bundeslade von Kirjath-Jearim nichts erwähnt worden, begreift man nicht, wozu Saul dieselbe herbeiholen lässt; beachtet man aber den ganzen Zusammenhang, sieht man, wie Saul v. 37–42 das heilige Loos befragt, bedenkt man das אסף ידך, v. 19, und vergleicht man 23, 9; 30, 7, so muss man sich für die Lesarten der R [G^B], האפוד anstatt לפני, und היה ארון האלהים, anstatt הוא נשא האפוד ארון האלהים anstatt ובני, entscheiden. Saul will (ganz wie David in den andern Stellen) das heilige, in dem Brustschilde des *Ephod* aufbewahrte, Loos fragen, was zu thun sei, ob er mit den Seinen gegen die Philister aufbrechen solle, oder nicht. . . . Nachdem einmal אפוד 1° in ארון verschrieben war, bildete sich das Uebrige der traditionellen Lesart durch Conjectur."[1]

[1] *Die Bücher Samuels*, 1842, p. 53; second edition 1864, p. 60; third edition, revised by Löhr, 1898, p. 59.

Keil: "In v. 18 fällt die Angabe: 'Bring her die Lade Gottes, denn die Lade Gottes war an jenem Tage bei den Söhnen Israels,' sehr auf, da in jener Zeit die Bundeslade in Kirjath-Jearim deponirt war und die Anwesenheit derselben in dem kleinen Kriegslager Sauls höchst unwahrscheinlich ist, auch beim Erfragen des göttlichen Willens durch den Hohepriester sonst nirgends der Bundeslade Erwähnung geschieht, sondern nur des Ephod. . . . Hiezu kommt, dass für die Bundeslade, die kein Gegenstand war, den man ohne weiteres hin- und herreichte, das הגישה nicht recht passt, dieses Verbum dagegen der geläufige Ausdruck für das Herbeiholen des Ephod ist, vgl. 23, 9; 30, 7. Alle diese Umstände machen die Richtigkeit des masorethischen Textes höchst zweifelhaft, trotzdem dass *Chald. Syr. Ar.* und *Vulg.* für denselben zeugen, und empfehlen die Lesart der LXX." [1] One can almost hear, גם אתה ברוטס!

Wellhausen quotes Thenius as above and adds: "Dieser Ausführung Thenius' mich anschliessend, verweise ich zur Bestätigung des griechischen Textes noch auf קרב אפודא des Chald. v. 19 [in place of אסף ידך]." [2] And elsewhere: "In 1 Sam. 14, 18 ist wegen 7, 1; 2 Sam. 6, 1 ff statt ארון [ה]אלהים *die Lade Gottes* zu lesen האפוד *das Ephod*, ebenso 1 Kön. 2, 26 wegen 1 Sam. 23, 6, und zwar beruht die Lade auf dogmatischer Correktur." [3]

Reuss: "L'arche pouvait avoir été cherchée à Qirjat-Ie'arîm pour cette expédition (chap. 7, 1); cependant on ne lit nulle part ailleurs qu'elle servait aux oracles, et la comparaison de chap. 23, 9 et 30, 7 fera sans doute préférer la leçon du Septante." [4]

Klostermann: "LXX τὸ ἐφούδ; notwendig, denn die Lade Jahves ist in Kirjath-Jearim (7, 2), und der, welcher v. 3 einsetzte, hat in v. 18 vom Ephod gelesen, diesem Mittel, zu göttlicher Aufklärung und Entscheidung zu gelangen." [5]

Driver: "We must certainly read, with LXX, הגישה האפוד, cf. v. 3, and especially 23, 9 הגישה האפוד; 30, 7 הגישה נא לי האפוד.

---

[1] *Die Bücher Samuels*[1], 1864, p. 103.
[2] *Der Text der Bücher Samuelis*, 1872, p. 89.
[3] Bleek-Wellhausen, *Einleitung in das Alte Testament*[4], 1878, p. 642.
[4] *La Bible*, 1877, ad loc.
[5] *Die Bücher Samuelis und der Könige*, 1887, p. 47.

I SAMUEL 14, 18   21

The ephod, not the ark, was the organ of divination; and, as the passages cited show, הגיש is the word properly applied to bringing the ephod into use."¹

H. P. Smith: "The text of G is to be adopted unconditionally.... Historically we could hardly object that the presence of the Ark at Kirjath Jearim would decide against this text, because our author may not have known of its detention at Kirjath Jearim. But the Ephod is elsewhere the means of giving the oracle, and if original here may have been displaced by a scrupulous scribe who was aware of its dangerous resemblance to an image." And again: "The difficulty in retaining the words הגישה ארון האלהים is *prima facie* a historical one. The Ark had been settled at Kirjath Jearim, and if brought to Saul we should have been told of the transfer.... Even if we suppose this author not to know of the detention of the Ark at Kirjath Jearim, it remains true that we nowhere else hear of it in connection with Saul, and the presumption is therefore against it here. The second difficulty is that, so far as we know, the Ark was not used in consulting the oracle."²

Nowack: "Schon Thenius hat nachgewiesen, das in diesem Zusammenhang die Lade keine Stelle hat, dass es sich vielmehr hier um das heilige Loos handelt.... In der That hat LXX hier einen entsprechenden Text."³

Budde: "Von der Lade kann nach 7, 1 gar keine Rede sein. LXX bietet den ganz durchsichtigen, durch v. 3 bestätigten Text."⁴

Kittel: "MT augenscheinlich sinnlos; lies nach G. Die Lade ist (gegen 7, 2; 2 Sam. 6, 2 ff) hereingekommen weil man am Ephod Anstoss nahm."⁵

Dhorme: "Avec G, lire האפוד au lieu de 'l'arche de Dieu' qui ne sert pas pour les consultations. On a alors הגישה האפוד comme

¹ *Notes on the Hebrew Text of the Books of Samuel*, 1890, pp. 83 f; second edition 1913, p. 110.
² *Critical and Exegetical Commentary on the Books of Samuel*, 1899, pp. 111 f.
³ *Handkommentar zum Alten Testament*, 1902, ad loc. Cf. the same author's *Lehrbuch der hebräischen Archäologie*, 1894, II, p. 93.
⁴ *Kurzer Hand-Commentar zum Alten Testament*, 1902, ad loc. Cf. *Sacred Books of the Old Testament*, 1894, p. 62; and *Die Bücher Richter und Samuel*, 1890, p. 206.
⁵ In Kautzsch's *Heilige Schrift des Alten Testaments*³, 1909, ad loc.

dans 23, 9; 30, 7. Le ה de האפוד étant tombé par haplographie, une première confusion a remplacé אפוד par ארון, ce qui a nécessité l'adjonction de האלהים. A partir de כי, nous avons une glose qui suppose déjà la substitution de ארון האלהים à האפוד."[1]

It is apparent from this rehearsal of critical opinion that the rejection of the reading ארון האלהים in favor of האפוד of the Greek rests entirely on two assumptions of historical fact: (1) The ark which had once belonged to the sanctuary of Shiloh was, after its capture and release by the Philistines, deposited in the house of Abinadab on the height above Kirjath-jearim (1 Sam. 7, 1.) and remained there until David removed it thence to his newly occupied capital of Jerusalem (2 Sam. 6); it cannot, therefore, have been in the camp of Saul near Gibeah of Benjamin at the battle of Michmash (1 Sam. 14, 18). And (2) the instrument of priestly divination among the ancient Israelites, which is clearly demanded by the context of our passage, was not the ark, but the ephod.[2]

The second assumption need not detain us, since it begs the question. What was the instrument of divination among the ancient Israelites, is the very question at issue, *with the presumption by no means in favor of the ephod.* For we do know that in two undisputed passages of the older literature (1 Sam. 2, 18; 2 Sam. 6, 14) — to

---

[1] *Les Livres de Samuel*, 1910, p. 118. See also Schlögl, *Die Bücher Samuelis*, 1904, p. 88; and *Libri Samuelis*, 1905, p. xxxv. A similar position regarding our passage is adopted uncompromisingly in all the recent works on the Religion of Israel which mention it. So Smend, *Lehrbuch der alttestamentlichen Religionsgeschichte*[2], 1899, p. 136; Kautzsch, article "Religion of Israel" in the Extra Volume of Hastings' *Dictionary of the Bible*, 1904, p. 649; and in the posthumous German edition under the title, *Biblische Theologie des Alten Testaments*, 1911, pp. 96, 118; Stade, *Biblische Theologie des Alten Testaments*, 1905, p. 117; Kayser-Marti, *Geschichte der israelitischen Religion*[5], 1907, pp. 36 f, 54; König, *Geschichte der alttestamentlichen Religion*, 1912, p. 214.

[2] The lame theory put forward by several scholars to account for the entry of ארון האלהים into the Masoretic text, namely, that some scribe knew the ephod was an idol or other heathenish fetich and so replaced it with the ark, has already been disposed of above: a Pentateuchal Jew could not have objected to the presence of the High Priest's ephod with Ahijah, while an earlier editor could have made no changes in the text without affecting the Septuagint. The pyramid of successive scribal alterations assumed by Dhorme, and less explicitly by Thenius, is not amenable to discussion.

say nothing of P in Ex. 28, 6-12; 29, 5; 39, 2-7; Lev. 8, 7 — the ephod is a ceremonial garment which has no relation to divination; whereas we admittedly do not know what the historical ark — as distinguished from the fiction of Deuteronomistic and Jewish imagination — really was. If therefore the first assumption of historical fact, regarding the whereabouts of the ark during the events of 1 Sam. 14, 18, can be shown to be untenable or irrelevant, nothing stands in the way of our discarding the second, and deciding in favor of the ark as the specific instrument of divination. The crux of the whole matter lies in the first assumption and its attendant implications.

As long ago as 1835, Vatke [1] based upon the Masoretic text of 1 Sam. 14, 18 the opinion that the ark was, *like the ephod*, employed for purposes of divination; and his view has been revived in recent times by Holzinger [2] upon the same basis. But neither Vatke nor Holzinger made any attempt to reconcile the authenticity of the reading ארון האלהים in 1 Sam. 14, 18 with the fact that the ark was at the time in question comfortably reposing in the house of Abinadab at Kirjath-jearim. If the Hebrew reading of our passage is to be maintained, such a reconciliation must be forthcoming.

That the ark of Yahwe which finally rested in the temple of Solomon in Jerusalem was at Kirjath-jearim during the battle of Michmash cannot be disputed. For if the story of 2 Sam. 6 is not historical, there is no history anywhere in the Old Testament; and if 2 Sam. 6 is historical, the fact recorded in 1 Sam. 7, 1 must also be historical. The historical ark of these narratives was accordingly in the house of Abinadab at Kirjath-jearim from some time before the accession of Saul until after the accession of David to the throne of all Israel a generation later.[3] But — *why may not the ark of 1 Sam. 14, 18 be another ark?* In point of fact, we shall see that it was.

[1] *Die Religion des Alten Testaments*, I, pp. 320 ff.
[2] *Kurzer Hand-Commentar zum Alten Testament; Exodus*, 1900, p. 123.
[3] The entire reign of Saul — the story of Samuel must be disregarded — and the rule of David as king of Judah in Hebron fall in the interval. 1 Sam. 7, 2, although of questionable origin, will not be very far astray on the matter of time; since Abinadab, who has a grown son in 1 Sam. 7, 1, is presumably still alive in 2 Sam. 6, 3. Other-

V

The opinion that there was more than one ark of Yahwe among the Hebrews is an ancient Jewish heresy,[1] originating with a certain Judah ben Laqish, a Palestinian rabbi of unusual sanity and insight, who flourished at the close of the second century A.D.[2] The following is translated from the Jerusalem Talmud:[3]

"It is related that Rabbi Judah ben Laqish[4] said, Two arks journeyed with the Israelites in the wilderness[5]; one in which the Law was deposited, and one in which the fragments of the (broken) tables of stone were deposited.[6] That in which the Law was de-

---

wise the house would probably have been called בית פ' בן אבינדב in the latter passage. His son Eleazar may have died in the interval.

[1] Not exactly a "tradition," as H. P. Smith, *l. c.*, p. 112.

[2] Cf. Bacher, *Die Agada der Tannaiten*, II, pp. 494 f.

[3] *Sheqalim* 49c; cf. *j. Soṭa* 22bc. I use the Bomberg edition, Venice 1523–4.

[4] So the Bomberg edition, both in *Sheqalim* and *Soṭa;* and the text of the latter contained in the *Jerushalmi Fragments from the Genizah*, edited by Ginzberg, I, p. 213. The Tosephta, *Soṭa* vii, 18 (ed. Zuckermandel, p. 308), also attributes the doctrine to Judah ben Laqish. Abravanel, *l.c.*, fol. 85b, cites the section from *Sheqalim* with יהודה בר אלעאי instead of יודה בן לקיש throughout; but his numerous paraphrases and important omissions show conclusively that he was quoting from memory. Buxtorf the younger, who had Abravanel's commentary as well as the Jerusalem Talmud before him, gives a mixed text, with יהודה בן לקיש the first and second times the name occurs, but יהודה בר אלעאי the third time; and calls him *R. Jehuda ben Elai* from the first in his Latin translation; *Historia Arcae Foederis*, Basel, 1659, p. 33. The reading בר אלעי which the Jitomir edition of the Jerusalem Talmud (followed by the Piotrkow edition) inserts in parentheses in the text of *Sheqalim* (but not in that of *Soṭa*) rests, not upon manuscript evidence, but upon a suggestion of the Gaon Elijah of Wilna; and this latter, though buttressed with an erroneous argument, was probably not wholly independent of Abravanel's misquotation.

[5] From this passage Graetz, *Geschichte der Juden*, I, 1874, p. 160, quoted שני ארונות היו in support of his contention that a second ark — lacking the tables of stone, of course, so that one fails to see what object it was to serve — was constructed by the Aaronic priesthood of Nob to take the place of the one lost to the Philistines. Which recalls the sermon against the vanity of ladies' top-knots, from the text, "top not come down." The Talmud has שני ארונות היו מהלכין עם ישראל במדבר.

[6] The orthodox *haggadah* placed the fragments of the first two tables of stone, which were broken by Moses, beside the second two in the single ark; see *b. Baba Bathra* 14b; *b. Berachoth* 8b. The present text of Siphre § 82, however, reflects the opinion of Judah ben Laqish in its comment on the statement וארון ברית יהוה נוסע

posited was kept in the Tent of Meeting; concerning this it is written, *And the ark of the covenant of the LORD and Moses did not move from the midst of the camp* (Numbers 14, 44). That in which the fragments of the tables of stone were deposited went in and out with them (in war); and twice it appears with them (in the biblical narrative: 1 Sam. 14, 18; 2 Sam. 11, 11).[1] But the Rabbis affirm, There was only one ark,[2] and it went forth only once, in the days of Eli, and then it was captured. A text of Scripture supports the Rabbis: *Woe unto us! who shall deliver us from these mighty gods?* (1 Sam. 4, 8) — a thing which they (the Philistines) had never seen before. (On the other hand) a text of Scripture supports Rabbi Judah ben Laqish: *And Saul said to Ahijah, Bring hither the divine ark* (1 Sam. 14, 18). Was there not an ark at Kirjath-jearim? How do the Rabbis dispose of this passage? (Answer: Saul meant) Bring me the ציץ (the High Priest's golden plate, Ex. 28, 36).[3] Another text of Scripture supports Rabbi Judah ben Laqish: *The ark and Israel and Judah are living in booths* (2 Sam. 11, 11). Was there not an ark in Zion? How do the Rabbis dispose of this passage? (Answer:) It (the ark in Zion) was indeed in a booth (when Uriah spoke), for it was under an awning[4] (cf. 2 Sam. 7, 2), since the Temple had not yet been built."[5] We moderns must admit that Rabbi Judah had the best of the argument.

---

[1] ארון זה שיצא עמהם במחנה היו בו שברי לוחות שנאמר לפניהם of Numbers 10, 33: וארון ברית יהוה ומשה לא משו מקרב המחנה. ופעמי' הוא מתרה עמהן. Ugolinus, *Thesaurus antiquitatum sacrarum*, XVIII, col. 112 f, renders *et aliquando praemonebat eos*, reading פעמים as plural and מתרה as if from תרה. The same misunderstanding underlies the Tosephta version: פעמים היה מדבר עמהם, though the latter interprets פעמים correctly as dual. Before עמהן, מתרה can only be an Aramaizing equivalent of נראה. Buxtorf and the Jitomir edition actually read מתראה. Aptowitzer, *l. c.*, p. 49, bases a characteristically muddled argument upon a misinterpretation of this sentence.

[2] Here and elsewhere Schwab, *Le Talmud de Jérusalem*, V, pp. 298 f, attempts to harmonize and mistranslates.

[3] Note that the Talmudic authorities do not connect this passage with the ephod. For "l'arche contenant les vêtements sacrés pour consulter l'oracle" of Schwab's rendering one has to come down to Abravanel.

[4] For בקירוי read בקירוי, as in *j. Soṭa* 22c.

[5] Abravanel, who accepts the orthodox rabbinical view, points out that Uriah's excuse was factitious, since by the same token he would never in his life have been free to go home; *l. c.*, fol. 86b.

The Jewish scholars of the Middle Ages gave themselves less concern over the subtle, tell-tale testimony of 1 Sam. 14, 18 and 2 Sam. 11, 11 regarding the historical ark, than they did over the explicit contradiction bequeathed to them by the redactors of the Pentateuch regarding the fictitious ark of Jewish dogma. Exodus 37, 1 ff, it will be recalled, asserts that the ark was manufactured in costly fashion by Bezaleel, from specifications delivered to Moses (Ex. 25, 10 ff), after the latter's descent from the mount with the second two tables of stone (Ex. 34, 29); whereas Deuteronomy 10 affirms that Moses himself constructed it of plain shittim wood just before he went up into the mount to receive the second two tables of stone. Accordingly, some held that the Israelites carried away two arks from Sinai, one made by Bezaleel and containing the two sound tables of stone, and another made by Moses and containing the fragments of the broken tables. The first ordinarily remained in the sanctuary, while the second regularly marched ahead of the people through the wilderness, and accompanied them into battle after their settlement in Canaan. On one occasion the ark of Bezaleel was carried into battle without divine authority, when the irregularity was punished by the capture of the ark and the defeat of the people at the hands of the Philistines. The prevailing opinion, however, held that the ark which Moses made was in use only temporarily, until the completion of the more costly one manufactured by Bezaleel, when it was stowed away in a sort of pristine *genizah*; and that both sets of tables, the sound and the broken, were preserved in the single ark of Bezaleel. This alone accompanied the Israelites away from Sinai and into the land of Canaan.[1]

So far as it concerns our present enquiry, the doctrine of Judah ben Laqish and his heretical successors of the Middle Ages falls far short of the truth; which — to return to the atmosphere and language of modern historical science — may be stated as follows: *The historical ark of Yahwe was not a unique but a manifold object, attach-*

---

[1] See Abravanel, *l. c.*, fol. 85 f. Abravanel's exhaustive discussion is reproduced with characteristic lucidity by Buxtorf the younger in chapter 3 of the valuable work already cited: *An arca haec quam Bezaleel fecit sola inter Israelitas fuerit? An vero praeter eam adhuc alia quam Moses fecerit quamque Israelitae secum in bellum eduxerunt?*

ing to every Palestinian sanctuary that possessed a consecrated priesthood; and the theory of a single ark, corresponding to that of a single legitimate sanctuary, is the last surviving Deuteronomistic conceit in the theological science of the present day.[1] Not only was the ark of 1 Sam. 14, 18 a different ark from the one detained at Kirjath-jearim, but the one mentioned by Uriah the Hittite as encamped with the army of Joab at the siege of Rabbath Ammon (2 Sam. 11, 11) was perhaps still another; the " ephod " with which Abiathar accompanied David on his wanderings (1 Sam. 23, 6 9; 30, 7; cf. 1 Kings 2, 26) was certainly another; that in the sanctuary of Nob (1 Sam. 21, 10) was perhaps still another; that of Micah and the Danites (Judges 17 f) was certainly another; and that of Gideon (Judges 8, 27) was still another. What is more, 1 Sam. 14, 18 is far from being the only passage in the Old Testament where the scribes have failed to conceal the true state of the case. On the contrary, the ancient records contain hardly a single surviving reference to the ark which does not by its very language, when critically examined, betray the fact that the object was manifold and not unique.

VI

At this point it will be well for us to abandon the obsolete term " ark," which to our sensibilities has acquired something of the dignity of a proper name, and employ henceforward the plain English " box," which reproduces exactly the classical sense of the Hebrew word ארון.

And first attention must be directed to a point of grammar which has been sadly overlooked in this connection.[2] It has been generally assumed that, the object being unique, the Old Testament expressions ארון יהוה, ארון אלהים, and ארון האלהים were, to all intents and purposes, proper names, with identical, or at least equivalent sema-

---

[1] This thesis, it is hardly necessary to say, must not be confounded with such an opinion as that of Schwally (*l. c.*, pp. 14 f), to the effect that the ark was indeed a unique national institution in the historical period, but that before the other Israelitish tribes had allied themselves with Joseph, one and another of them may have had a corresponding tribal palladium of its own, consecrated perhaps to another deity than Yahwe.

[2] In a measure, it has been tacitly anticipated in my translations above.

siological value. So that whether a Hebrew author employed the one or the other, depended upon the impulse of the moment, the exigencies of style, or at best on his individual habit; the sense would be the same. Some recent critics have gone so far as to analyse the old narratives of 1 Sam. 4–6 and 2 Sam. 6 into two distinct sources: a J source, employing ארון יהוה, and an E source, employing ארון האלהים or ארון אלהים, to designate the same object and expressing the same idea.[1] Even the few scholars who have recognized that the genitive in ארון האלהים has adjectival rather than substantive force, and that the phrase should be rendered *the sacred box* rather than *the box of God* — *die Gotteslade* rather than *die Lade Gottes* — have failed to perceive any material difference between its actual connotation and that of the expression ארון יהוה. Still less, so far as I am aware, has any critic ever dreamed of a material difference between ארון אלהים and ארון האלהים. It has been universally assumed that the only difference between these two expressions is that in the one case God is called אלהים, and in the other he is called האלהים.[2] The fact is, however, that not only do they both differ in meaning from ארון יהוה, but ארון אלהים and ארון האלהים have *diametrically opposite syntactical values*.

In classical Hebrew, such a phrase as ארון אלהים is an *indeterminate appellative*, the genitive אלהים being employed generically and adjectivally; and the expression as a whole signifies neither *the box of God*, nor yet *the sacred box*, but distinctly *a sacred box*. This may

---

[1] So, for example, Dhorme affirms that 2 Sam. 6 is " une double narration. L'une (v. 2–4, 6–8) comprenant l'épisode d'Ouzzâ et se terminant par le nom de Pérès-Ouzzâ, appartient à E. Nous n'y voyons figurer que *l'arche de Dieu* (v. 2, 3, 6, 7). L'autre, qui ne parle que de *l'arche de Iahvé*, contient l'entrée de l'arche à Jérusalem, après une station chez Obédédom et l'épisode de Mîcal. On sait que les passages relatifs à Mîcal appartiennent à J." *L.c.*, p. 334; cf. p. 7.

[2] This erroneous assumption, explicitly avowed (p. 82), characterizes the entire treatment of Hebrew compounds with אלהים in Baumgärtel's *Elohim ausserhalb des Pentateuch*, Leipsic, 1914; and very seriously impairs the value of a painstaking and otherwise laudably methodical contribution toward the scientific solution of the question of the divine names in Genesis. The fact is, that even when standing alone, אלהים and האלהים are not employed indiscriminately in the older literature — least of all in Genesis.

be seen not only from such abstract and semi-abstract parallels as דעת אלהים, *religious practice*; יראת אלהים, *religious scruple*; חסד אלהים, *sacred faith*; פחד אלהים, *divine awe*; חרדת אלהים, (a) *tremendous panic*; אש אלהים, (a) *miraculous fire*; רוח אלהים, (a) *divine spirit* (for which the corresponding unqualified expressions would be דעת, יראה, חסד, פחד, חרדה, אש, רוח; not הדעת, etc.); but also from such distinctly unitary concrete parallels as בית אלהים, *a sanctuary* (Judges, 17, 5; Gen. 28, 22); מלאך אלהים, *an angel* (Gen. 28, 12, where אלהים is clearly not a surrogate for יהוה); נזיר אלהים, *a religious devotee* (Judges 13, 5); איש אלהים, *a divine agent* (1 Kings 17, 24). And when, in classical Hebrew, the article is prefixed to the genitive of such a compound, it indicates, not that the writer is employing indiscriminately an alternative adjectival genitive, האלהים, but that the whole compound, and specifically the construct noun, is *consciously determined*. No greater mistake can be made than to suppose that classical Hebrew could employ interchangeably בית אלהים and ארון האלהים, איש אלהים and איש האלהים, בית האלהים and ארון האלהים. To a certain, very limited extent, the distinction has been obscured by textual corruption and by the fact that the Hebrew idiom sometimes employs the determinate where we should employ the indeterminate;[1] but of the validity of the principle there can be no doubt whatever. By the ancient Hebrews themselves ארון האלהים was never employed without the distinct consciousness that it was the determinate form of an antecedent indeterminate ארון אלהים.

This proposition is of such fundamental importance that it is worth our while to demonstrate it conclusively by an exhaustive survey of the Old Testament usage with regard to one such compound which occurs often enough in the pre-exilic literature to preclude the possibility of our result being vitiated by chance phenomena or textual corruption. I will be pardoned if, in order to secure the precision demanded in such a matter, I employ the prefix "deity" with a hyphen, to represent the adjectival אלהים of the

---

[1] So in 2 Sam. 14, 17 the woman of Tekoa says to David, כמלאך האלהים כן אדני המלך; just as Amos (5, 19) says, כאשר ינום איש מפני הארי ופגעו הדב. Cf. Gesenius-Kautzsch § 126 r.

Hebrew compound, rather than the more elegant but misleading suffix " of God " or the ambiguous adjective " sacred."

1 Sam. 2, 27, *a (strange) deity-man*, איש אלהים, comes to Eli. 1 Sam. 9, 6, Saul's servant says to him, " Behold, there is *a deity-man* (איש אלהים) in this city "; thereafter *the (aforesaid) deity-man* is איש האלהים, v. 7, 8, 10. 1 Kings 13, 1, *a deity-man*, איש אלהים, comes to Bethel from Judah; thereafter *the (aforesaid) deity-man* is איש האלהים, v. 4, 5, 6, 7, 8, 11, 12, 14, 21, 26, 29, 31. 1 Kings 20, 28, *a (strange) deity-man*, איש אלהים, steps up to the king of Israel. 2 Kings 4, 7, Elisha, who is already the subject of the narrative, is *the deity-man*, איש האלהים; similarly in the sequel, 4, 21 22 25 27 42; 5, 14 15; 6, 6 9 10 15; 7, 2 17 18 19; 8, 2 4 7 8 11; 13, 19. 2 Kings 23, 16 f, *the deity-man* of the episode of 1 Kings 13 is איש האלהים. 1 Kings 12, 22; 2 Kings 5, 8 20; Jer. 35, 4, *the deity-man*, in apposition to a proper name, is איש האלהים. 1 Kings 17, 18; 2 Kings 1, 9 11 13; 4 16 40, the vocative, *O deity-man*, is, in accordance with correct Hebrew idiom, איש האלהים. On the other hand, in the predicate: 1 Kings 17, 24, " I know that thou art *a deity-man* " — איש אלהים. 2 Kings 1, 10, " If I be *a deity-man* " — איש אלהים; and so without doubt originally in verse 12, where the Masoretic text now reads איש האלהים, but G^B has ἄνθρωπος θεοῦ. 2 Kings 4, 9, " I know that he is *a holy deity-man* " — איש אלהים קדוש. Judges 13, 6, the Masoretic text again exhibits the erroneous איש האלהים where the context demands *a deity-man*, but again G^B has ἄνθρωπος θεοῦ; with which contrast τὸν ἄνθρωπον τοῦ θεοῦ, reproducing the correct איש האלהים, *the deity-man*, of the sequel in verse 8.[1]

The above survey exhibits the undeviating usage of classical Hebrew. The only case in the Old Testament where that usage would seem to have been violated by the author himself is 2 Chron. 25, 7, where we have ואיש האלהים בא אליו, though the context demands an indeterminate subject. But this is the exception which proves the rule. For, to the Chronicler, the determinate איש האלהים of the

---

[1] If G^B of Judges represents a late Greek translation of the fourth century A.D. (Moore, *Commentary*, p. xlvi; but cf. Thackeray, *Grammar of the Old Testament in Greek*, I, p. 9), it indicates that, as late as that, the Hebrew text of Judges 13, 6 still exhibited the correct איש אלהים.

sequel in verse 9 does not signify *the deity-man*, but *the man of the Deity* = *the man of God*; and hence איש האלהים of verse 7 is neither *the deity-man* nor *a deity-man*, but *a man of the Deity* = *a man of God*. In other words, for the Chronicler, the genitive is determinate, and not adjectival but substantive. And the same will be the construction intended in all other cases where the title is bestowed by an epigone who had no understanding of the historical institution. So משה איש האלהים, Deut. 33, 1; Joshua 14, 6; Psalm 90, 1 (title), as well as 1 Chron. 23, 14; 2 Chron. 30, 16; Ezra 3, 2 (Chronicler), is *Moses the man of God*; and דויד איש האלהים, 2 Chron. 8, 14; Neh. 12, 24 36 (Chronicler), is *David the man of God*. In 2 Chron. 11, 2 the author is copying 1 Kings 12, 22.

The Chronicler's use of the divine names has occasioned so much perplexity and misunderstanding (cf., for example, Kittel, *Handkommentar zum Alten Testament*, pp. 63 f) that a few observations on the subject may not be out of place. (1) He employed יהוה — much as we employ " viz." for " namely " — only as the ideogrammatic spelling of *Adonai*, his favorite divine name. This is the simple explanation of the vast preponderance of יהוה over (ה)אלהים in the writings of the Chronicler. (For the statistics, see Baumgärtel, *l. c.*, pp. 68 f) It is noteworthy that, except in two passages copied from Nehemiah's memoirs, the spelling אדני occurs nowhere in Chron.-Ezr.-Neh. (2) He employed האלהים as a determinate appellative = *the Deity* κατ' ἐξοχήν. (3) He employed the old generic title אלהים, *Deity*, as the equivalent of *Adonai* (יהוה). So are to be explained such phrases as בית אלהים (ii. 34, 9), ברית אלהים (ii. 34, 32), דבר אלהים (i. 17, 3; cf. 2 Sam. 7, 4), פי אלהים (ii. 35, 22) — all determinate, and equivalent *in meaning* to דבר יהוה, ברית יהוה, בית יהוה, and פי יהוה respectively. This substantive אלהים must be distinguished from the adjectival אלהים of such indeterminate stereotyped phrases as רוח אלהים (ii. 15, 1; 24, 10), פחד אלהים (ii. 20, 29), and מחנה אלהים (i. 12, 22), which the Chronicler probably never stopped to analyse. (4) He employed יהוה אלהים to represent the double name *Adonai Elohim*, and hence used it when reproducing אדני יהוה of the older literature, which he pronounced *Adonai Elohim;* cf. i. 17, 16 17 with 2 Sam. 7, 18 19. (5) When not copying mechanically (as in i. 11, 9; 17, 7 24 = 2 Sam. 5, 10; 7, 8 26 respectively), he reproduces יהוה צבאות by יהוה alone; cf. i. 13, 6 with 2 Sam. 6, 2, and i. 16, 2 with 2 Sam. 6, 18. This indicates that his oral surrogate for יהוה צבאות, as well as for the simple יהוה, of the older literature was *Adonai*. See p. 147 below for evidence that certain Septuagint translators followed a similar practice.

For the period with which we are concerned, when the people still possessed the historical institution of the sacred box, or, at all events, a living tradition of what it had been, the rigid observance of the linguistic usage I have indicated has been abundantly demonstrated. Just as it is no accident that the expression נזיר אלהים, which is found in the Old Testament only in the predicate (Judges 13, 5 7; 16, 17), occurs every time without the article, so we may confidently assume that in the mouth of the ancient Hebrews ארון אלהים always signified *a sacred box*; and ארון האלהים signified neither *the box of God* nor *the Sacred Box* κατ' ἐξοχήν, but merely *the sacred box* — either already mentioned, or about to be identified by means of a relative clause, or unmistakably defined by the context.

It remains to remind ourselves that even ארון יהוה, though grammatically defined for the given context, does not by any means, in pre-Deuteronomic thinking, imply that the object so designated is intrinsically unique. In this respect ארון יהוה carries the same implications — no more and no less — that are involved in the expression מזבח יהוה in the story of Elijah (1 Kings 18, 30; cf. מזבחתיך, 19, 10); or in the term בית יהוה of the early codes (Ex. 23, 19; 34, 26), the story of Samuel (1 Sam. 1, 7 24), and the history of David (2 Sam. 12, 20).[1] To speak familiarly, "the pen of John Smith" is not necessarily John Smith's only existing pen, in the absence of a law forbidding the possession of more than one pen.

With these preliminary observations, we pass to the testimony of the records.

VII

And we may begin by affirming that the very employment in the records of such an appellative as ארון אלהים, whether determined or not, is evidence that the Hebrews were acquainted with a plurality of such objects; just as the employment of the appellative איש אלהים is evidence that the Hebrews were acquainted with a plurality of such functionaries. An object designated ארון יהוה might possibly

---

[1] Budde's objection to the reading בית יהוה in 2 Sam. 12, 20 (*Kurzer Hand-Commentar*, p. 257), like Steuernagel's to the same reading in Joshua 6, 24 (*Handkommentar*, p. 174), is not well taken. The term בית argues nothing at all as to the character of the attendant structure, whether היכל (1 Sam. 1, 9), אהל (1 Kings 2, 28), or merely מצבה (Gen. 28, 22).

be unique in the religion of Israel as well as peculiar to it; an object designated ארון אלהים was pretty certainly neither the one nor the other. There was of course more than one מלאך אלהים, איש אלהים, בית אלהים, נזיר אלהים, not merely in the world of the ancient Hebrews, but also in the service of Yahwe. So, presumably, there was also more than one ארון אלהים in his service. Nor is anything gained for the traditional theory by maintaining that the employment of the appellative points to a plurality of such objects only in the broader field of common Canaanitish institutions, but not in the narrower field of specifically Israelitish religion. For if the sacred box was, to the consciousness of the early Israelitish writers, a common Canaanitish institution, then presumably it was not one which their ancestors brought with them from the desert of Sinai. And we should be going far out of our way to assume that, after their dispersion in Canaan and before their unification under the monarchy, the Israelites adopted a plural Canaanitish institution, but managed nevertheless to impose upon it a gratuitously singular character.

If, however, we draw the natural conclusion, that the use of the appellative ארון אלהים argues acquaintance with a plurality of sacred boxes, Yahwistic as well as non-Yahwistic, then it becomes exceedingly significant that the appellative is found again and again in the most ancient narratives in the Old Testament, which actually deal with historical conditions and events in Canaan (1 Sam. 4, 4 [1].11 13 17 18 19 21 22; 5, 1 2 10; 1 Sam. 14, 18; 2 Sam. 6, 2 3 4 7 12; 2 Sam. 15, 24 25 29), although it is conspicuously absent in the imaginative compositions concerning the olden time when all Israel lived and journeyed together as a single company with a single portable sanctuary (Numbers 10, 33–36; 14, 44; Joshua 3–8).[2]

It must be admitted that these general considerations, added to the solid testimony of 1 Sam. 14, 18, go far towards establishing the contention that the Israelites possessed more than one sacred box. And, in view of the doctrine which has prevailed in the Jewish church

---

[1] The Deuteronomistic gloss ברית is of course disregarded.

[2] If the narratives concerning the sacred box could be analyzed into two distinct sources characterized by the use of ארון יהוה and ארון (ה)אלהים respectively—which they can not — the "Elohistic" source would have to be assigned the earlier date.

34   EPHOD AND ARK

from the very beginning concerning the box of Yahwe, and the drastic measures which we have seen reason to believe were adopted by the early scribes to destroy the traces of its plural character, it would not be at all surprising if we could discover no additional evidence in support of that contention. But in fact, as already intimated, the direct evidence of a manifold sacred box yielded by the surviving references in the early literature of the Old Testament is abundant and unmistakable.

There are, to be sure, some references to the sacred box in the later pre-exilic literature which are neutral — compatible with either of the two opposing hypotheses. Such are, for example, the notices in the story of the Mosaic journeyings, and in the pre-Deuteronomic stratum of the story of Joshua. These we shall of course interpret finally in the light of the hypothesis demanded by the less equivocal passages. On the other hand, there is not a single pre-exilic reference — not even in Deuteronomy and Kings [1] — which is actually incompatible with the hypothesis of a manifold box; whereas there are no less than five passages, besides 1 Sam. 14, 18, which are irreconcilable with any other hypothesis. These passages are **1 Sam. 3, 3**; **1 Sam. 4, 3 f**; **2 Sam. 6, 2**; **1 Kings 2, 26**; and **Jer. 3, 16**. In addition, there are several passages which become thoroughly intelligible only upon the hypothesis of a manifold sacred box employed for purposes of divination; namely, **2 Sam. 11, 11**; **2 Sam. 15, 24 ff**; and **Judges 20, 27**. We will examine all these passages in the order given.

VIII

In **1 Sam. 3, 3** the Masoretic text reads: ושמואל שכב בהיכל יהוה אשר שם ארון אלהים. As this text stands — and there is no good reason for questioning it — it can only mean, *and Samuel was asleep in the temple of Yahwe, where there was a sacred box.*[2] A like rendering

---

[1] 1 Kings 8, 9. 21 and the interpolations in Deut. 10, 1—5 are disregarded for the present; cf. page 5, note 1.

[2] For the loose relative with שם cf. Gen. 2, 11. Since Eli is presumably asleep in another apartment of the same building, היכל יהוה must be the single chamber used as a sanctuary. An earlier writer would probably have taken it for granted that the sanctuary contained a sacred box.

is demanded by the preceding clause, נר אלהים טרם יכבה; not *the lamp of God had not yet gone out*, but *not a single temple lamp had yet gone out* — all the lamps were still burning.[1] Both נר אלהים and ארון אלהים could be determinate only if the expressions were exceptions to the grammatical principle we have been at pains to establish, that is, only if אלהים is not an adjectival genitive but a constructively determinate surrogate of the name *Yahwe*. Such an assumption is utterly unwarranted. Nowhere in the story of Eli (1 Sam. 1–6), either in the earlier or later sections, is אלהים employed as the surrogate of *Yahwe*. On the contrary, Yahwe is uniformly called by his proper name, and actually so in the very sentence we are discussing. אלהים throughout 1 Sam. 1–6 is invariably an appellative. As such it occurs: (*a*) In the construct: of Dagon, אלהינו (5, 7), אלהיכם (6, 5); of Yahwe, אלהי ישראל (1, 17; 2, 30; 5, 7 8 10 11; 6, 3 5); besides אלהינו in the song of Hannah (2, 2). (*b*) In apposition without following genitive, יהוה האלהים הקדוש הזה (6, 20). (*c*) Of " deity " in general, not specifically Yahwe: of the category in contradistinction to Yahwe (2, 25); in the expression מקללים אלהים (so the correct reading), *guilty of sacrilege* (3, 13); in the common Palestinian adjuration, כה יעשה לך אלהים וכה יוסיף (3, 17); in the mouth of the Philistines, בא אלהים אל המחנה, *Deity has arrived in the camp* (4, 7). (*d*) In compounds: איש אלהים (2, 27); נר אלהים (3, 3); ארון אלהים (3, 3; 4, 4 11 13 17 18 19 21 22; 5, 1 2 10); יד אלהים (5, 11). (*e*) Distinctly in the plural, *gods:* only in the scribal interpolation 4, 8![2] With this array of facts before us, we must insist upon the adjectival character of אלהים in 1 Sam. 3, 3, and upon the rendering *a sacred box* rather than *the box of God*.

However, precisely for that reason, we can afford to be generous on the question of the authenticity of the indeterminate readings נר אלהים and ארון אלהים of the Masoretic text. That the Septuagint has ὁ λύχνος τοῦ θεοῦ and ἡ κιβωτὸς τοῦ θεοῦ is not to be

---

[1] 1 Kings 7, 49 and Ex. 25, 37 give us no reason to believe that important sanctuaries were served by a single light.

[2] The perpetrator of this interpolation was bound to have the Philistines talk like the unmitigated heathen they were. The author himself knew very well that אלהים could be construed as a singular by any Hebrew-speaking inhabitant of Canaan.

wondered at, in view of the determinate interpretation of the indeterminate Masoretic text which prevails universally at the present day. But even if we concede that the Greek translator had נר האלהים and ארון האלהים, and that these were the authentic readings, we should not have altered the fact that אלהים is adjectival. The only difference would be the substitution of the reading *the sacred box* for *a sacred box;* which is much as if one should say, regarding the chancel of a modern church building, " where the communion table was," instead of " where there was a communion table " — hardly evidence, in either case, that all Christendom has but one communion table. At the worst, this verse would take its place in the second group of passages we have enumerated. For the fact should not be overlooked that the author's mention of the presence of the sacred box in the room where Samuel slept is much more to the point if both he and his readers thought of it as a box from which the priests of Shiloh ordinarily extracted the oracular responses of Yahwe. And if it was that, it was of course not unique. Meanwhile we shall do well to bear in mind the exact meaning and unquestionable purport of the Masoretic text of 1 Sam. 3, 3; as well as the fact, that while it is very easy to account for the reading of G as arising from M, it is difficult to imagine how the text of M, could arise from that assumed for G.[1]

IX

Our next passage is **1 Sam. 4, 3 f.** It is commonly recognized that the story of the sacred box in which this passage occurs was not originally composed as a continuation of chapter 3, but is part of a distinct writing of much earlier date which has been imbedded in the setting furnished by the opening chapters. Such being the case,

---

[1] In 1 Sam. 4, 11, on the contrary, ארון אלהים cannot be the original; for, the sacred box having been introduced in verse 3, the compound appellative in verse 11 must be ארון האלהים, as regularly elsewhere in the narrative. The scribal emendation was, however, very far from intending a substantive construction for אלהים (cf. Budde, *Kurzer Hand-Commentar*, p. 35); it was merely concerned with avoiding at all costs, regardless of grammar, the vocal sequence האלהים נלקח, a scruple which will account also for the odd gender bestowed upon נלקח in verse 17.

the notice of the sacred box in 4, 3 f is an *initial mention*; and, since the box is not referred to incidentally but forms the subject of the narrative, the language of the text must, if our contention be correct, identify in some way, for the benefit of the reader, the particular sacred box whose history is about to be rehearsed. A careful attention to details will show that it does that very thing.

In 1 Sam. 4, the Israelites, having rashly engaged in a pitched battle with the Philistines in the open plain, are thoroughly beaten, and retire to their camp, leaving about four thousand men upon the field. Whereupon the chiefs take counsel: ויאמרו זקני ישראל למה ננפנו יהוה היום לפני פלשתים נקחה אלינו משלה את ארון (ברית) יהוה ויבא בקרבנו וישענו מכף איבינו: וישלח העם שלה וישאו משם את ארון (ברית) יהוה צבאות (ישב הכרבים). The textual difficulties are not very serious. In a document of this early date, the Deuteronomistic gloss ברית may be struck out without much ado in both verses (cf. G^B). That leaves, as the only textual question to be considered, the concluding phrase ישב הכרבים, which is ostensibly in apposition to יהוה צבאות.

Now, of course, no sacred box was actually designated ארון יהוה צבאות ישב הכרבים in current speech. צבאות was itself enough of a qualification of יהוה, without adding an adjectival clause to qualify in turn י. צבאות. Moreover, at the time here represented, the cherubim, which were designed by Solomon's Phoenician artisans to overshadow the sacred box in the cella of his temple,[1] were not in existence. Dibelius, to be sure, finds the cherubim carved upon the box (or rather, throne) itself from the very beginning; wherefore, and without respect to the cherubim of Solomon's temple, Yahwe was called ישב הכרבים, "*der über den Keruben thront.*"[2] But ישב הכרבים does not mean *he that sits over the cherubim*, any more than ישב ירושלם means *he that sits over Jerusalem*. The idiomatic Hebrew for *he that sits upon the cherubim* — which is the point of departure for this interpretation — would be הישב על הכרבים; the preposition being essential even with the participle,

---

[1] 1 Kings 6, 23 ff; cf. 8, 6.
[2] *L. c.*, pp. 17, 22 f; cf. Eduard Meyer, *Die Israeliten und ihre Nachbarstämme*, pp. 214 f. The archaeology is original; but the philological blunder is as ancient as the Septuagint and as recent as the latest edition of Gesenius-Buhl.

which in turn would have to be determined by means of the article in this context; cf. especially 1 Kings 22, 19; Isa. 6, 1; 28, 6; 40, 22; Jer. 17, 25; Prov. 20, 8. ישב ירושלם is *the inhabitant of Jerusalem*; similarly, ישב הכרבים is *the occupant of the cherubim*. And we have only to repeat this last phrase to ourselves once to realize that it is what the rabbis of the Mishnic period called a כנוי, that is, a *circumlocution* designed to avoid the utterance of a particular expression.

I have elsewhere [1] called attention to the fact that when the name *Yahwe* began to be avoided in the fourth century B.C., it was not always found practicable to substitute *Adonai* or *Elohim* for the sacred name in the reading of the ancient documents. This was obviously the case where the name *Yahwe* was itself the subject of discourse, as in Ex. 3, 14; and also where, as both here and in 2 Sam. 6, 2, the name יהוה צבאות had to be unmistakably indicated. For *Adonai Ṣebaoth* was not in those days a construable expression; since the possessive suffix of *Adonai* had not yet faded from the Jewish consciousness. And while there are indications that *Adonai* alone was used sometimes as a surrogate of the compound יהוה צבאות as well as of the plain יהוה in the early synagogue,[2] it could not well serve the purpose here, where the point of the text is the precise designation of the sacred box. This was not ארון יהוה (= ארון אדני), but ארון יהוה צבאות. And it would have been equally misleading and confusing for the reader to call the box ארון אלהי צבאות. But *the box of the occupant of the cherubim* was too palpable a circumlocution to mislead, while it was at the same time perfectly unambiguous. For the historic *box of Yahwe Ṣebaoth* had actually symbolized the presence of Yahwe under the outspread wings of the cherubim in Solomon's temple; and it was as *Yahwe Ṣebaoth* that the God of Israel was worshipped in that holy place, as once he had been worshipped under the same title in the sanctuary at Shiloh.[3] The "occupant of the cherubim" was there-

---

[1] *Journal of Biblical Literature*, XXIV, 1905, pp. 140 ff.

[2] This probably accounts for the unqualified Κυρίου of G^B in 1 Sam. 4, 4. See further pages 31, 146 f.

[3] Cf. 1 Sam. 1, 3 11; Isa. 6, 3 5; 37, 16 (= 2 Kings 19, 15); Jer. 7, 2 3[N. B.] 10 12 14; Zech. 7, 3.

therefore none other than *Yahwe Ṣebáoth*. Without doubt, the *kinnûi* or surrogate יֹשֵׁב הכרבים was first inserted in the manuscripts as a supralinear gloss for the guidance of the reader,[1] and eventually dropped into the line through inadvertence.[2]

Omitting the rubric יֹשֵׁב הכרבים accordingly, we get the authentic text of our passage, which may be rendered as follows: *And the elders of Israel said, Why has Yahwe smitten us to-day before the Philistines? Let us procure the box of Yahwe from Shiloh, and let it come into our ranks and save us from the hand of our enemies. So the army sent to Shiloh, and caused to be transported thence the box of Yahwe Militant*.[3]

Our author realized that the deliberating elders of Israel had no need of reminding each other which particular box of Yahwe resided at Shiloh in their day. But he realized also that his own readers did stand in need of information on that point. For, long before his day and theirs, that box had been separated from Shiloh for ever. Accordingly, at his first mention of the box *in propria persona*, he takes care to identify it by means of its distinctive name, as *the box of Yahwe Militant*.[4] Having done so, however, he employs

---

[1] Both public and private; for it should be borne in mind in this connection, that reading to oneself without movement of the lips and sound of the voice is a comparatively modern process.

[2] An interesting parallel is supplied by Ps. 10, 3, where the author undoubtedly wrote ובצע נאץ יהוה. But the last two words being deemed unpronounceable (cf. the remedial gloss איבי in 2 Sam. 12, 14), the euphemistic surrogate ברך was inscribed above נאץ, and eventually dropped into the text; with an effect which may be appreciated by consulting the latest commentaries on the Psalter. In our passage the result was, of course, that in due season the reading of יהוה צבאית had to be faced anew; and then it was mechanically conformed to the practice elsewhere in the Old Testament. In 2 Kings 19, 15, where the original text was unquestionably יהוה צבאות אלהי ישראל אתה הוא האלהים (cf. Isa. 37, 16), the compound name was eventually read *Adonai*. On the other hand, in Ps. 80, 2; 99, 1 the *kinnûi* ישׁב (ה)כרבים is authentic, having by that time come to be employed as an epithet.

[3] For the justification of this rendering of the name *Yahwe Ṣebáoth*, see Excursus I at the end of this treatise.

[4] As will presently appear, this individual sacred box was called *the box of Yahwe Militant*, not merely because it was attached to the sanctuary where Yahwe was worshipped under that title, but also — and perhaps more proximately — because of the peculiar formula attending its use in divination.

thereafter only the more or less general terms, *the box, the sacred box*, and *the box of Yahwe*, with *the box of the god of Israel* as the equivalent of the latter in the mouth of the Philistines. If there is a lingering doubt in the mind of the reader as to the exact nuance intended in our passage, let him substitute both times for the word " box " in the above translation some neutral word like " shrine," or " statue," or " standard," and then re-read the whole; when I think he will be convinced that the interpretation I have given is not only natural, but necessary.

The identical sacred box of 1 Sam. 4–6 is not heard of again in this ancient writing until a generation later. The sacred box of 1 Sam. 14, 18 was known to the author to be another box. So also was the " ephod " of the sanctuary at Nob, and the " ephod " which Abiathar carried in the service of David, if our view of the matter is correct. But when next this same *box of Yahwe Militant* re-appears in the narrative, the author once more takes pains to identify it, if anything still more explicitly than here. We turn, then, to 2 Sam. 6, 2.

X

The ancient record of David's removal of the box of Yahwe Militant from Kirjath-jearim to Jerusalem, which is of supreme importance for our subject, has been so radically misinterpreted from the earliest times to the present day, that, at the cost of some disproportion, I venture to print the complete text of the original record, together with my own translation and a few pages of unavoidable comment.

Part of the existing misinterpretation is due to the fact that the story was violently separated from its original setting by a late editor,[1] who, besides numerous other insertions and expansions, interpolated the opening verse of chapter 6; thereby transforming what was in reality a mere incident of David's campaign against the Philistines, into a great national enterprise, involving the whole country, and enlisting the services of an army of *thirty thousand*

[1] In spite of the transpositions of 1 Chron. 13 and 14, however, it is quite certain that the Chronicler had before him 2 Sam. 5 and 6 in their present form.

chosen men. To secure the original setting, we must begin with the invasion of the Philistines in 2 Sam. 5, 17. And from that point to the end of chapter 6, the following elements of the Masoretic text must be discarded as unauthentic:

5, 20–24, entire. As this question has no very direct bearing on our subject, a few observations may suffice. With verse 20 compare 6, 8 and Judges 21, 15. Verse 21 knows the Philistines as "heathen." Verse 22 is a slavish copy of 17a and 18.[1] The elaborate instructions of verses 23 and 24 have in mind the oracles of prophecy; the author's priestly oracle could only answer a pointed question by a simple yes or no, or indicate a particular by means of a series of exclusions; cf. Judges 1, 2; 18, 5 f; 20, 28; 1 Sam. 14, 37 40 ff; 23, 9 ff; 30, 8; 2 Sam. 2, 1.

5, 25, the word כן. Compare G.

6, 1, entire.

6, 2, the initial ויקם; also the second שם and the phrase ישב הכרבים, which together constituted originally a supralinear lectional rubric parallel to שם יהוה צבאות. We may suppose that rubric to have been disposed upon the manuscript something like this:

Qrê: שם ישב הכרבים
Kethib: שם יהוה צבאות

6, 3, the final חדשה together with

6, 4, וישאהו מבית אבינדב אשר בגבעה. An accidental repetition from verse 3a; compare G^B.

6, 5, entire. Note כל בית ישראל, and the catalogue of musical instruments.

6, 6, the ח of וישלח. See the commentary below.

6, 8, entire. Compare 5, 20.

6, 9, entire. An insipid editorial annotation.

6, 13, entire. The editor's meaning is that an ox and a fatling were sacrificed at every six paces of the march. "All Israel" could afford them.

---

[1] Even the Chronicler felt the awkwardness of the repeated proper name, and wrote בעמק when reproducing verse 22 in 1 Chron. 14, 13.

6, 15, entire. כל בית ישראל again, although three months have elapsed since verse 5, and the editor has forgotten to reconvene the 30,000.

6, 17, the awkwardly appended ושלמים.

6, 18, העולה והשלמים.

6, 19, לכל המון ישראל למאיש ועד אשה.

6, 21, ושחקתי לפני יהוה. This clause, which has in mind verse 5, came into the text from the margin (of course without the ו), where it was intended as a euphemistic *Qrê* for the offensive expression נגליתי לפני יהוה, *I have exposed myself before Yahwe*, at the beginning of the verse. Ultimately, the forbidden word נגליתי was dropped from the text, leaving the language unconstruable. The Greek ὀρχήσομαι and εὐλογητὸς κύριος (the latter derived from a marginal injunction, בָּרֵךְ יהוה) represent two other scribal notations having the same object in view; neither expression can represent the word deliberately omitted from the Hebrew original. For a similar case of several euphemisms surviving in the different texts of the same passage, see 1 Sam. 3, 13.[1]

6, 23, entire. A gloating observation by the unctuous editor, who was especially interested in vital statistics.[2] The sympathies of the author, who was very much of an aristocrat, are with Michal.[3]

So much for the necessary excisions. On the other hand, besides נגליתי in 6, 21, two words which have been preserved by the Septuagint must be added to the existing Hebrew text.

In 6, 2 the Greek reads: καὶ ἀνέστη καὶ ἐπορεύθη Δαυεὶδ καὶ πᾶς ὁ λαὸς ὁ μετ' αὐτοῦ ἀπὸ τῶν ἀρχόντων Ἰούδα ἐν ἀναβάσει τοῦ ἀναγαγεῖν κ.τ.λ., which represents Hebrew: ויקם וילך דוד וכל העם אשר אתו מבעלי יהודה במעלה להעלות וג׳. As the phrase ἐν ἀναβάσει is utterly devoid of meaning in the Greek, it cannot be an intra-

---

[1] Cf. *Journal of Biblical Literature*, XXIV, 1905, p. 134.

[2] Cf. 2 Sam. 3, 2–5; 4, 4; 5, 13–16. The same editor is perhaps responsible for 2 Sam. 18, 18, which contradicts 14, 27 and 1 Kings 15, 2. 2 Sam. 6, 8 shows that עד היום הזה might be employed in unadulterated romance; and Josephus, *Antiquities*, vii, 243 f, knew " Absalom's Pillar " only from the Book of Samuel.

[3] The monkish drivel of chapter 7 is of a piece with this *midrash;* the historical document is continued in chapter 8.

Septuagintal addition, but must be the blind translation of an original במעלה confronting the translator in his Hebrew manuscript. And since במעלה, when inserted at that point is equally senseless in the Hebrew, so long, and only so long, as 6, 2 is read as the continuation of 6, 1, it is evident that the word was part of the authentic text; which, in spite of its incompatibility with the editorial framework, was preserved in the Hebrew prototype of G, but, because of that incompatibility, was dropped in the ancestor of M.

Another phrase which is lacking in the Hebrew, and which nevertheless cannot be spurious, is found in the Septuagint version of 6, 20; where the latter has καὶ εὐλόγησεν αὐτὸν καὶ εἶπεν. This represents, though not quite idiomatically, Hebrew ותברכהו ותאמר, as against the simple ותאמר of the Masoretic text, and is unquestionably authentic; cf. 2 Kings 10, 15. Apparently, some Jewish scribe, taking תברכהו too literally, decided that David might well dispense with the impious Michal's " blessing."

Inserting במעלה accordingly in 6, 2, ותברכהו in 6, 20, and נגליתי in 6, 21, we secure the original text of our narrative:[1]

2 Samuel 5, 17 — 6, 22

(5, 17) וישמעו פלשתים כי משחו את דוד למלך על ישראל. ויעלו כל פלשתים לבקש את דוד וישמע דוד וירד אל המצודה (18) ופלשתים באו וינטשו בעמק רפאים (19) וישאל דוד ביהוה לאמר האעלה אל פלשתים התתנם בידי ויאמר יהוה אל דוד עלה כי נתן אתן את הפלשתים בידך (25) ויעש דוד כאשר צוהו יהוה ויך את פלשתים מגבע עד באך גזר

(6, 2) וילך דוד וכל העם אשר אתו מבעלי יהודה במעלה להעלות משם את ארון האלהים אשר נקרא שם יהוה צבאות עליו · (3) וירכבו את ארון האלהים אל עגלה חדשה וישאהו מבית אבינדב אשר בגבעה

ועזא ואחיו בני אבינדב 'נהגים את העגלה (4) עם ארון האלהים ואחיו הלך לפני הארון (6) ויבאו עד גרן נכון וישל עזה אל ארון האלהים ויאחז בו כי שמטו הבקר (7) ויחר אף יהוה בעזה ויכהו שם האלהים על השל וימת שם עם ארון האלהים

---

[1] One trifling emendation in 6, 22, consisting of the addition of a single letter, will be mentioned in the commentary below.

(10) ולא אבה דוד להסיר אליו את ארון יהוה על עיר דוד ויטהו דוד בית עבד אדם הגתי   (11) וישב ארון יהוה בית עבד אדם הגתי שלשה חדשים ויברך יהוה את עבד אדם ואת כל ביתו

(12) ויגד למלך דוד לאמר ברך יהוה את בית עבד אדם ואת כל אשר לו בעבור ארון האלהים וילך דוד ויעל את ארון האלהים מבית עבד אדם עיר דוד בשמחה

(14) ודוד מכרכר בכל עז לפני יהוה ודוד חגור אפוד בד   (16) והיה ארון יהוה בא עיר דוד ומיכל בת שאול נשקפה בעד החלון ותרא את המלך דוד מפזז ומכרכר לפני יהוה ותבז לו בלבה

(17) ויבאו את ארון יהוה ויצגו אתו במקומו בתוך האהל אשר נטה לו דוד ויעל דוד עלות לפני יהוה   (18) ויכל דוד מהעלות ויברך את העם בשם יהוה צבאות   (19) ויחלק לכל העם לאיש חלת לחם אחת ואשפר אחד ואשישה אחת וילך כל העם איש לביתו

(20) וישב דוד לברך את ביתו ותצא מיכל בת שאול לקראת דוד ותברכהו ותאמר מה נכבד היום מלך ישראל אשר נגלה היום לעיני אמהות עבדיו כהגלות נגלות אחד הרקים   (21) ויאמר דוד אל מיכל נגליתי לפני יהוה אשר בחר בי מאביך ומכל ביתו לצות אתי נגיד על עם יהוה על ישראל   (22) ונקלתי עוד מזאת והייתי שפל בעיניך ועם האמהות אשר אמרת עמם אכברה

2 SAMUEL 5, 17 — 6, 22

(5, 17) *And the Philistines heard that they had anointed David king over Israel; and all the Philistines came up to attack David. And David heard of it and went down into the stronghold.* (18) *And the Philistines came and spread themselves in the Plain of Rephaim.* (19) *And David enquired of Yahwe, saying, Shall I go up against the Philistines? will thou give them into mine hand? And Yahwe said unto David, Go up; for I will certainly give the Philistines into thine hand.* (25) *And David did as Yahwe commanded him, and he smote the Philistines from Geba‘ to the approach of Gezer.*

(6, 2) *And David and all the troops that were with him of the men of Judah on the way back, went to bring up from thence* (that is, from Geba‘) *the sacred box which was especially dedicated to Yahwe Militant.* (3) *And they mounted the sacred box upon a new cart and conveyed it from the house of Abinadab, which was on the height* (haggib‘ah).

And Uzzah and Ahio (?), *the sons of Abinadab, were conducting the cart,* (4) *with the sacred box, Ahio* (?) *walking ahead of the box.* (6) *And they reached a rock threshing-floor. And Uzzah* (who was behind) *slipped against the sacred box and clutched at it; for the oxen had been dunging.* (7) *And the anger of Yahwe was inflamed against Uzzah, and the deity smote him there because of his slip; and he died there, by the sacred box.*

(10) *Thereupon David was unwilling to take the box of Yahwe home with him to the City of David; so David turned it aside to the house of Obed-edom the Gittite.* (11) *And the box of Yahwe remained in the house of Obed-edom the Gittite three months; and Yahwe blessed Obed-edom and all his house.*

(12) *And it was told king David, saying, Yahwe has blessed the house of Obed-edom and all that is his, on account of the sacred box. So David went and brought up the sacred box from the house of Obed-edom to the City of David with rejoicing.*

(14) *And David was dancing with all his might before Yahwe. And David was girded with a linen ephod* (apron). (16) *And as the box of Yahwe approached the City of David, Michal the daughter of Saul looked out of the window and saw king David leaping and dancing before Yahwe; and she despised him in her heart.*

(17) *And they brought the box of Yahwe and set it down in its place, inside the tent which David had spread for it. And David offered up burnt-offerings before Yahwe.* (18) *And when David had finished offering, he blessed the people with the name of Yahwe Militant.* (19) *And he distributed to all the people, to each person one roll of bread, one —— ? ——, and one fruit-cake. And all the people dispersed, each to his own house.*

(20) *And David returned to greet his household. And Michal the daughter of Saul went out to meet David; and she greeted him, and said, How honored to-day is the king of Israel, who has exposed himself to-day before the eyes of his servants' serving-women, like a common clown exhibiting his nakedness!* (21) *And David said to Michal, I have exposed myself before Yahwe, who preferred me above thy father and all his house, to appoint me ruler over the people of Yahwe, over*

Israel. (22) *And though I degrade myself even more, and become contemptible in thy sight, yet with the young women of whom thou speakest, with them I shall be held in honor.*

5, 17. המצודה is not Adullam (as Wellhausen, *Bücher Samuelis*, and others more recently), but the stronghold on the southeastern hill at Jerusalem, which David captured from the Jebusites and renamed the City of David. That he could "go down" into it on receiving news of the approach of the Philistines, is not at all strange; for we have been expressly told that he had no sooner occupied it than he began to extend the settlement *from the Millo northward* (2 Sam. 5, 9, ויבן דוד סביב מן המלוא וביתה).[1] The Millo — whatever it was — certainly lay between the מצודה on the south, and the hill later occupied by Solomon's temple on the north. It did not exist in the time of David; but it did exist for the writer of 5, 9, having been built by Solomon (1 Kings 9, 15; 11, 27),[2] and so, like the term ביתה, it served to mark the locality for the author's readers. If David was in the new town north of the Millo when he heard of the Philistine invasion, he would of course "go down" to the מצודה.

The nature as well as the exact location of the structure called המלוא — instrinsically a determinate appellative, *the Millo* κατ' ἐξοχήν — is still considered an unsolved problem of Hebrew archaeology.[3] In my judgment, however, there can be little doubt that it was *a huge causeway* or *embankment* connecting the City of David with the temple hill, *across a transverse gully which has since disappeared*. So 1 Kings 11, 27 becomes for the first time intelligible: Jeroboam did not object to the forced labor exacted from his North Israelites for the temple or the palace; but he rebelled when king Solomon, vying with nature, undertook *the building of the causeway, the closing of the gap of the City of David*, בנה את המלוא סגר את פרץ

---

[1] סביב must not be construed as a preposition with מן המלוא, but as an adverb; the phrase מן המלוא וביתה is analogous to מן היום ההוא ומעלה.

[2] In 1 Kings 9, 24 we must read אשר בנה לה אל המלוא; cf. GA. 2 Kings 12, 21b is obviously corrupt, and of doubtful authenticity.

[3] Cf., for example, Budde, *Kurzer Hand-Commentar*, on 2 Sam. 5, 9; Guthe, *Protestantische Realencyklopädie*³, VIII, p. 677; Buhl, *Geographie des alten Palästina*, p. 135; Benzinger, *Hebräische Archäologie*² p. 33.

עיר דוד.¹ The Chronicler too, though he may have known no more about the history of Hezekiah than the next man, apparently did know what the Millo was; for he is careful to tell us that Hezekiah *built* the broken wall, and *erected* the towers,² but *strengthened* the causeway at the City of David (ויחזק את המלוא עיר דוד, 2 Chron. 32, 5). He doubtless had in mind its eastern retaining-wall. The etymology of מלוא, literally *a filling*, is in perfect accord with this interpretation. For the rest, the unfilled easterly end of the original gully was still a prominent feature of the city in the days of the Chronicler, who calls it המקצוע, *the Cut*,³ and leaves us in no uncertainty as to its location (Neh. 3, 24 f; 2 Chron. 26, 9). It lay in immediate proximity to the city walls, and just south of *the angle* (הפנה) formed by the wall running north on the easterly side of the City of David, and the wall running southwest from *the great projecting tower* (המגדל הגדול היוצא) on the Ophel. Since the situation of that tower and the direction of its adjacent wall are known,⁴ the Old Testament data on the subject may be represented as in the diagram on the next page.

In this connection it should be recalled that as long ago as 1881, Guthe, conducting excavations on the southeastern promontory, found that immediately to the north of a line drawn due west from the Virgin's Fountain, the native rock lay some thirty feet lower than it did twenty yards further south, in spite of the downward slope of the present surface from north to south. He inferred that the south-

¹ Construe the preceding שלמה as appositive to המלך, and the verbs as infinitive absolute. Note the absence of the conjunction before סגר: the two phrases are synonymous.

² Read ויעל את המגדלות.

³ Cf. Arabic *maqṭaʿ*. Even in Exodus and Ezekiel מקצע is not *corner*, but *edge*. In Neh. 3, 19 המקצע, after the determinate הנשק, must be a gloss or else accusative of direction; and in either case מן המקצע of 3, 20 is interpolated.

⁴ Both tower and wall were discovered by Warren in 1868; see *Recovery of Jerusalem*, pp. 300 ff (American edition, pp. 228 f); *Survey of Western Palestine*, Jerusalem volume, pp. 228 f, and plates III, VII, XI. It should be added that העפל of the Chronicler was not the southeastern promontory, the ancient מצודת ציון (as G. A. Smith, *Jerusalem*, I, pp. 152 f), but the shoulder of the temple hill immediately to the north of the מקצוע. Josephus attaches the Aramaicized name 'Οφλᾶ(ς) to the same locality; see especially *Jewish War*, v, 145.

eastern ridge was originally separated from the temple hill by a ravine or gully, running from the Tyropoeon to the valley of the Kidron; and pointed out that unless such a depression lay along its

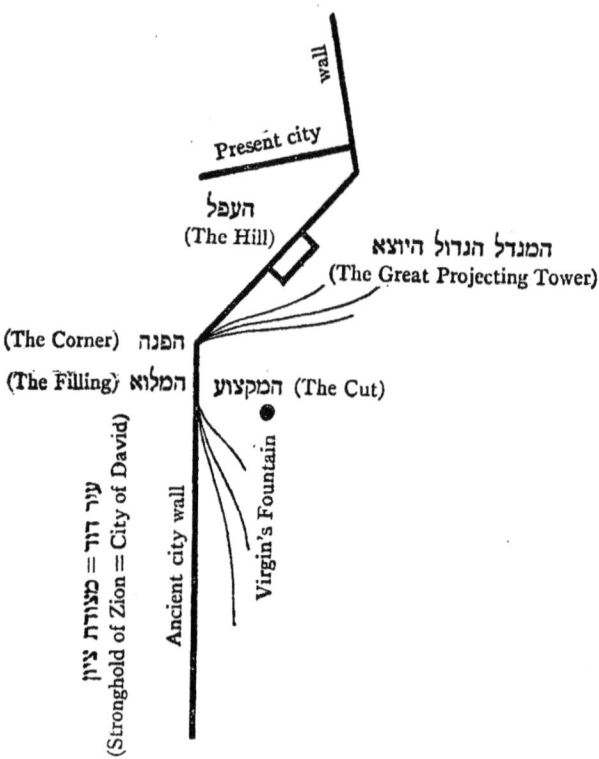

northern boundary, the City of David could hardly have been much of a stronghold.[1] Though Guthe has steadfastly adhered to his well-grounded opinion,[2] it has not been generally accepted by other archaeologists.[3] Nevertheless, if the Old Testament records are to

[1] *Zeitschrift des Deutschen Palästina-Vereins*, V, 1882, pp. 166, 317.
[2] See *Protestantische Realencyklopädie*³, VIII, pp. 668 f, 675.
[3] Cf. G. A. Smith, *l. c.*, I, pp. 139, 154. The evidence of "only two shafts" may not be so good as that of six or seven shafts; but it is infinitely better than the *a priori* opinion of any number of authorities. The view of Guthe is favored by Benzinger, *l. c.*, p. 31; and Paton, *Jerusalem in Bible Times*, p. 47. Dalman, *Palästinajahrbuch*, XI, 1915, pp. 61 f, thinks Guthe's shafts may have descended into some old pit or stone-quarry; or possibly the native rock contracts at that point into a narrow saddle connecting the promontory and the temple hill.

be believed, both " the Cut " of the Chronicler and " the Filling " of Solomon only await the spade of the excavator to prove their existence.

I may add that history actually tells us where Solomon got the notion of this bold enterprise, which cost his successors the greater part of the kingdom. Dius, a Greek writer on the history of Tyre, says of Hiram, the contemporary and friend of Solomon: οὗτος τὰ πρὸς ἀνατολὰς μέρη τῆς πόλεως προσέχωσεν καὶ μεῖζον τὸ ἄστυ ἐποίησεν καὶ τοῦ Ὀλυμπίου Διὸς τὸ ἱερὸν καθ' ἑαυτὸ ὂν ἐν νήσῳ χώσας τὸν μεταξὺ τόπον συνῆψε τῇ πόλει.

This statement of Dius is quoted, quite innocently, by Josephus (*Against Apion*, i, 113; *Antiquities*, viii, 147), who had not the least idea of what the Millo of Solomon really was, as may be seen from his paraphrase of 1 Kings 9, 15, *Antiquities*, viii, 150. Josephus was well aware that the southeast promontory was originally separated from the temple hill by a considerable ravine; but he was under the delusion that the latter remained entirely unbridged until the days of the Maccabees; see *Jewish War*, v, 138 f, where the word ἄντικρυς, be it pointed out for the benefit of the multitude of disputants on the topography of Josephus, does not mean *opposite* (καταντικρύ), but *straight in line with*. The correct interpretation of this passage disposes also of the theory of G. A. Smith, *l. c.*, I, pp. 154, 159 ff, that the southeast hill or City of David was originally higher than at present, and was shaved off under the Hasmoneans. The southeast hill was, according to Josephus, ταπεινότερος φύσει; there was no need of lowering it. The shaving was done on that part of the temple hill called העפל, which thereby ceased to exhibit a noticeable " mound ", though it retained the name; and the material was dumped into the ravine to the south of it, the Chronicler's מקצוע, which thereby ceased to exist.

5, 18. עמק רפאים is not the modern *Buqai‘a*, on the Bethlehem road, southwest of Jerusalem (as Buhl, *l. c.*, p. 91, and most writers), but the *lofty plateau* northwest of the city.

The literary data to be reckoned with in determining the question are fewer than at first sight appears. Jerome's " vallis Allofylorum ad septemtrionalem plagam Ierusalem," *Onomasticon*, 147, merely reproduces the statement of Eusebius, κοιλὰς Ἀλλοφύλων κατὰ βορρᾶν Ἱερουσαλήμ, *Onomasticon*, 288; which latter in turn is without value, the reference to the Philistines showing that the definition is based entirely upon inference from the allusions in the Old Testament. Equally valueless, on the other side, is the supposed identification of Josephus, *Antiquities*, vii, 312; where, in paraphrasing the legend of 2 Sam. 23, 13–17, he harmonizes verses 13b and 14b as follows: τῆς δὲ τῶν ἐχθρῶν παρεμβολῆς ἐν τῇ κοιλάδι κειμένης, ἣ μέχρι Βηθλεέμης πόλεως διατείνει σταδίους Ἱεροσολύμων ἀπεχούσης εἴκοσιν. The story of the three heroes, as Josephus interpreted its conflicting statements, demanded that the plain in which the Philistines were encamped, and which the heroes should break through, be located between Jerusalem (ἐν Ἱεροσολύμοις ὄντος τοῦ βασιλέως) and the well at Bethlehem; so perforce he identifies it with the plain southwest of Jerusalem. But it is noticeable that in this passage, when locating the plain, he avoids the name κοιλὰς τῶν Γιγάντων, which he had given in vii, 71 (paraphrasing 2 Sam. 5, 18), and had described, in the absence of any guidance from the text, with becoming vagueness as τόπος οὐ πόρρω τῆς πόλεως. It is evident that he knew of no locality bearing such a name in his own day; and that the identification of vii, 312, was suggested to him for the first time when he reached the story of 2 Sam. 23.

In the Old Testament, besides 2 Sam. 5, 18 22, the Plain of Rephaim is mentioned in 2 Sam. 23, 13; 1 Chron. 11, 15; 14, 9 13 (בעמק); Isa. 17, 5; Josh. 15, 8; 18, 16. But 2 Sam. 5, 22, we have already seen, was copied from verse 18. The references in 1 Chron. 11, 15; 14, 9 13 are of course merely reproductions of 2 Sam. 23, 13; 5, 18 22 respectively. And 2 Sam. 23, 13b–14a, which disturbs the context and confuses the otherwise perfectly coherent story of verses 13–17, is in turn unquestionably the interpolation of some muddled scribe drawing upon 2 Sam. 5, 17b–18. On the other hand, Isa. 17, 5b, והיה כמלקט שבלים בעמק רפאים, though an independent allusion (whether authentic or not), yields no evidence either way; since ears of corn were doubtless gathered in ancient times, as at present, both north and south of Jerusalem. The passages upon which we must rely are therefore Josh. 15, 8; 18, 16; and 2 Sam. 5, 18.

The references in Joshua distinctly locate the plain northwest of the city. In 15, 8 the author is describing the northern boundary of the territory of Judah. He has traced the line from the mouth of the Jordan westward, up to Debir and across to En-shemesh, emerging at En-rogel, southeast of Jerusalem. Thence, he tells us, the boundary ascended up the Valley of Hinnom to the southern shoulder of the Jebusite (the southwest hill of Jerusalem); whence *the border ascended to the head of the ridge which faces the Valley of Hinnom on the west, situated at the northern end of the Plain of Rephaim*: ועלה הגבול אל ראש ההר אשר על פני גי הנם ימה אשר בקצה עמק רפאים צפונה. The usual interpretation of the clause I have overscored, which understands it to mean that the southern end of the ridge bordered upon the northern edge of the Plain of Rephaim, (1) misconceives the import of the word ראש; which is not the *top* of the ridge to one crossing it at right angles, but the *upper end* to one ascending it longitudinally. (2) It misconstrues the final relative clause; which attaches, not to ההר — the first relative attaches to that — but to ראש (determined by the genitive ההר); to assume any other construction, is to attribute to the author a slovenliness of composition at this point for which his usual style affords no warrant. And (3) it overlooks the fact that the Valley of Hinnom is mentioned in order to identify the ridge — which is not the only ridge north of the plateau — and does identify it beyond the possibility of question; whereas the mention of the *Buqai'a* could serve no such purpose, for a reader who was presumably a resident of Jerusalem. For the rest, the southern end of the ridge, where it merges with the *Buqai'a*, falls well within the territory of Judah, and is therefore utterly irrelevant to the author's business; whereas the northern end is a point on the boundary, from which he continues his description in the following verse: ותאר הגבול מראש ההר אל מעין מי נפתוח, *And from the head of the ridge the border turned to the spring of Mê-neftôḥ* (the present *Lifta*, in the *Wâdi Bêt Ḥanîna*, beyond the watershed). All of which is strikingly confirmed by the language of Josh. 18, 16; where the same author, describing the southern boundary of the tribe of Benjamin, and following the same line in the reverse direction, comes *first* to the *northern end* of the same ridge (not ראש ההר this time, as in 15, 8, but actually קצה ההר), and *then* descends southward through the Valley of Hinnom to the southwest hill of Jerusalem, and on down to En-rogel: וירד ני הנם אל כתף היבוסי ננבה וירד עין רגל.[1] The " head " or " end " of the ridge will be the point, about a mile and a half north of the present city wall, where this section of the main watershed turns off to the southwest, and lifts itself above the plateau stretching away to the southeast.

The same location for the Plain of Rephaim is demanded by 2 Sam. 5, 18. I do not press the use of the verb עלה in verse 19, although it is most naturally understood as purporting the reverse of ירד in verse 17; since the *Buqai'a*, as well as the northwest plateau, is higher than the southeast promontory. But (1) the pursuit of the Philistines after the battle *from Geba' to the approach of Gezer*, demands a location north of the city for the Plain of Rephaim, where they had spread their camp and were attacked by David. And (2) Kirjath-jearim, where David stopped on his way back to secure the box of Yahwe, certainly lay northwest of Jerusalem.

5, 25. גבע, quasi proper name for the גבעה or *eminence* belonging to the town of Kirjath-jearim; cf. 6, 3 and 1 Sam. 7, 1. So in 1 Sam. 14, 2 5 16, גבעת בנימין (proper name) = הגבעה (determinate appellative) = גבע (quasi proper name). The גבעה of Kirjath-jearim was evidently a familiar feature of the highway leading from Jerusalem to the Philistine lowlands and the sea, so that there was no need of defining it more exactly in this context; just as, at the present day, a certain station on the carriage road to Jaffa is spoken of as *Bâb el Wâd* instead of *Bâb Wâdi 'Ali*. The Philistines, we may be sure, retreated the same way they came; and they of course came by the commonly travelled road. But at no time in history did a road from the maritime plain to Jerusalem lead up the *Wâdi Isma'în*;[2] and not until after the Muhammedan conquest and the rise of Ramleh did such a road lead up the *Wâdi 'Ali*.[3] If only for

---

[1] In verse 16a, for וירד of the Masoretic text read ותאר, as in 15, 9 (cf. Holzinger, *Kurzer Hand-Commentar zum Alten Testament, ad loc.*), and for בעמק רפאים read בקצה עמק רפאים with G.

[2] Cf. G. A. Smith, *Jerusalem*, I, p. 9 f.

[3] See below.

this reason, therefore, Kirjath-jearim was neither *Khirbet 'Erma*[1] nor *Qaryet el 'Enab*.[2]

On the site of Kirjath-jearim, and the related question of the identity of the road upon which it lay, there has been much darkening of counsel from the earliest times. The confusion began with the interpolation of 2 Sam. 6, 1; which caused the Chronicler — and our modern critics as well — to misinterpret בעלי יהודה of verse 2 as a local proper name synonymous with קרית יערים (1 Chron. 13, 6). The same misinterpretation of this important narrative led to a series of scribal interpolations in the Book of Joshua; where the Judahite town of קרית בעל or בעלה has been systematically and erroneously identified with the Benjamite town of קרית יערים. The true state of the case is best exhibited in tabular form.[3]

Josh. 15, 9	בעלה (היא קרית יערים)
15, 10	בעלה
15, 60	קרית בעל (היא קרית יערים)
18, 14	קרית בעל (היא קרית יערים) עיר בני יהודה
18, 15	[M substitutes קרית יערים] G correctly: קרית בעל

The last passage, where the distinguishing בעל has actually been struck out in the Masoretic text and יערים substituted, shows conclusively — what indeed hardly needs showing, since the author would have said קרית יערים in the first place had he meant it — that the identification with קרית יערים is in every case the work of a glossator. *Per contra*, the glossator having identified קרית יערים with קרית בעל or בעלה, which the text of Josh. 18, 14 explicitly, and that of 2 Sam. 6, 2 ostensibly, declared to belong to Judah, it became necessary to mutilate the text of Josh. 18, 28; where the author — consistently enough, as we shall see — had enumerated קרית יערים among the cities of Benjamin. The result was, that in this latter passage two construct nouns were left hanging in the air, and

---

[1] Conder, *Survey of Western Palestine*, III, pp. 43 ff.
[2] Robinson, *Biblical Researches*, II, pp. 334 ff.
[3] The table includes every mention of this town in the Old Testament. In Josh. 15, 11, בעלה is another place of the same name west of Ekron; and in Josh. 15, 29, still another in the Negeb.

the sum total of cities enumerated was raised from thirteen to fourteen. A comparison of the Septuagint shows that the text originally read, ערים שלש עשרה : ‎וגבעת קרית יערים. Nor, in view of all these facts, can we doubt that ביהודה of Judges 18, 12 is likewise a gloss, of a piece with the topographical information (?) which follows it.

Both the Chronicler and the glossator of Joshua 15 and 18 were of course perfectly familiar with the whereabouts of Kirjath-jearim, though 2 Sam. 6, 2 may have upset them on the question of its supposed tribal affiliation in early times.[1] What they seem not to have known, was a town actually bearing the name קרית בעל or בעלה in their own day. Possibly the בעל had already been dropped and the name reduced to הקריה or קריתא. However that may be, the Kirjath-baal of the author of Joshua 15 and 18 was a Judahite city (18, 14), situated on the northern boundary of Judah (15, 9 f), and marking the southwest angle of the territory accredited to Benjamin (18, 14 f). For all we know, therefore, it may well have been identical with the modern *el Qaryeh* or *Qaryet el 'Enab*, otherwise known as *Abu Ghôsh*.

Kirjath-jearim, on the other hand, lay well within the territory assigned to Benjamin by the author of Joshua 15 and 18, and may be located with mathematical certitude some three miles northeast of *Qaryet el 'Enab*. For according to Eusebius it was still in existence under that name in the fourth century A.D., and was situated nine Roman miles from Aelia (Jerusalem) on the highway to Diospolis

[1] As a matter of fact, Kirjath-jearim was inhabited neither by Benjamites nor by Judahites, but by Gibeonites, who had been received into the Israelitish confederation and had adopted the worship of Yahwe; Josh. 9, 17; 1 Sam. 6, 21; 7, 1; 2 Sam. 21, 2 6. The only one of the four cities mentioned in Josh. 9, 17 from which the Gibeonites had been expelled was Beeroth (2 Sam. 4, 2b-3), and that presumably by Saul (cf. 2 Sam. 21, 1-5) in connection with the occupation of גבעת שאול — a new name, like עיר דוד, signalizing the seizure of an old place. (Philologically, there is no more reason for rendering גבעת שאול *Gibeah of Saul* than there is for rendering עיר דוד '*Ir of David*.) For the rest, Beeroth was certainly not the present *Bireh*, east of Ramallah, but a settlement πλησίον Αἰλίας κατιόντων ἐπὶ Νεάπολιν [so, with Jerome] ἀπὸ ζ´ σημείων (Eusebius, *Onomasticon*, 233, 83); that is, it must be sought on the *Nâblus* road, but some three or four miles south of *Bireh*, and east of *el Jib*. In the description of Gibeon itself, *Onomasticon*, 243, 6 ff, we probably should read: πλησίον Βηρὼθ πρὸς δυσμάς, ὡς ἀπὸ σημείων δ´. Similarly in that of Rama, 287, 1 f: ἀπέναντι Βηρώθ.

(Lydda).¹ Beyond the shadow of a doubt, therefore, it must be identified with the modern village of *el Qubêbeh*, which lies on the Roman road to Lydda, at the exact distance from Jerusalem indicated by Eusebius.²

This identification would have been adopted universally long ago, but for the persistent and quite inexcusable misplacing of the Roman road leading from Aelia to Diospolis referred to by Eusebius.³ The method which has been employed of late for the identification of this road, is exhibited with engaging naïveté by P. Thomsen, in his elaborate article on *Palästina nach dem Onomasticon des Eusebius*.⁴ "Nach Westen," he writes, "kommt vor allem die Strasse nach Διοσπολις in Betracht. Allein welche heute noch existierende Strasse Eusebius meint, lässt sich schwer feststellen. Zunächst [why?] denkt man an die heutige *jāfā*-Strasse. Dafür spricht, dass nach Eusebius am Wege nach Διοσπολις and zwar 9 oder 10 Meilen von Jerusalem entfernt Καριαθιαρειμ lag, das man gewöhnlich in *ḳarjet el-'ineb* gesucht hat." ⁵ That is, Kirjath-jearim having been located at *Qaryet el 'Eneb* because the present Jaffa road is assumed to be the road in question, the present Jaffa road is the road in question because Kirjath-jearim has been located at *Qaryet el 'Enab*. To be sure, Thomsen goes on to mention some of the difficulties in the way of that view; but he concludes, all the same, by inserting the present Jaffa road in his "map of Palestine according to the

¹ *Onomasticon*, 271, 40 ff. Elsewhere (234, 96) Eusebius gives the distance more roughly as "about ten miles." His more precise expression must of course be preferred. The very divergence, however, shows that he was speaking of his own knowledge, and not copying from a manuscript itinerary. A life-long resident of Caesarea, he had doubtless often passed that way.

² That the site is ancient, is universally recognized. On the other hand, the name *el Qubêbeh*, literally, "the little dome," is pure Arabic, and therefore not ancient. It is very fair Arabic for הגבעה, however.

The Latin tradition which for some centuries has identified this site with the Emmaus of Luke 24, 13 — it lies at *about* the specified distance of 60 stadia from Jerusalem on the road once regularly travelled by the pilgrims — bids fair, as the result of the heated controversies of the last twenty-five years, to become a dogma; but it will never become a fact. If the Evangelist had not in mind the present *'Amwâs*, as Eusebius and Jerome imagined, he had in mind another place bearing the name Ἐμμαοὺς; and *el Qubêbeh* was demonstrably not such a place, down to the days of Eusebius at any rate.

³ The road is mentioned, *Onomasticon*, 211, 93; 234, 95; 271, 42.

⁴ *Zeitschrift des Deutschen Palästina-Vereins*, XXVI, 1903, pp. 97–188.

⁵ *L. c.*, pp. 180 f.

Onomasticon of Eusebius."[1] Buhl, in his article on "Roads and Travel" in Hastings' *Dictionary of the Bible*,[2] affirms flatly, "The present road from Jerusalem to Jaffa or Lydda is first mentioned a few times by Eusebius."[3] It would be nearer the truth to say that the present road from Jerusalem to Jaffa is first mentioned unmistakably by Nâsir-i-Khusrau, who relates how in 1047 A.D., that is, some three centuries after the founding of Ramleh, he travelled from the latter city to Jerusalem past *Lâṭrûn* and *Qaryet el 'Enab*.[4] Not only does Eusebius make no mention whatever of the present Jaffa road, but both he and Jerome furnish affirmative evidence that no such road existed in their day. For according to Jerome's Onomasticon (89, 29), to go from Nicopolis (*'Amwâs*) to Jerusalem one travelled northeast past Ajalon (*Yâlo*).[5] And Eusebius would certainly not have contented himself with defining Beth-horon as " 12 miles from Jerusalem, toward the (cross) road to Nicopolis" (233, 71), if there had been a road running straight from Jerusalem to a point on the south of that same Nicopolis and only one mile distant.[6] The fact is, the Jaffa road is not an ancient road.[7] Nor,

[1] In a later publication, *Loca Sancta*, 1907, p. 78, Thomsen remarks briefly, "Die Angabe des Eusebius [concerning Kirjath-jearim] führt vielleicht auf *bēt 'anān*."

[2] Extra volume, p. 371a.

[3] The same error characterizes the labored and in large part irrelevant argument of Lauffs, "Zur Lage und Geschichte des Ortes Kirjath Jearim," *Zeitschrift des Deutschen Palästina-Vereins*, XXXVIII, 1915, pp. 249–302.

[4] *Palestine Pilgrim Texts*, IV, No. 9, p. 22. The distances given by Ibn Khordâdbeh in the ninth century A.D. — 18 miles between Ramleh and Jerusalem, and 8 miles between Ramleh and Jaffa (De Goeje, *Bibliotheca geographorum arabicorum*, VI, pp. 78 f) — are inconclusive; though it is probable that the new route had been established by that time. Ramleh was founded by the Omayyad Khalif Sulêmân, while he was still governor of the province of *Filasṭîn*, at the beginning of the eighth century; and by the middle of the tenth century it had grown to be the largest city in the province, not excepting Jerusalem; cf. Le Strange, *Palestine under the Moslems*, pp. 28, 303 ff.

[5] The testimony of Jerome's "Hebraei" as to the whereabouts of Ajalon, and the way by which one travelled from Nicopolis to Jerusalem, is quite as good as that of Eusebius, *pace* Thomsen, *l. c.*, p. 181.

[6] Nor can the 22 miles which the Bordeaux Pilgrim gives as the distance between Jerusalem and Nicopolis (*Corpus scriptorum ecclesiasticorum latinorum*, XXXVIIII, p. 25) be squeezed into the Jaffa road; although his data should perhaps not be taken too seriously.

[7] Cf. *Survey of Western Palestine Memoirs*, III, p. 56. The very existence of the old Roman road which curves from *Qaryet el 'Enab* to *Yâlo* is enough to show that no

II SAMUEL 6

with Ramleh off the map, would any one think of reaching Lydda by the roundabout route of *Qaryet el 'Enab* and the *Wâdi 'Ali*.

If now the reader will take a map of Palestine and draw a straight line from Jerusalem to Lydda, he will find that line practically coinciding with an ancient road which runs with remarkable directness from the Damascus Gate to Lydda, past *Bêt Iksa, Biddu, el Qubêbeh, Bêt 'Anân, Bêt Liqyeh, Berfilyeh,* and *Jimzu*; and which bears distinct evidence of Roman construction. A Roman mile-stone has actually been found by the road side about half a mile east of *el Qubêbeh.* All of which is plainly indicated on the *Large Map* of the Palestine Exploration Fund, sheets XIII, XIV, XVII. There can be no manner of doubt that this is the Aelia-Diospolis road to which Eusebius refers. And if so, not *Qaryet el 'Enab* but *el Qubêbeh* is " the long-lost city Kirjath-jearim."[1] This location fits perfectly all the Old Testament references which must be reckoned with, namely, Josh. 9, 17; 18, 28; Judges 18, 12; 1 Sam. 6, 21; 7, 1; 2 Sam. 5, 25; 6, 3; Jer. 26, 20.

Bêt 'Anân is obviously the place which Eusebius identified with the Αἰνάν of the Septuagint text of Gen. 38, 14 21. His words are worth quoting, for no better confirmation of our conclusion could be desired:. ἔρημος νῦν τόπος ἐστὶν ἡ Αἰνάν, παρακείμενος τῇ Θαμνὰ εἰς δεῦρο οἰκουμένῃ μεγίστῃ κώμῃ, κειμένῃ μεταξὺ Αἰλίας καὶ Διοσπόλεως. πηγὴ δὲ ἔστιν ἐν τῷ Αἰνὰν λεγομένῳ τόπῳ, παρ' ἣν εἴδωλον ἦν παρὰ τῶν ἐγχωρίων τιμώμενον (*l. c.*, 211, 91 ff). With this compare the following description of *Bêt 'Anân* in the *S. W. P. Memoirs*, III, p. 16: " A small village on the top of a flat ridge; near a main road to the west are remains of a Khân with water, and about a mile to the east is a spring." In the middle of the last century Guérin found *Bêt 'Anân* a village of 600 inhabitants; *Judée*, I, p. 348. With the question of Eusebius' identifications we are not here concerned; although עינים in Gen. 38, 14 — without the article and followed by אשר — is necessarily a proper name, and, if derived from עין *spring*, is necessarily dual; which in Aramaic, how-

Roman road ran thence through the *Wâdi 'Ali* to *'Amwâs*. On the Roman mile-stone reported found near *'Ên ed-Dilbeh*, southeast of *Qaryet el 'Enab* (Benzinger, *Mittheilungen und Nachrichten des D. P. V.*, 1905, pp. 26 f) see Vincent, *Revue Biblique*, 1905, pp. 97 f; who shows that the stone had been moved a considerable distance at least once, and probably oftener.

[1] Cf. Guthe, *Zeitschrift des Deutschen Palästina-Vereins*, XXXVI, 1913, pp. 81 ff. It may perhaps be of interest to note that the above discussion was written before Guthe's article came to my notice.

ever, becomes עַיִן = Αλυάν. Nor yet are we concerned with the bearing of this testimony on the location of the Θάμνα of Josephus, *Antiquities*, xiv, 275; *Jewish War*, iii, 55; iv, 444; although Eusebius clearly takes it for granted that his readers will be familiar with the history of this important site; while the Madaba Mosaic shows the same Θάμνα between Jerusalem and Diospolis, and *south* of Beth-horon. It is enough for us that the name Αλυάν still clings to the locality he described, to render unmistakable his "road from Aelia to Diospolis."

-5, 25. עד באך גזר, *until you approach Gezer*; a vague expression, denoting little more than the final direction of a long pursuit beyond Kirjath-jearim; by no means the equivalent of *as far as Gezer* (as H. P. Smith and Nowack, *ad loc.*). Had he intended *as far af Gezer* (1 Chron. 14, 16) the author would have written ועד גזר, if not indeed ועד שערי גזר; cf. 1 Sam. 17, 52.[1] He does imply, however, that David pursued the Philistines far into the Plain of Ajalon[2]; which we may reasonably assume was reached from Kirjath-jearim (*el Qubêbeh*) by the same route that was followed in later times by the Roman road — by way of the ridge past *Bêt 'Anân* and *Bêt Liqyeh*, and down the *Wâdi Selmân*, rather than by way of the *Wâdi el Quṭneh*, past *Bêt Nûba* and *Yâlo*. The indefinite phrase עד באך גזר, it should be noted, cannot possibly furnish the antecedent for the definite משם of 6, 2.

6, 2. בעלי יהודה, *the fighting men of Judah*; cf. בעלי יריחו, Josh. 24, 11; בעלי שכם, Judges 9, 2 ff; בעלי מגדל שכם, Judges 9, 46 f (contrast with the expression אנשי מגדל שכם of verse 49, where women are included); בעלי קעילה, 1 Sam. 23, 11 f; בעלי הפרשים,

---

[1] Needless to say, I cite this story only for the Hebrew idiom. Compare further Gen. 10, 19, where באך and the simple עד are actually used in contrasted senses: באכה גררה עד עזה, *in the direction of Gerar* (= *southwestward*), *as far as Gaza*. The language of this passage is misinterpreted by both Gunkel, *Handkommentar zum Alten Testament*[3], p. 91, and Holzinger, *Kurzer Hand-Commentar*, p. 103. Skinner fails to realize the author's geographical and literary problem, when he asserts, "The rendering '*in the direction of* Gerar, as far as Gaza' would only be intelligible if Gerar were a better known locality than Gaza"; *Commentary on Genesis*, p. 217. It is not a question of which locality was better known. Both were well enough known. Granted, however, that the author desired to indicate the extension of Canaanitish territory, first to the southwest, and then to the southeast, he could hardly begin by saying, "in the direction of Gaza, as far as Gaza." And how else was he to express himself?

[2] Cf. G. A. Smith, *Historical Geography of the Holy Land*[3], pp. 209 ff.

the cavalry-men,[1] 2 Sam. 1, 6. David apparently did not attempt to engage all the forces of the Philistines (כל פלשתים, 5, 17) with the small number of men constituting the garrison of Jerusalem, or even with such an army as he could muster from the tribe of Judah alone, but summoned to his assistance the North Israelites as well. Perhaps he owed his decisive victory to a well-laid plan, in accordance with which the Israelites fell upon the camp of the Philistines from the north, at the same time that he and the men of Judah attacked from the south. In any case, naturally only that part of the army made up of men of Judah (העם אשר אתו מבעלי יהודה) would be returning with him toward Jerusalem and the south country after the battle.

במעלה, testified to by ἐν ἀναβάσει of the Septuagint, must of course be pointed with the article; and in this context *on the ascent* is equivalent to *on the return*, the march from the Plain of Ajalon to the highlands of Judea at *el Qubêbeh* involving a climb of some seventeen hundred feet.

ארון האלהים אשר נקרא שם יהוה צבאות עליו. On the excision of the second שם and ישב הכרבים of the Masoretic text, see pages 37 ff and 41 above. After what has been said on the meaning of the compound appellative ארון אלהים, it is unnecessary to labor the point that the expression ארון האלהים in this passage is a consciously determined appellative, with the article pointing to the identifying relative clause which follows: *that particular sacred box which*, etc. The construction is exactly the same as in כל הגוים אשר נקרא שמי עליהם, Amos 9, 12; בבית אשר, Jer. 25, 29; בעיר אשר נקרא שמי עליה, נקרא שמי עליו, Jer. 7, 30; 32, 34; 34, 15. And whatever may be the precise meaning of this relative clause, its mere presence in this connection proves that the author thinks of the sacred box (ארון אלהים) as a plural institution. The point of the clause is of course the name יהוה צבאות: every Israelitish sacred box was a box אשר נקרא שם יהוה עליו; the peculiarity of this box, which serves to identify and distinguish it, is that it was *the box* אשר נקרא שם יהוה צבאות עליו.

---

[1] See *Journal of Biblical Literature*, XXIV, 1905, p. 52.

On the question of the intrinsic meaning of the relative clause the Old Testament usage is sufficiently clear — more so than Kautzsch's labored and much-quoted mystification, " obige Formel bedeutet, dass die nach einem bestimmten Namen benannte Person oder Sache zu dem Träger des Namens in einem Verhältniss der Unterordnung und Zugehörigkeit steht " [1]; which with all its vagueness is not quite correct. If anybody in the world, a man's own son stands to him "in einem Verhältniss der Unterordnung und Zugehörigkeit"; yet a son was the one person in the world of whom this formula could never be employed. The fact is, Kautzsch's definition applies better to the formula נקרא בשם פ׳ (in which נקרא is a participle; Isa. 43, 7; 48, 1; cf. Gen. 48, 16) than to נקרא שם פ׳ עליו. For this last does not describe a state, as Kautzsch implies, but an occurrence; הבית אשר נקרא שם יהוה עליו, for example, is not *the house which is* (habitually) *called after Yahwe*, but rather *the house over which the name of Yahwe was* (once upon a time) *proclaimed* — that is, *the house which was dedicated, consecrated*, or *devoted to Yahwe*. So the formula is employed *of a sanctuary* dedicated to the deity, 1 Kings 8, 43 (= 2 Chron. 6, 33); Jer. 7, 10 11 14 30; 32, 34; 34, 15; *of a city,* Jer. 25, 29; Dan. 9, 18 f; *of a person*, Jer. 15, 16; and *of a people,* Deut. 28, 10 (cf. the language of verse 9); Isa. 63, 19; Jer. 14, 9; Amos, 9, 12; 2 Chron. 7, 14; Dan. 9, 19.[2] Nor is the connotation essentially different when the name is that of a human being, though our own idiom may require a different rendering. In 2 Sam. 12, 28, ונקרא שמי עליה refers perhaps to a custom of crying the name of the commander when carrying a place by assault (cf. ליהוה ולגדעון, Judges 7, 18 20); which, however, might entail the *re-naming* of the captured stronghold if it was permanently occupied, as in the case of גבעת שאול,[3] and עיר דוד. Even Isa. 4, 1, רק יקרא שמך עלינו, has in view the act of taking in marriage rather than the married state.

---

[1] *Zeitschrift für die alttestamentliche Wissenschaft*, VI, 1886, p. 18.

[2] In the case of a sanctuary or a person the sense is literal; in the other cases it will be figurative.

[3] See page 54, note.

II SAMUEL 6

Accordingly, אשר נקרא שם יהוה צבאות עליו in our passage is literally, *over which the name of Yahwe Militant had been cried*, and this is idiomatic Hebrew for *which was dedicated to Yahwe Militant*. Just what the ceremony of dedication consisted in, besides the crying of the divine name in the presence of the object dedicated, we cannot say. But of this we may be sure: whatever form of name had been employed in dedicating a sacred box, the same was subsequently employed when invoking the divine oracles through the instrumentality of that box. In the case of this box, then, not יהוה אלהי ישראל, as in 1 Sam. 14, 41 (G); 23, 10, but יהוה צבאות or יהוה צבאות אלהי ישראל; cf. verse 18 of our chapter.

6, 3. עגלה חדשה. Not necessarily one that had never been used, as in 1 Sam. 6, 7; although even that might be had in so important a place as Kirjath-jearim. חדש may signify no more than *in perfect condition*, relatively *new*; cf. Josh. 9, 13; Judges 15, 13; 2 Sam. 21, 16 (*sc.* שריה?); 1 Kings 11, 29 f. The cart was employed, not because of the weight or size of the sacred box,[1] but merely for processional purposes. Later on, when David comes to fetch the box from the house of Obed-edom, as well as in 1 Sam. 4, 4, there is no mention of a cart. Perhaps the fate of Uzzah recommended a return to "the good old way."

בית אבינדב אשר בגבעה. The sanctuary of Kirjath-jearim may have been an open-air high place, and the house of Abinadab the nearest dwelling. The family of Abinadab was presumably of Gibeonitish origin; cf. Josh. 9, 17.

אחיו. Wellhausen, following G, construes this word as an appellative, אָחִיו, *his brother*; and we must admit that it hardly looks like an old Hebrew proper name.[2] But the context in both verses

---

[1] The dimensions of P's imaginary box of Yahwe (Ex. 25, 10; 37, 1) have no relation to the subject; cf. Holzinger, *Exodus*, pp. 123 f.

[2] In 1 Chron. 8, 31; 9, 37 it may be borrowed from our passage. אַחְיוֹ cannot be "another form of אחיהו" (as H. P. Smith, Nowack, Budde, and Driver[2]). אחיהו could yield אחיה and even אחי, but not אחיו; for at the end of a name the element 'yahu never became yô, and in the Old Testament at least, it is never even spelled יו (= yau); cf. Jastrow, *Journal of Biblical Literature*, XIII, 1894, p. 101; Nöldeke, *Encyclopaedia Biblica*, col. 3279. The name אִישִׁיוֹ, cited as a parallel by Nowack, Budde, and Driver, does not exist. In 1 Sam. 14, 49 Ιεσσιουλ of G^B, which represents

3 and 4 demands a proper name. If, therefore, אחיו is not a proper name, *it has been substituted for one.* In which event it not improbably conceals the Gibeonitish origin of Zadok; who appears at the court of David for the first time after this episode, and whose ancestry is never disclosed. Besides — since we are already speculating — under what influence *did* the youthful Solomon make a pilgrimage to the chief sanctuary of the Gibeonites soon after his accession? And what priest was responsible for the oracle of 2 Sam. 21, 1? Abiathar the son of Ahimelech had reason to remember a far greater sacrilege than the slaughter of the Gibeonites. And just what is the author of Josh. 9, 22–27 concerned to refute?

6, 4. עם ארון האלהים = *in attendance upon,* or *in charge of, the sacred box.* The clause relates to the sons of Abinadab, not to the cart; cf. verse 7 and 1 Sam. 4, 4.

6, 6. נכון is of course not a proper name; which could serve no purpose here. Neither the author nor his readers would be familiar with the name of the owner of every threshing-floor between Kirjath-jearim and Jerusalem. Obviously the adjective, like the substantive נרן itself, has some bearing on the misadventure about to be narrated. I have taken נכון to signify in this connection, *firm, hard, permanent,* that is, a threshing-floor of bare rock, as distinguished from one made of levelled and hardened earth.[1] It is possible, to be sure, that the author intends נכון in the alternative sense of *prepared,* that is, smoothed and swept, and made ready for the season's threshing. In the latter case, the description would fix the season of the year as late in June or early in July. For the rest, the phrase ויבאו עד seems to imply that the procession had not travelled very far when the accident happened. Nor was a threshing-floor likely to lie across the path when once the highway had been gained.

the Hebrew letters ישיעל, points to אשבעל as the original of the corrupt ישוי of the Masoretic text, but furnishes no evidence of an intermediary אשיו (as Wellhausen). It should be added, however, that a name אחיו occurs several times in the Elephantine papyri.

[1] "The threshing-floor is usually a smooth plot of ground near the village, beaten hard. Very often a natural rock floor may be utilized." Elihu Grant, *The Peasantry of Palestine*, p. 136.

וישלח(ח). עזה אל ארון האלהים ויאחז בו. The reading וישלח of the Masoretic text — *and Uzzah sent to the sacred box* — is impossible. On the other hand, the Chronicler's וישלח עזא את ידו לאחז את הארון (1 Chron. 13, 9) is plainly not a transcription, but an interpretation and paraphrase of the text of Samuel. If his manuscript really exhibited את ידו, as is assumed by all modern critics, there was no reason in the world why he should not transcribe את וישלח עזה את ידו אל הארון ויאחז בו. The paraphrase only indicates that the text of his source seemed difficult; which of course cannot be affirmed of the Hebrew just quoted. Nor, if את ידו had ever stood in the text of Samuel, is it conceivable that it should have permanently dropped out. The testimony of the Septuagint points to the same conclusion. The repeated addition of κατασχεῖν αὐτήν betrays the fact that there too we are dealing with the labored elucidation of an enigmatical text. For these reasons we must conclude that both the Chronicler and the Septuagint translator read our text as we have it — and misinterpreted accordingly. The clause כי שמטו הבקר, however, leaves no doubt that, not את ידו has been omitted from the authentic text, but ח has been added to the author's וישל. Moreover, whatever it was that Uzzah did in verse 6, that he was punished for in verse 7; and השל of verse 7 has no ח. The reading וַיִּשַּׁל (imperfect of נשל, *to slip*; cf. Deut. 19, 5 [1]) at once makes the whole passage intelligible.

שמטו, literally *dropped* (transitive), euphemism for *dunged*. שמט is never instransitive; and nowhere has it the meaning *stumble, slip, fall, be mired, be refractory, run away, shake, tilt, knock over,* or anything else that has been conjectured by interpreters ancient and modern to meet the supposed demands of this passage. It invariably means *to drop* something, either physically, as here (= 1 Chron. 13, 9); 2 Kings 9, 33; Ps. 141, 6 [2]; or figuratively, in the sense of *to relinquish* a claim, as in Ex. 23, 11; Deut. 15, 2 f; Jer. 17, 4.

---

[1] In Deut. 19, 5 ונשל הברזל מן העץ does not mean *the axe-head slips from the helve,* but *the axe glances from the tree;* הברזל and העץ have the same meaning as in the preceding clause.

[2] The text of this psalm is disordered; but נשמטו בידי סלע evidently charges that certain persons *have been hurled from a cliff;* cf. verse 7.

6, 7. ויכהו שם האלהים. The verdict of the bystanders, accepted by the tradition, and transmitted by the author in good faith. In point of historical fact, the unfortunate man doubtless cracked his skull on the bare rock of the threshing-floor in falling. האלהים is not a " change of the divine name " (H. P. Smith), nor is there any reason for omitting it (as Nowack and Budde). It is a determinate appellative referring to יהוה. The style would be exactly paralleled by ויחר אף דוד בעזה ויכהו שם המלך; cf. 2 Sam. 9, 2; 20, 3. It is true that the renewed mention of the subject at this point strikes us as superfluous; but it is thoroughly characteristic of the author's style, cf. 5, 17a 18a 19a 25a; 6, 2a 10b 11b 12b 14a 14b 18a 21a.

שׁל, *slip*, noun, apparently of the form *qtal* from the root נשׁל. Cf. the infinitive שׁל in Ruth 2, 16; where we perhaps should point שַׁל תִּשְׁלוּ, and in any case must interpret, *be sure to let slip*. There is no Hebrew verb שׁלל *to draw out* (as Brown-Driver-Briggs, following Gesenius, *Thesaurus*), nor if there were, would it give a satisfactory sense in that passage. At best we might assume a root שׁלל cognate to, and not clearly differentiated from, נשׁל; but the form שׁל for the infinitive absolute would remain anomalous; cf. Gesenius-Kautzsch § 67 o. Of the meaning of the word שׁל in our passage, whatever its proximate derivation, there can be no doubt whatever.[1]

6, 10. להסיר אליו, *amener chez lui*, rather than *faire pénétrer chez lui* (Dhorme).

6, 14. אפוד. Compare pages 7 f above.

6, 16. והיה ארון יהוה בא. We must not alter the initial והיה to the usual introductory ויהי, with the Chronicler and all recent commentators. The case is not the same as in 1 Sam. 1, 12; 10, 9, etc. (Driver). The subject here is not the following sentence, but the noun ארון; and what the author predicates of the box is not that it *had arrived* or *used to arrive* (היה בא), but that it *was about to arrive* (והיה בא = יהיה בא). Nowack is mistaken when he affirms, " es handelt sich um die Erzählung einer einmaligen Handlung."

---

[1] The judicious reader will apprehend that the above is written in the prevailing jargon. שׁל is not really " derived " from either נשׁל or שׁלל; " related to " would better answer to the fact, the biliteral stem being antecedent to both the פ״ן and the ע״ע verb.

6, 17. ויצגו, *deposited* upon the ground; cf. Deut. 28, 56; Judges 6, 37 [1]; used elsewhere of the sacred box: 1 Sam. 5, 2; 2 Sam. 15, 24 (where we must of course read ויצגו for the senseless ויצקו of the Masoretic text); as well as in the parallel to this passage, 1 Chron. 16, 1. It is no accident that the same verb, which never means *to set up* or *to hang up*, and is never employed of either an idol or a garment, is used of the " ephod " of Gideon, Judges 8, 27.

6, 18. ויכל דוד מהעלות. The last word is Hiphil infinitive, not determinate plural of the noun עולה; cf. ויכל מהתנבות; 1 Sam. 10, 13. Nor does the verb העלה require an object; cf. 2 Kings 16, 12.

ויברך את העם בשם יהוה צבאות. He dismissed the assembly with the words יברככם יהוה צבאות, instead of the customary יברככם יהוה.

6, 19. אשפר. With the שלמים of the Masoretic text of verses 17 and 18 discarded, this strange word can hardly be anything but the name of some fruit, the unit of which would be an adequate individual portion — that is, provided the consonants have been correctly transmitted. One thinks of the *quince*; cf. Cant. 2, 5, where אשישות are coupled with תפוחים, *apples*. The quince is not mentioned elsewhere in the Old Testament, although there is reason to believe that it was extensively cultivated in Palestine in early times.[2] Several of the commonest vegetables, it should be remembered, happen to be mentioned only once in the Old Testament (Numbers 11, 5).[3] On the other hand, the Septuagint of this

---

[1] In Ex. 10, 24 יצג is used figuratively of something *deposited* as a pledge.

[2] Cf. Hehn-Schrader, *Kulturpflanzen und Hausthiere*[7], pp. 245 ff. In the tenth century A.D. a rhyme of Al Muqaddasi boasts that no grapes are so large and no quinces so excellent as those of his native city of Jerusalem; and elsewhere he actually reckons the quince (which he calls *al muʻannaqa;* cf. Dozy) among the seven kinds of produce unknown outside of Palestine (ed. De Goeje, pp. 166, 181; cf. Le Strange, *l. c.*, pp. 16, 85). In Arabia the quince was formerly very abundant, and was highly prized for its supposed therapeutic and stimulating qualities (see Lane, *s. v. safarjal*). The statement of Kennedy (*Encyclopaedia Biblica*, col. 1573) that " it can scarcely have been eaten raw, but only when made into a preserve," is not justified. At the present day the quince is habitually eaten raw, after being stored a little while to mellow, both in the East and among the peasantry of Italy.

[3] The Hebrew of the Mishna has a fruit called פריש, which the Jerusalem Talmud, *Maʻseroth* 48d, defines with איספרגל, Aramaic for *quince*, Arabic *safarjal;* cf. Löw, *Aramäische Pflanzennamen*, pp. 25, 144, 460. The Talmud goes on to explain that

passage has ἐσχαρίτην, which is of course a makeshift based on אשכר. And this, if authentic, would be *a cup of wine* (שכר); not an improbable sense in Ez. 27, 15 and Ps. 72, 10 as well.

אשישה, a small *brick* of pressed dried fruit. אשישי ענבים of Hosea 3, 1 argues that the אשישה was not always made of ענבים. It may have consisted of figs, like the Arabic *malban* (מלבן), a sweetmeat "made of figs pressed into the form of small bricks."[1] In that case it will have differed from the דבלה in being more of a confection.

6, 20. ותברכהו, merely *greeted him*. The "blessing" was nothing more than the conventional form of salutation; cf. 1 Sam. 13, 10; 25, 14; 2 Kings 4, 29; Ruth 2, 4.

אמהות עבדיו is rhetoric; cf. לרחץ רגלי עבדי אדני, 1 Sam. 25, 41.

כהגלות נגלות. By means of the infinitive absolute the idea of the verb is intensified from mere *disclosure* to wilful *exhibition*. The grammatical form נגלות has occasioned needless perplexity. The traditional reading should be retained without change. The "infinitive absolute" (which is of course not the absolute form of the "infinitive construct," but a wholly independent verbal noun with distinctly abstract sense) could not in this case occupy any other position than immediately before the genitive אחד; which it accordingly introduces by means of a construct form of its own. For the rest, the statement of Kautzsch (Gesenius-Kautzsch § 113 a, footnote), " Ganz ausgeschlossen ist die Verbindung des Inf. absol. mit einem Genetiv oder mit einem Pronominalsuffix," is justified only as regards a pronominal suffix, and that on logical grounds: a pronominal suffix *ipso facto* makes the act specific and concrete, and contradicts the very idea of the infinitive absolute or abstract. But no such reason exists why the infinitive absolute may not be joined to an indefinite genitive[2]; as it unmistakably is in שְׁתוֹת יין, not *a certain drinking of certain wine*, but *the act of wine-drinking* in itself, Isa. 22, 13. That expression, employed in the same verse with the unqualified form שָׁתֹה, shows that the construction of the

the quince was called פריש because it is the only tree-fruit *separated* (פרש) for the kettle (cooked). The identification may be no better than the etymology.

[1] Quoted from Maimonides by Le Strange, *l. c.*, p. 20, cf. p. 296.
[2] Even of the object; against König, *Syntax*, p. 119.

formally ambiguous parallel phrases, חרג בקר *killing of cattle*, שחט צאן *slaughtering of sheep*, is that of noun with genitive, rather than verb with accusative (as Gesenius-Kautzsch § 113*e*).

אחד הרקים. For the force of this formula when used in derogation cf. אחד הנבלים, *a common rake*, 2 Sam. 13, 13; אחד האדם, *an ordinary man*, Judges 16, 7.11. On the other hand, in approbation: אחד הצבים, *a veritable gazelle*, 2 Sam. 2, 18.

6, 21. נגליתי. On the reading see page 42 above.

6, 22. עיניך. So we must necessarily read, with G, against the Masoretic עיני.

עמם. The author probably wrote עמן.

XI

It has, I think, been shown that the ancient record of David's transfer of the box of Yahwe Militant from Kirjath-jearim to Jerusalem testifies unequivocally to the existence of a plurality of sacred boxes among the Hebrews, both in the age of David and at the time when that narrative itself was composed. Equally emphatic and indisputable, for the same period and the same author, is the testimony of the next passage we have to consider, namely **1 Kings 2, 26**.

Here we are told that Solomon, when banishing Abiathar from Jerusalem for his adherence to the cause of Adonijah, made use of the following language: ענתת לך על שדיך כי איש מות אתה וביום הזה לא אמיתך כי נשאת את ארון (אדני)[1] יהוה לפני דוד אבי וכי התענית בכל אשר התענה אבי, *Get thee to Anathoth to thine estate; for thou art under sentence of death; but for the present I will not put thee to death, because thou didst bear the box of Yahwe before David my father and didst share all the sufferings which my father suffered.* The natural sense of this statement is that there was a period in the life of David when Abiathar attended him as priest, carrying the box of Yahwe [2];

[1] אדני, lacking in G and in the Peshita, is not " a mistaken repetition of ארון " (Burney, *Notes on the Hebrew Text of the Books of Kings*, p. 23; cf. Kittel, *Handkommentar zum Alten Testament*, p. 19 f), but merely a Qrê indicating the reading ארון אדני instead of ארון יהוה.

[2] With the phrase נשאת את ארון יהוה לפני דוד אבי, compare הוא נשא ארון האלהים ביום ההוא לפני ישראל, 1 Sam. 14, 18 (as restored, p. 16).

and that during that period they had together suffered extraordinary and prolonged hardship.

Now there was never such a period in the life of David after the box of Yahwe Militant (of Shiloh and Kirjath-jearim) came into his possession (2 Sam. 6). To be sure, David suffered great hardship and humiliation when he fled from Jerusalem on the occasion of Absalom's rebellion. But 2 Sam. 15, 29 explicitly tells us that no sacred box accompanied him on that occasion, and that Abiathar too was left behind, to act as his spy at the court of Absalom; nor by any stretch of the imagination can the ensuing experiences of Abiathar in Jerusalem be held to justify the term התענית. There was one period, and only one, in the life of David when he endured protracted hardship in the company of Abiathar; and that was before he came to the throne, when for many months he led the life of a hunted outlaw on the southern border, in such consant fear of death that he finally sought safety in the service of the arch-enemy of his nation, the Philistine king of Gath (1 Sam. 22-30). Throughout that period and those trials, Abiathar, likewise a fugitive from the vengeful fury of Saul, was ever at David's side, ministering to him, in moments of perplexity or danger, the sacred oracles of Yahwe (1 Sam. 22, 20 ff.; 23, 6 9; 30, 7). If Solomon and our author knew what they were talking about — as presumably both of them did — the object which, in those troublous times, Abiathar carried with him, as at once the badge and the instrument of his sacred office, was *the box of Yahwe*. And that "box of Yahwe" was necessarily a different box from the "box of Yahwe Militant" which all through that period, and for years afterwards, was lodged in the house of Abinadab at Kirjath-jearim (1 Sam. 7, 1; 2 Sam. 6, 3). 1 Kings 2, 26, accordingly, offers independent and conclusive proof of the existence of more than one box of Yahwe in the age of David, and to the knowledge of the author of this unimpeachable source.

On the theory of a single sacred box this passage raises difficulties which commentators have never succeeded in overcoming. Rashi understands כי נשאת את ארון אדני יהוה to refer to the episode of

2 Sam. 15, 24 ff (where David, Abiathar, and the sacred box are met together by the side of the Brook Kidron for a few brief moments), and התענית has in mind the hunger, weariness, and thirst (העם רעב ועיף וצמא במדבר, 2 Sam. 17, 29) subsequently endured by David and his followers (but not by Abiathar). Levi ben Gershon also sees in the mention of the box of Yahwe an allusion to the experience of 2 Sam. 15, 24 ff, though he apparently realizes the strained character of that explanation; for he adds that Abiathar stayed with David on that occasion until the latter desired the box taken back to Jerusalem. The "suffering" was endured both during the early period of outlawry and during Absalom's rebellion. So already David Qimḥi, who follows Rashi in quoting 2 Sam. 17, 29. The view that the entire statement relates to the episode of 2 Sam. 15, 24 ff, is put forward by J. H. Michaelis,[1] Böttcher,[2] and Kittel.[3] More sensible and straightforward was the attitude of Clericus: "Vix crediderim respici ad id quod habetur 2 Sam. 15, 24 29; tunc enim noluit David Arcam secum auferri; sed potius ad bella quae gessit David [after 2 Sam. 6], quamvis haec circumstantia antea non sit memorata." And on התענית: "In exsilio semper fuerat cum Davide, ex quo ad eum confugerat, 1 Sam. 22, 20 21 et seqq."[4]

Burney, who retains the reading ארון יהוה, divorces the two halves of Solomon's declaration: Abiathar was one of the bearers when the box of Yahwe was removed from the house of Obed-edom to the City of David "with rejoicing" (2 Sam. 6, 12); whereas the affliction referred to is that which he had shared with David in their joint wanderings as outlaws some years earlier.[5] That is, Solomon recalls two experiences of diametrically opposite character; in one of which, moreover, we have (in spite of 1 Chron. 15, 11) no evidence that Abiathar shared. It does not help the matter that the paraphrase of Josephus, Θανάτου μὲν ῥύεταί σε τά τε ἄλλα ὅσα

---

[1] *Biblia hebraica cum annotationibus, ad loc.*
[2] *Neue exegetisch-kritische Aehrenlese*, II, p. 11.
[3] *L. c.*, p. 19.
[4] *Veteris Testamenti libri historici*, p. 367.
[5] *L. c.*, p. 22.

τῷ πατρὶ συνέκαμες καὶ ἡ κιβωτός, ἣν σὺν αὐτῷ μετήνεγκας,[1] may imply a similar interpretation. On the other hand, the comprehensive exegesis of Keil sees in the utterance of Solomon a reference to all available occasions — the transfer of the box of Yahwe from the house of Obed-edom, as related in 1 Chron. 15, and also the episode of 2 Sam. 15, 24 ff; the sufferings of the days of outlawry, as well as those caused by Absalom's rebellion.[2]

Thenius was the first to seek relief in textual emendation. As an "Oberpriester," Abiathar had nothing to do with the portage of the sacred box, while the text obviously alludes to his exercise of the priestly function. In accordance, therefore, with 1 Sam. 2, 28; 14, 3; 14, 18 (G), we should very probably read אפוד in place of ארון. ("Very probably," in this case, doubtless because the Septuagint does not support the proposed emendation.) The resulting combination אפוד אדני יהוה he thinks sufficiently justified by the circumstance that the sacred oracles were attached to the ephod, as may be seen from 1 Sam. 14, 41.[3] Against this reading, which is apparently adopted by Benzinger,[4] it is sufficient to point out that the combination אפוד יהוה is an impossible one.[5] Even the unique ephod of the High Priest could no more be called אפוד יהוה than his robe could be called מעיל יהוה. Much the same criticism applies to the doubly conjectural אפוד אלהים which Klostermann offers as the authentic text of this passage. According to that critic, an original אפוד אלהים (which he curiously calls "ungewöhnlich") was first altered to ארון אלהים, "da sonst der Ephod vor Jahve, nicht vor Menschen getragen wird"; then glossed with יהוה as a variant to אלהים, resulting in the conflate reading ארון אלהים יהוה; and finally the latter was corrected to ארון אדני יהוה.[6]

---

[1] *Antiquities*, viii, 10. [2] *Die Bücher der Könige*[1], pp. 26 f.

[3] *Die Bücher der Könige*[1], 1849, p. 18. In the second edition, 1873, he reasserted his opinion against the criticisms of Böttcher and Keil.

[4] *Kurzer Hand-Commentar zum Alten Testament*, p. 12.

[5] It is not quite correct to say that the expression "never occurs" (as Burney, and before him Böttcher); for its Greek equivalent is found in the Septuagint text of 1 Sam. 23, 9; which, however, merely constitutes additional evidence that אפוד is not authentic in that passage.

[6] *Die Bücher Samuelis und der Könige*, p. 271.

The obstacle of the possessive יהוה is avoided by Wellhausen[1] and Stade,[2] who substitute the determinate האפוד for the whole phrase ארון יהוה. In view of the present text of 1 Sam. 23, 6 9; 30, 7, this is the most rational alternative to the retention of the Masoretic text with the interpretation I have given. But the objections to this drastic emendation are insurmountable. In the first place, the reading ארון יהוה of the Masoretic text is, in so far forth,[3] supported by all the manuscripts and editions of all the ancient versions; and, after what has been said in discussing the problem of 1 Sam. 14, 18, it is evident that this is more likely to be a case where the original ארון has been preserved unaltered, than one where an original אפוד has been changed to ארון, of which the Old Testament offers no demonstrable instance. Secondly, there is the material objection urged against the emendation to האפוד in 1 Sam. 14, 18, namely, that nothing is achieved by the proposed alteration but the substitution of a major difficulty for a minor one. Instead of a second sacred box, which, though it conflicts with Jewish tradition, is perfectly intelligible, we are burdened with a cryptic vocable which cannot, in this context, have a meaning in the least resembling its well-attested sense elsewhere in the Old Testament.[4] And third, the displacement of an original האפוד by ארון יהוה (as distinguished from that of אפוד by ארון) cannot be the result of careless copying, but only of deliberate falsification — as indeed is contended by Wellhausen. And so we confront again the untenable hypothesis, that an editor or scribe who (if he lived in the Second Temple) thought of the ephod as an essential article of the High Priest's apparel, and whose historical books (in any event) showed him that a similar garment was worn by such divine favorites as Samuel and David, found the mere mention of it in connection with Abiathar so intolerable that he wilfully substituted for it " the box of Yahwe," which (by hypothesis) he knew was the unique object domiciled at Kirjath-jearim throughout the period

---

[1] Bleek-Wellhausen, *Einleitung in das Alte Testament*[4], p. 642.
[2] *Sacred Books of the Old Testament*, pp. 3, 70.
[3] G represents ארון (ברית) יהוה.
[4] See pages 9, 16.

here in question. To be sure, it is assumed that the tinkering scribe knew or suspected that the ephod here mentioned, unlike that of the High Priest, was an idol; but it still remains to be proved that the ephod was ever an idol, or that the Jewish scribe ever lived who thought it was.

Far simpler is the contrary view, which accepts the universally authenticated genitive יהוה as evidence that the construct which precedes it was never other than ארון; and that here, as in the Masoretic text of 1 Sam. 14, 18, the authentic reading has been preserved in spite of its incompatibility with the later Jewish theory of the single box of Yahwe. For it is one thing to leave unaltered an ancient text which does not accord with current doctrine — what were our Old Testament science today but for the abundance of such laxity? — and quite another to make positive alterations which are repugnant to that doctrine. There can, of course, be no serious question that the object spoken of by Solomon in 1 Kings 2, 26 was the same as that mentioned by the narrator of 1 Sam. 23, 6 9; 30, 7. But sound criticism is not governed by a count of verses. If ארון of our passage is emended to אפוד, the confusion is only increased; whereas if אפוד of the other passages is replaced by ארון, all is at once made plain.

XII

The last Old Testament passage we have to adduce as intrinsically irreconcilable with the theory that the box of Yahwe was unique is **Jer. 3, 16**. This verse occurs in a prophecy of Jeremiah which is attributed, professedly by the prophet himself (3, 6), to the reign of Josiah. Some three hundred years have elapsed since the author lived from whose priceless history the last passages were drawn. The separate monarchy established by Jeroboam has been swept away; and in the surviving kingdom of Judah the time has long since passed when the king sought supernatural guidance of the priest with his portable instrument of divination. Where Saul and David enquired of Yahwe through an Ahijah or an Abiathar, Hezekiah and Josiah enquired only of an Isaiah or a Huldah, through whose living voice the spirit of the Deity made known his articulate and certain message. For king and counselor and royal priest, the naïve institution of the early days is now little more than a blend of outworn superstition and pious memory. Nevertheless the institution is not quite extinct; for superstitions die hard. In remoter circles, and among people less highly placed, the primitive oracle is still preserved. Particularly, it would seem, among the wretched remnant of North Israel, now for three generations subject to foreign rule, disintegrated, unshepherded, and fast falling away from the family of Yahwe — at the old high places and in the sacred groves of Canaan, side by side with images of *baalim* and symbols of other strange divinities, the box of Yahwe continues to be cherished and invoked. It is to these North Israelites that the prophet Jeremiah addresses his words:

(3, 14) שובו בנים שובבים נאם יהוה כי אנכי בעלתי בכם ולקחתי אתכם אחד
מעיר ושנים ממשפחה והבאתי אתכם ציון: (15) ונתתי לכם רעים כלבי ורעו אתכם
דעה והשכיל: (16) והיה כי תרבו ופריתם בארץ בימים ההמה נאם יהוה לא
יאמרו עוד ארון (ברית) יהוה ולא יעלה על לב ולא יַזָּכְרוּ בו ולא יפקדו ולא יעשה עוד.

(3, 14) *Return, you wandering children, declares Yahwe, for I am your owner. And I will take you, one from a city, and two from a clan, and will bring you to Zion* (for instruction); (15) *and I will give you shepherds after my own heart, and they will feed you with knowledge and discretion.* (16) *And it shall come to pass, when you increase and multiply in the land in those days, declares Yahwe, that men will no longer speak of "the box of Yahwe," nor will it enter their minds, nor will they invoke it, nor will they resort to it; neither will it be manufactured any more.*

עוד must of course be given the same meaning in the clause לא יעשה עוד which it has in לא יאמרו עוד; and in the latter it cannot possibly have the meaning *again = a second time*.[1] Otherwise the

---

[1] Giesebrecht is obliged to render, " dann wird man nicht *fürder* sagen: ' die Lade des Bundes Jahves ' "; but represents the last clause by " und sie wird (auch) nicht *wieder* gemacht werden " (*Handkommentar zum Alten Testament*[2], p. 20). Similarly Cornill: " und keine neue anfertigen wollen " (*Das Buch Jeremia erklärt*, p. 41); and Erbt: " noch sie wieder anfertigen " (*Jeremia und seine Zeit*, p. 130). Other critics follow a sounder philological instinct, in spite of the fact that the resultant rendering

text calls for few comments. ברית is the usual Deuteronomistic gloss, never more clearly out of place than here. לא יזכרו עוד is quite meaningless if we adhere to the desperate pointing of the synagogue. Nowhere in the Old Testament is זכר בְּ Hebrew for *remember*, as is assumed, for this passage alone, by all the commentaries and lexicons.[1] We must point the verb as Hiphil, which, with ב of the object, is idiomatic Hebrew for *invoke*. Only in this sense is זכר used with the preposition ב, either with or without a complementary שֵׁם. So in the following: ובאלהי ישראל יזכירו, parallel to הנשבעים בשם יהוה, Isa. 48, 1; לבד בך נזכיר, Isa. 26, 13 (where שמך is a gloss); אלה ברכב ואלה בסוסים ואנחנו בשם יהוה אלהינו נזכיר, Ps. 20, 8; בשם אלהיהם לא תזכירו, Amos 6, 10; הס כי לא להזכיר בשם יהוה, Josh. 23, 7. Compare further Ex. 3, 15; 23, 13; 2 Sam. 14, 11; Isa. 49, 1; 62, 6 f; Hos. 2, 19.[2] On יפקדו compare Judges 15, 1.

The testimony of the last three clauses in this utterance of Jeremiah could not be more plain. The box of Yahwe here referred to is not an individual object, but an institution. Neither the fictional Sinaitic box of Jewish dogma, nor yet the supposedly unique historical box of Solomon's temple, was resorted to and invoked in the days of Jeremiah by the people of North Israel. Evidently, too, the object which the prophet has in mind had been reproduced again and again in the past, and might conceivably be multiplied indefinitely in the future; so that he cannot be alluding to a box whose essential character consisted in its harboring an ancestral fetich of the age of Moses. Nor should we overlook the significant implication of the context; it is as the cherished instrument of divine guidance that the sacred box is to be superseded by the ministrations of

---

does not accord with their own assumption that the reference is to the restoration of the lost box of the Solomonic temple. So Duhm: "noch wird sie mehr angefertigt werden" (*Das Buch Jeremia übersetzt*, p. 10; cf. *Kurzer Hand-Commentar*, p. 40); and Driver: "neither shall it be made any more" (*The Book of the Prophet Jeremiah*, p. 17; cf. *Introduction*, new edition, p. 251).

[1] The Septuagint οὐκ ὀνομασθήσεται comes very much closer to the correct interpretation.

[2] להזכיר in the title of Psalms 38 and 70 has nothing to do with the אזכרה of the Levitical ritual; it merely characterizes the psalm as adapted *for invocation* (in distress).

prophecy. For the rest, it is apparent that Jeremiah had never heard of the fiction of 1 Kings 8, 9 regarding the Solomonic box, and that it would have been quite foreign to his temper to sympathize with it. To his mind, the box of Yahwe was a pagan excrescence which could not be too thoroughly eradicated.

I am of course aware that the authenticity, and when not the authenticity the pre-exilic date, of the above-quoted words has been questioned by able and conscientious critics.[1] Quite generally, too, it has been denied that the words are addressed to the inhabitants of North Israel. It might be replied, that for the purposes of the present argument it makes little difference by whom and just when they were uttered, if only they were uttered in good faith; that, in fact, granted the philological correctness of the above interpretation, the later their date the better. Nevertheless, it must be pointed out that correct exegesis precedes literary criticism, and that the adverse judgments passed upon this passage are all based upon an exegesis now shown to be totally erroneous. If our interpretation of the words is correct, it is quite impossible to imagine their being penned after the publication of the Pentateuch at the end of the fifth century, and not easy to imagine their being uttered much later than the time of Jeremiah. Nor is there any positive reason left for holding them to be subsequent to the destruction of Jerusalem (and the disappearance of the Solomonic box).

As regards the question of the addressee, we cannot too energetically resist the impression sought to be conveyed by the patently polemical and malevolent statements of 2 Kings 17, 6 18 23 24—41.[2] We have the authority of Sargon himself for the fact that he deported from the kingdom of Samaria in the year 722 not more than 27,290 persons; and that he left the rest in possession of their holdings, installed an Assyrian governor over them, and imposed upon them the same yearly tribute which he had formerly exacted from

---

[1] See Stade, *Zeitschrift für die alttestamentliche Wissenschaft*, IV, 1884, p. 152; Kuenen, *Onderzoek*², II, pp. 171 f; Giesebrecht, *l. c.*, pp. xv f, 17; Smend, *Lehrbuch der alttestamentlichen Religionsgeschichte*², pp. 247 f; Duhm, *Kurzer Hand-Commentar*, pp. 36 ff; Cornill, *l. c.*, pp. 40 f.

[2] Cf. Torrey, *Ezra Studies*, pp. 326 ff.

the kings of Samaria.¹ The last fact alone is enough to show that the country was very far from being transformed into a howling wilderness, pending the arrival of the foreign settlers imported by Sargon. These settlers, moreover, cannot have been so very numerous proportionally, and will hardly have affected the character of the population more seriously than did the deported Israelites that of the regions into which they were removed — which, in the long run, was not at all. Jeremiah must not be credited with the absurd notions of the post-exilic anti-Samaritans and exclusivists. He might very well suppose himself summoned to " see what apostate Israel was doing " (3, 6).² And we may be quite certain that in his day, and for a long time after, the majority of the people of central and northern Palestine still considered themselves and were generally acknowledged to be of Israelitish blood and, in some sort, worshippers of Yahwe. They were not very faithful, to be sure, nor very exclusive — Jeremiah is perfectly aware of that; but, if the prophet Hosea is to be believed, they were just drifting along the path upon which their more prosperous ancestors had entered long before the termination of the monarchy.

¹ See *Keilinschriftliche Bibliothek*, ii, pp. 54 f; Rogers, *Cuneiform Parallels to the Old Testament*, p. 331, cf. p. 326.

² " Seltsam ist Jahves Frage an Jeremia, ob er gesehen habe, was (Nord-)Israel that. Als ob Jeremia nicht hundert Jahr nach dem Untergange Nordisraels gelebt hätte! " — Duhm, *l. c.*, p. 36. The text of Jer. 3, 6 ff is of course not devoid of editorial expansions and interpolations. But when once it is realized that the foundation is just what it pretends to be, a genuine prophecy of Jeremiah, ascribed by himself to the early years of his ministry, and addressed to North Israel, there is little difficulty in detecting the spurious material. The prophecy beginning with 3, 6 apparently makes reference (verse 7a) to an earlier utterance of the same tenor. This was doubtless the long address contained in chapter 2. My own judgment is that we have in 2, 4—3, 5 and 3, 6–22 two successive prophecies of Jeremiah addressed to the North Israelites. 3, 22b–25 is unmistakably the rumination of a post-exilic Jew; and, besides that, the following sections must clearly be discarded as spurious: 2, 11aβ 15 f 26b 28b; 3, 3a 7b–11 תחת כל עץ רענן in 13b 17–19. It is possible that the original continuation of 3, 16 was destroyed when verses 17 ff were inserted.

XIII

We turn now to the three additional passages which we said are thoroughly intelligible only upon the hypothesis of a manifold sacred box employed for purposes of divination.[1] It hardly needs stating that if the sacred box was the ordinary instrument of priestly oracles, it was necessarily plural at a time when sanctuaries and priestly establishments were plural. And since its plural character has, moreover, been amply demonstrated from other passages in the Old Testament, we are concerned only with the corroborative evidence which these three passages afford that the sacred box was in fact the organ of divination.

The first of these passages is **2 Sam. 11, 11**. Here the sacred box is mentioned quite casually, in the course of a rhetorical question relating to a wholly different subject. The evidence yielded by the passage is therefore inferential. Nevertheless, it is not altogether negligible. Uriah the Hittite, explaining to David his reluctance to repair to his own house in Jerusalem during his enforced absence from the army besieging Rabbath Ammon, is represented as saying: הארון וישראל ויהודה ישבים בסכות ואדני יואב ועבדי אדני על פני השדה חנים ואני אבוא אל ביתי לאכל ולשתות ולשכב עם אשתי.[2] *The box and Israel and Judah are* (at this very moment) *lodged in booths, and my lord Joab and the servants* (retainers) *of my lord* (the king) *are encamped in the open field; and shall I go home, to eat and to drink and to lie with my wife?*

The casual nature of this allusion to the sacred box is significant. Uriah is not informing David of its presence with the Israelitish army, any more than he is informing David that the army is engaged in a military campaign. David is aware that the box is there. Not

---

[1] See page 34.

[2] Budde (*Kurzer Hand-Commentar*), following S. A. Cook (*American Journal of Semitic Languages*, XVI, 1900, p. 156), rejects the words וישראל ויהודה ישבים בסכות as editorial. But 1 Kings 20, 12 16 shows the officers of a besieging army occuping סכות in the environs of Samaria; and the sacred box is more fittingly associated with the people of Yahwe who are mustered in his service (cf. את יואב ואת עבדיו עמו ואת כל ישראל in verse 1) than with Joab and the mercenary soldiers of the king.

only so, but the reader also is supposed to be aware of it. The author himself, in his account of this and the preceding expedition against Rabbath Ammon, has nowhere mentioned the transfer of the sacred box to the scene of operations from Jerusalem or elsewhere.[1] In rehearsing the conversation between David and Uriah he obviously takes it for granted, therefore, that his readers will know well enough that the box of Yahwe would be found at the headquarters of an Israelitish army. And although, as the symbol and organ of Yahwe, the box is given first place in the utterance of Uriah, it is apparently so customary a concomitant of every military expedition, that the speaker does not even trouble to describe it as "the box of Yahwe" or "the sacred box." He refers to it merely as "the box"[2]; much as we might speak of "the staff." Our current English translation, "the Ark," lends an element of distinction to the word which is quite foreign to the expression in the original. From all of which it is evident that this "box" so uniformly accompanied an Israelitish army on its campaigns, that we should never have learned of its presence before Rabbath Ammon on this occasion, but for David's adultery and the report of his chance conversation with the injured husband.

The question then is, What was the function of the box which, according to the evidence of 2 Sam. 11, 11, habitually accompanied an Israelitish army? In other words, must the casual reference to the box of Yahwe in this ancient source be interpreted in the light of 1 Sam. 4, 3 ff, or in the light of the Masoretic text of 1 Sam. 14, 18 f? Was the box of Yahwe essentially a wonder-working palladium

[1] Klostermann, followed by Budde, H. P. Smith, and Nowack, reads ארון אלהינו for ערי אלהינו in 2 Sam. 10, 12. This conjecture is certainly wrong. Smith observes that the cities of Israel were in no danger. But that is taking the rhetoric of Joab altogether too seriously. Was there ever a war of conquest in which the aggressor did not fight in defence of his territory, liberty, existence, or something of the sort? Military claptrap is as old as warfare. Yet even if Klostermann's emendation be accepted, we should only have an earlier casual mention of the box of Yahwe in the mouth of one of the actors. On the other hand, the suggestion of the same critic that we read את יואב ואתו ארן אלהי צבאות in 10, 7 is rightly dismissed as fantastic.

[2] The Lucianic reading ἡ κιβωτὸς τοῦ θεοῦ, followed by Jerome, is certainly unauthentic; as may be seen from the divergent expansion of the Peshîta.

which the Israelites carried into battle? or was it simply the instrument of the priestly oracles? These are the alternatives; and they are sufficiently distinct.

Scholars have hitherto adopted the former of these alternatives in explaining our passage. But the situation underlying 2 Sam. 11, 11 has nothing at all in common with the events recorded in 1 Sam. 4. In the latter case we have to do with an apparently unprecedented, and certainly extraordinary, use of a particular sacred box. The Israelites have been routed; and in their extremity and bewilderment they send to Shiloh for the box especially dedicated to *Yahwe Militant*, that by carrying it with them into the fight they may triumph over their terrible opponents. Here, on the contrary, the Israelites, far from being in extremity or danger, are themselves the aggressors and the victors. They have defeated the Ammonites and their Syrian allies in open battle; they have devastated the enemy's country up to the gates of his capital, and are engaged in reducing his last refuge; it is but a matter of time when the city must surrender to them or be taken by assault. There has been no need and no thought of desperate expedients. The box accompanied the expedition as a matter of course when it first set out, and is safely lodged at headquarters at the time of speaking. Clearly, not 1 Sam. 4, 3 ff but 1 Sam. 14, 18 f supplies the parallel required. For in this latter passage likewise, the presence of the sacred box at army headquarters from the beginning is taken for granted. The first mention of it is in the quoted command of Saul to Ahijah, " Bring hither the sacred box." [1] The author's parenthesis, " for he carried the sacred box before Israel that day," explains, not the presence of the box, but the mention of Ahijah. The box is consulted as a matter of course before the military operation is undertaken, and is presumably left in the rear when the army proceeds to the attack. In fact, so perfectly does 1 Sam. 14, 18 f supply the background required for the allusion in 2 Sam. 11, 11, that one wonders how it happens that the emendation of ארון to אפוד in the latter passage has never been suggested. There can be no reasonable doubt that

---

[1] On the mention of the " ephod " in 14, 3a, compare pages 14 f, above.

the object spoken of in the two narratives was the same. In 1 Sam. 14, 18, however, the object is the instrument of divination and nothing else. In 2 Sam. 11, 11 likewise, therefore, the "box" can hardly be anything else.

That this conclusion is correct becomes quite certain from a critical study of the next passage which mentions the sacred box in connection with military operations, namely 2 Sam. 15, 24 ff.

XIV

I say, in connection with military operations. For it was as a valued auxiliary in war that the sacred box was carried out by the priests of David when the latter fled from Jerusalem before Absalom; and for purely military reasons that both priests and box were finally left behind.

The text of 2 Sam. 15, 24–29 is admittedly corrupt.[1] Ancient translators and early commentators wrestled unsuccessfully with the difficulties which it presents; while recent critics invariably emend the text at one or more points. It is not necessary, however, to review all the explanations and emendations which have been adopted or proposed. I may state my own conclusions regarding the less important critical questions involved, and reserve a more detailed discussion for the single clause with which we are principally concerned, and which, though perfectly authentic, has proved most troublesome to interpreters and critics.

In verse 24 the words וכל הלוים אתו are reminiscent of the Pentateuch (Num. 1, 50; 3, 31; Deut. 10, 8), and certainly spurious; cf. 1 Chron. 15, 2. On the other hand, the verbs נשאים and יצקו (sic) require a plural subject; and both verse 27 (בניכם אתכם) and verse 29 (צדוק ואביתר) leave no doubt that the authentic reading at the beginning of verse 24 was והנה גם צדוק ואביתר. The original ואביתר is preserved in the meaningless ἀπὸ Βαιθαρ which follows the first clause of the verse in most manuscripts of the Septuagint. Doubtless, the word was entered upon the margin of a Hebrew manu-

---

[1] Cf., for instance, Budde, *Kurzer Hand-Commentar*, p. 273: "Den absichtlich veränderten und obendrein beschädigten Text können wir nur annähernd herstellen."

script from which it had been omitted, and was then misplaced at the next copying. The similarly dislocated ויעל אביתר of the Masoretic text of 24b, however, is probably of different origin (see below).

ברית, absent in the sequel, is the usual Deuteronomistic gloss. τὴν κιβωτὸν διαθήκης Κυρίου of G^B and congeners represents a more logical alteration of ארון האלהים to ארון ברית יהוה, limited likewise to verse 24a.

ויצקו, *poured*, must of course be corrected to ויצגו, *set down;* cf. page 65, above.

ויעל אביתר. This phrase disturbs the unity of verse 24b and is obviously misplaced, as was recognized already by Rashi. But it is equally out of place anywhere else in the verse. On the other hand, some such phrase — that is, אביתר preceded by a *jussive* — is imperatively demanded, and has certainly fallen out, after the words שבה העיר בשלום in verse 27. וְיַעַל אביתר is not impossible at that point, since the conversation takes place in the valley of the Kidron, with the city of Jerusalem on the height above; but וְיֵשֵׁב אביתר would be more natural in the context. Like ואביתר in the first half of verse 24, this clause will have been deliberately omitted from verse 27 in transcribing, and subsequently re-inserted from the margin at the wrong place and in erroneous form. Possibly it was this strayed and misconstrued וישב אביתר which, under the influence of Aramaic אתר, yielded the superfluous καὶ καθισάτω εἰς τὸν τόπον αὐτῆς of the Lucianic text of verse 25a. On the other hand, the phrase καὶ ἀνέβη Ἀβιαθάρ, corresponding to the Masoretic text of verse 24b in G^B and G^A, but lacking in the Lucianic manuscripts, is probably a Hexaplaric addition on the basis of the Hebrew. Verse 27, it should be observed, was not originally so far removed from verse 24; for

Verses 25 and 26 are interpolated entire. The formula ויאמר המלך אל צדוק הכהן of verse 27 is stylistically impossible after ויאמר המלך לצדוק of verse 25.[1] Either 25 f or 27 f, therefore, is interpo-

---

[1] The solecism was noticed by Abravanel, who explains (*l. c.*, fol. 163, col. b) that the formula is repeated in verse 27 because the first statement related to the return

lated. But 27 f is authenticated, not only by its pragmatic content, as against the unctuous irrelevancies of 25 f, but also by the corroborative evidence of verses 35 f and the story related in 17, 15–22. On the other hand, both the matter and the language of 25 f stamp it as spurious. It is obviously written from the point of view of a pious Jew, to whom the box, rather than the priests who bear it, must perforce be the object of David's chief concern; and in any case it furnishes no really adequate reason for David's extraordinary procedure. The sentiment expressed is more congenial to the bathos of 2 Sam. 7 than to the virile realism of our narrator. The style likewise betrays the diaskeuast. The writer seems not to have been quite clear in his own mind regarding the reference of the suffix in נוהו; and the word itself is a euphuistic affectation — נוה is properly *sheepfold;* elsewhere in Samuel only ii. 7, 8(!) — which, whether it relates to the dwelling of Yahwe or of the box, can hardly be ascribed to a classical writer of vernacular Hebrew prose. Nor is the incongruity of ואם כה יאמר לא חפצתי בך lessened by Driver's citation[1] of 1 Sam. 14, 9 and Gen. 31, 8, which are by no means in the same case. Finally, it may be observed that ויאמר המלך אל צדוק of verse 27 is more in accord with our author's usage than ויאמר המלך לצדוק of verse 25. If, therefore, we are compelled to choose between 25 f and 27 f — and I think we are — there can be no question as to which must be retained.

Verse 28. עברות. We must read ערבות, with the *Qrê* and the ancient versions, here as well as in 2 Sam. 17, 16. The Hebrew for both *ford* and *pass* is מעבר or מעברה. There is no word עברה in either sense. In 2 Sam. 19, 19 העברה may be *the transport*, denoting the instrument or the agents, but it certainly is not *the ford*. Moreover, *fords of the wilderness*, the prevalent rendering in our passage,

---

of the box, while the second relates to the return of Zadok and Abiathar. Klostermann, *Die Bücher Samuelis und der Könige*, p. 202, intimates that the first utterance was spoken aloud for the benefit of the bystanders, and the second in the ear of Zadok. If so, our author's own powers of expression must have been singularly impaired at this point. Cook, *American Journal of Semitic Languages*, XVI, 1899, p. 161, attributes verses 25 f to another " source."

[1] *Notes on the Text of Samuel*[2], pp. 107, 316.

is without meaning; the fords would be those of Jordan, not of the wilderness. Nor had David any occasion to scatter his followers along several fords. *Passes of the wilderness* would be intrinsically less objectionable, if עברה were the word for *pass*. On the other hand, the Masoretic tradition has everything in its favor. Compare especially 2 Kings 25, 4 f, where Zedekiah in similar case flees from Jerusalem דרך הערבה, and is overtaken בערבות ירחו. The ערבות המדבר are those parts of the ערבה, the modern *Ghor*, which adjoin המדבר, *the Wilderness* κατ' ἐξοχήν, stretching between the Judean and Ephraimite hill country and the Jordan valley;[1] just as the ערבות מואב are those parts of the Arabah which attach to the territory of Moab on the other side, *the lowlands of Moab*, and the ערבות ירחו are those parts of the Arabah which surround the city of Jericho, *the lowlands of Jericho*. According to Num. 22, 1, the ערבות מואב lie immediately across the Jordan from Jericho; and *per contra*, when one has crossed the Jordan from thence to the western bank, he finds himself in the ערבות ירחו, Josh. 4, 13 (cf. 4, 19; 5, 10). David indicates only that he will stay on the westerly side of the Jordan valley. The assumption that, on his outward journey, he finally crossed the Jordan near its mouth (Driver), is not justified. The commonly travelled road northward to Mahanaim ran up the Arabah west of the Jordan for a considerable distance; cf. 2 Sam. 2, 29; 4, 7. Even on his return, as far as can be judged from the confused text of chapter 19, he crossed the Jordan north of Gilgal.

The authentic text of the passage with which we are concerned is accordingly the following:

(15, 24) והנה גם צדוק ואביתר נשאים את ארון האלהים : ויצגו את ארון האלהים עד תם כל העם לעבור מן העיר : (27) ויאמר המלך אל צדוק הכהן הרואה אתה שבה העיר בשלום וְיָשֹׁב(?) אביתר ואחימעץ בנך ויהונתן בן אביתר שני בניכם אתכם : (28) ראו אנכי מתמהמה בערבות המדבר עד בוא דבר מעמכם להגיד לי : (29) וישב צדוק ואביתר את ארון האלהים ירושלם וישבו שם.

(15, 24) *And behold also Zadok and Abiathar bearing the sacred box. And they set the sacred box down* (on the ground) *until all the*

---

[1] Cf. *American Journal of Semitic Languages*, XXVIII, 1912, p. 280, note 28.

people had finished passing over from the city. (27) *And the king said unto Zadok the priest, Art thou a seer? Return to the city in peace, and let Abiathar* (also) *return, and Ahimaaz thy son and Jonathan the son of Abiathar, your two sons, with you.* (28) *See, I will linger in the lowlands of the Wilderness until word came from you to inform me.* (29) *So Zadok and Abiathar took the sacred box back to Jerusalem and remained there.*

It is to be observed that the phrase הרואה אתה, which I have rendered *Art thou a seer?* contains the pith of David's utterance, and is indispensable to the sense of the paragraph. We, who are acquainted with the sequel and the motive of Zadok's return to Jerusalem, are apt to overlook the fact, that to one who reads the narrative for the first time, the language of verse 28 is not of itself sufficiently informing. What was it David desired the priests and their sons to tell him? That verse is palpably defective unless the reason for David's command was already pregnantly conveyed in the expression הרואה אתה of verse 27. Moreover, since this same expression has always proved a stumbling-block to interpreters and commentators, it is hardly conceivable that it should have been inserted as an explanatory gloss, or be the result of textual corruption in the direction of a simpler and more familiar reading.

If only for such reasons as these, there can be no thought of rejecting the Masoretic text in favor of the supposed original of G^B and congeners, ἴδετε σὺ ἐπιστρέφεις (or ἐπιστρέψεις) εἰς τὴν πόλιν = ראו אתה שֻׁב העיר, or of the Lucianic βλέπε σὺ ἀνάστρεφε εἰς τὴν πόλιν = רְאֵה אתה שֻׁבה העיר. Neither ἴδετε σύ nor βλέπε σύ contains the substance demanded by the context; and it is difficult to imagine ראו or ראה being altered to the troublesome הרואה either by design or accident. Besides, הרואה אתה שבה העיר — whatever may be the point of it — is excellent Hebrew syntax, whereas ראו אתה שב is no syntax at all. Nor is ראה אתה שבה very much better; for the interjectional ראה must introduce a statement of fact,[1]

---

[1] Actual or (as in Ex. 4, 21; Josh. 8, 4) constructive. 2 Kings 6, 32, בא ראו המלאך סגרו הדלת, is hardly a case in point; but, anyhow, one cannot imagine ראו סגרו הדלת. The least objectionable reconstruction of our passage on the basis of the Greek texts would be רְאֵה אתה שֻׁב.

which שבה העיר does not supply. The presence of the pronoun σύ is sufficient to show that ἴδετε does not reproduce the original Hebrew of the preceding word, but is only a makeshift, suggested perhaps by the initial ראו of verse 28, in the face of a text which baffled the understanding of the translator. The reading βλέπε σύ will then be merely a stylistic revision of ἴδετε σύ; cf. the Lucianic ἰδού for ἴδετε in verse 28. As will presently appear, more than one desperate commentator in later times has been driven to the same far-fetched rendering of the existing Hebrew text.

Similar considerations compel the rejection of the text of the Peshiṭa, which omits the word הרואה altogether, and transposes אתה to the end of the following clause: "Go back (h'fukh zel) to the city in peace, thou and Ahimaaz thy son." This too leaves us at a loss to account for the existence of the Masoretic text, and fails to meet the requirements of the narrative. It is clearly nothing but a translator's counsel of despair.

On the other hand, both the Targum of Jonathan, חזויא¹ את חוב לקרתא בשלם, and the Latin of Jerome, *O Videns, revertere in civitatem in pace*, reproduce, though not very instructively, the Masoretic consonantal text.

Accordingly, unless we are to give up the passage as hopelessly corrupt and incomprehensible, we must extract a satisfactory and fairly weighty sense from the traditional Hebrew text. Yet this is precisely what exegetes, blinded by the age-long error regarding the nature of the sacred box and the function of the priests in relation to it, have thus far wholly failed to do; while the mere number of mutually discordant proposals on the subject goes far to show that an essential element in the situation is being universally ignored.

¹ So the Codex Reuchlinianus (ed. Lagarde) both here and in 1 Sam. 9, 9 11 18 19, as well as for Hebrew חֹזֶה in 2 Sam. 24, 11. Jacob ben Chayyim and the Amsterdam Rabbinical Bible have חֲזַוָּיא (properly, *visions*) in 1 Sam. 9 and here, but חֲזוָיָא in 2 Sam. 24, 11. The Antwerp Polyglot has חֲזַוָּיא in 1 Sam. 9, but חֲזוִיאָה in 2 Sam. 15, 27, and חֲזָאָה in 24, 11. The correct spelling and vocalization in all these passages is of course חֲזָיָא. Buxtorf's Rabbinical Bible and the London Polyglot employ throughout the participial form חָזֵיָא, which is the only permissible alternative. The variant does not affect the question we have in hand.

The rabbinical commentators abide by the Masoretic pointing with interrogatory ה, but construct רואה as a participial verb: הרואה אתה = *does thou see?* So Rashi, who understands the verb ראה in the rabbinical sense of *to entertain or accept a view*, and paraphrases accordingly: אם רואה אתה שעצה נכונה היא שוב העיר, *If thou art of the opinion that it is a good plan, return to the city.* This strained interpretation is no worse than most.

David Qimḥi follows Rashi, though with halting step: אם רואה אתה בעיניך כלומר בעצתך, *If such is thy view; that is, thy judgment.* He seems not entirely satisfied with the explanation, however; for he goes on to quote the rendering of the Targum, חזויא את, which he affirms is the equivalent of נביא אתה, *thou art a prophet.* This will have been addressed to Zadok because David saw that the Holy Spirit had descended upon him, and he was being answered by Urim and Thummim. The allusion is to the *haggadah* that it was on this occasion Abiathar was deposed from the High Priesthood, because of his failure to obtain oracular responses, and Zadok elevated to that office in his stead.[1] Qimḥi understands חזויא את as affirmative, and the noun as indeterminate; but the Aramaic is ambiguous in both respects.

The same construction, הרואה אתה = *dost thou see?* underlies the finespun exegesis of Levi ben Gershon: ר״ל ואתה רואה אלו העניינים לאי זה תכלית פונים שתלך עמנו להגיד לנו זה בודאי צריך אתה לזה לקחת עצה בדברים לפי מה שיגלה מעניינם ולזה טוב שתשוב העיר בשלום. The purport of which appears to be: "The meaning is, *Dost thou then see the outcome of these events, that thou shouldst go with us to inform us?* For that purpose it decidedly behooves thee to take counsel in the circumstances, as they may be shaped by future developments; and therefore it is well that thou *return to the city in peace.*" No wonder Ralbag's loquacious but discerning student, Abravanel, is silent on this passage.

Christian scholars have been equally unsuccessful in arriving at a plausible explanation, although they have not always been equally

---

[1] See *Seder ʿOlam Rabba*, § 14; *b. Yoma* 73b; Rashi, on 2 Sam. 15, 24; Abravanel, *l. c.*, fol. 163, col. a.

mindful of Hebrew linguistic usage. So Sebastian Münster interprets: "*An non tu es Videns?* — h. e. summus Sacerdos, qui ex Urim et Thummim advertere poteris responsa Divina."[1] But the "*non*" which is essential to this sense is conspicuously absent in the Hebrew. Vatablus is guilty of the same error, as regards both Hebrew and Aramaic, in the first of his alternative interpretations: "*Nonne Videns es?* i. Propheta, ut quidam exponunt; et etiam Chaldaeus paraph. *Nonne Propheta es?* q. d. Si Dominus responderit tibi redeundum in urbem, redito. Alii, *Videsne tu?* i. Valesne consilio? q. d. Si valeas consilio, revertere, plus enim mihi profueris redeundo quam manendo."[2] The second interpretation seems to be based upon a misunderstanding of Qimḥi. Grotius, too, imagines himself to be opposing the exact Hebrew text to the rendering of the Vulgate: "*O Videns* — Rectius, *Nonne vides?* quo loco sunt res scilicet.*"[3]

Otherwise Sebastian Schmidt: "*Num Videns tu?* Chaldaeus interpres *Videntem* accepit pro *Propheta*. Et aliquando in scriptura sic usurpatur; cf. 1 Sam. 9. Sed non quadrat interrogatio; nec in scriptura dicitur quod Zadok propheta fuerit. . . . Putamus nihil aliud velle quam quod alias dicitur ראה, *vide*, quod admonentis et excitantis est. Sed hic interrogative loquitur ad augendam emphasin."[4] That is, הראה אתה must be construed as an emphatic interjection, "*Do* you see?" or "*Will* you see?" = "See!" It is to be noticed that this sense is being attributed to the existing Hebrew text, with no thought of any alteration on the basis of the Septuagint.

Clericus is, as usual, more critical: "הראה אתה, *an tu es videns?* — ראה dicitur Propheta 1 Sam. 9, 9, verum hic ejusmodi significationi locus non est. Itaque *speculatorem* vertimus, qui *videt* quid rerum agatur alicubi, idque ad suos perscribit, aut curat iis dici. ה, quod voci ראה praefigitur, existimavimus emphaticum esse, non interrogationis notam; quae hic minus convenit, quamvis ita cen-

---

[1] *Critici Sacri*, II, col. 2426.
[2] *Ibid.*, col. 2428. Our own Revised Version offers the same two alternatives.
[3] *Ibid.*, col. 2430. [4] *In Librum Posteriorem Samuelis commentarius*, pp. 704 f.

suerint Massorethae. . . . Vulgatus vertit, *O videns*, sed Tsadokus nusquam Propheta fuisse dicitur."[1] He renders accordingly, *Speculator tu (mihi es)*, that is, "Thou art the (= my) spy." This rendering has at least the double merit of conforming to Hebrew syntax[2] and recognizing the demands of the context. Only, רואה is not the Hebrew for *spy*; cf. in particular Gen. 42, 9.

J. H. Michaelis echoes the opinion of Sebastian Schmidt: "*Anne videns es? viden'?* admonentis et excitantis est, ut v. 28, q. d. videsne statum rerum praesentem et quid in illo factu opus sit?"[3] And doubtless the same influence is to be recognized in the renderings of J. D. Michaelis[4] (*Merke!*) and Dathe[5] (*attende*); both of which are offered without comment. Dathe smooths out the redundancy by adding *inquam* to the *attendite* of verse 28.

Among later scholars, Böttcher is one of the very few who retain the Masoretic pointing: "*Siehest Du es ein* (was ich eben gesagt habe)?"[6] Another is Reuss, for whom the problem is minimized by the accident of French idiom: "*Vois tu, retourne en paix à la ville.*"[7] But the great majority alter either the pointing or the consonantal text itself.

Ewald adopts the rendering of Jerome, which had been followed in Luther's German version: "Für הָרוֹאֶה ist zu lesen הָרוֹאֶה als Ausruf: *du Seher!* d. i. du Prophet, da ein Hohepriester allerdings diesen höhern aber zugleich altertümlichen Namen tragen konnte."[8] Similarly Keil: "*Du Seher, Kehre um in die Stadt in Frieden.* — הרואה אתה mit ה *interr.* gibt keinen passenden Sinn, da ה hier nicht für הלוא stehen kann, weil es sich nicht um eine Sache handelt, die der Angeredete nicht leugnen kann. Daher ist הָרֹאֶה (mit dem Artikel) zu vocalisiren und als Vocativ zu fassen. ראה *Seher* ist

---

[1] *Libri historici Vet. Test.*, p. 325.
[2] Assuming that he intends, "The spy is what thou art," rather than, "It is thou who art the spy."
[3] *Biblia Hebraica, ad loc.*
[4] *Deutsche Uebersetzung des Alten Testaments*, V. 2, p. 158.
[5] *Libri historici Vet. Test.*, p. 362.
[6] *Neue exegetisch-kritische Aehrenlese*, I, p. 189.
[7] *La Bible, in loc.*
[8] *Geschichte des Volkes Israel*¹, II, p. 649; 3d ed., III, p. 244.

so viel als Prophet. So nennt er Zadok als Hohepriester, der mittelst des Urim göttliche Offenbarungen empfängt. Der Sinn ist: Du Zadok stehst einem Propheten gleich, darum ist dein eigentlicher Platz in Jerusalem. Dort sollte Zadok mit Ebjathar und den Söhnen beider gleichsam auf der Warte stehen, um die Ereignisse zu beobachten und dann durch die Söhne ihm Nachricht in die Jordanaue senden."[1] But a רואה, in spite of 1 Sam. 9, 9, was not the same as a prophet; and, in any case, Zadok was not a prophet; neither was Jerusalem the special abode of prophets; nor was a prophet especially competent for the business of spying. Moreover, this construction really leaves אתה unaccounted for, the pronoun being as difficult to connect with the preceding vocative as with the following imperative.[2]

Under the circumstances, it is not surprising that other commentators have been constrained to question the authenticity of the consonantal text. The first to yield to this temptation was Thenius. Upon the basis of the expressions ויפן ויבא (Ex. 7, 23), ויפן ויצא (Ex. 10, 6), לא הפנו (Jer. 47, 3), coupled with the fact that in the Septuagint of Ez. 8, 3; 9, 2; 2 Chron. 4, 4 the participles פונה and מפנה are represented by βλέπων, while βλέπε appears as an alternative reading for ἴδετε in our passage, Thenius alters the text to הפנה אתה שבה וג׳, *Wende dich! Du* (antithetical to אנכי in verse 28) *kehre zurück*, u. s. w.[3]

Wellhausen's remedy is even more drastic. He first emends הרואה to הראש, which he combines with the preceding הכהן in apposition to צדוק: "Lies הכהן הראש statt des unverständlichen הרואה." But the title "Chief Priest" of course cannot be authentic in this connection; hence "Der Ausdruck stammt von dem Bearbeiter."[4]

To this provocation Klostermann responds by separating הכהן

---

[1] *Die Bücher Samuels*[1], p. 305.

[2] The pronoun would precede the vocative, and in a case like the above, would follow the imperative.

[3] *Die Bücher Samuels*[2], p. 222. Löhr, in the third edition of this book, omits Thenius and rehearses Wellhausen and Budde.

[4] *Der Text der Bücher Samuelis*, p. 198. I hardly need observe that the opinion of Wellhausen is quoted as matter of history. There is no reason for supposing that

itself from the preceding צדוק and attaching it to the following clause, obtaining thus the (authentic) nominal sentence הכהן הראה אתה, *Du bist der Seherpriester;* — a title whose novelty and incongruity are not lessened by pretending that it was the equivalent of "mantischer Priester" or "Orakelpriester." He points out that as "oracle-priest" Zadok would be immune from harm at the hands of Absalom, and would, moreover, be the first to discover the latter's military designs.[1] But every כהן was an "oracle-priest" (1 Sam. 2, 28; 22, 18); and if the Hebrew of the period had occasion for so tautological a compound, כהן ראה would be the last expression to serve the purpose. A slight variation of this confusion is advocated by Schlögl, upon the basis of the same Hebrew reading: "*Der Priester und* [!] *Seher bist du,* d. i. der Priester, welcher durch die Urim und Thummim den Willen Gottes erforscht."[2]

Most recent critics, however, fall back, in one form or another, on the easy but empty text of the Septuagint. So Budde: "הרואה giebt keinen Sinn. . . . Für הרואה wird man im Anschluss an LXX ἴδετε רְאֵה lesen dürfen, weiter versuchsweise אתה ואביתר שֻׁבוּ, also: *Merk auf, du und Ebjatar kehret zurück* u. s. w. Das אתה verlangt geradezu eine Ergänzung, die Einleitung mit רְאֵה ein vorhergegangenes Gespräch."[3] Nowack: "*Sehet, du und Ebjatar, kehret zurück in die Stadt.* — הרואה ist unverständlich. LXX hat ἴδετε, las also רְאוּ, und diese Lesart verdient um so mehr Erwägung, als das am Schluss des Verses sich findende שני בניכם אתכם beweist, dass hier zwei Personen angeredet sind. Offenbar ist auch hier Ebjatar

---

the veteran critic would in every case re-assert at the present time the judgments he expressed half a century ago.

Ehrlich, *Randglossen*, III, p. 313, accepts Wellhausen's initial emendation, but not the consequent excision. He thinks the title may very well have been employed of Zadok by the original writer. "Captain" of a company of two would be something of an oddity, however.

[1] *Die Bücher Samuelis und der Könige*, p. 202.
[2] *Die Bücher Samuels*, II, pp. 86 f. In his Latin commentary, *Libri Samuelis*, p. xciii, he renders, with Klostermann, "*Sacerdos videns* (*i.e.* vaticinans) *tu es.*"
[3] *Kurzer Hand-Commentar*, p. 274; cf. *Sacred Books of the Old Testament*, pp. 43, 92. We have seen that the authentic text contained no antecedent conversation.

II SAMUEL 15, 24–29

eliminirt, daher wird man wohl zu lesen haben: ראו אתה ואביתר שובו."¹
Kittel: "Der MT. ist unverständlich; lies nach G ראו wie in V. 28
und setze dann Abjathar ein: *Merket: du und Abjathar kehrt ruhig
nach der Stadt zurück.*"² Dhorme: "On voit que הראה ne donne
pas de sens. . . . D'après G ἴδετε on peut lire רָאוּ. Le pluriel n'a
rien pour nous étonner d'après בניכם אתכם de la fin. Ici encore
ואביתר a été supprimé après אתה. On lira donc ensuite שֻׁבוּ. Le
verset est ainsi parfaitement équilibré. — *Voyez! toi et Abiathar,
retournez en paix à la ville.*"³

Driver is not quite so positive: "הרואה אתה = *Seest thou?* (Ez.
8, 6)⁴ *i.e.* dost thou see how matters are? But the text excites
suspicion. . . . LXX has ἴδετε, which may either represent רְאוּ,
or be a misreading of רְאֵה; and as the plural pronouns at the end
of the verse and in verse 28 show that Abiathar and Zadoq are
both present, either רְאֵה or רְאוּ may have been used here, according
as David began by addressing Zadoq in particular, or both together. With the text otherwise as it stands, אתה must go with
what follows: *return thou;* but in view of the plural following and
especially of verse 29a, it is highly probable that for אתה שבה we
should read אתה ואביתר שֻׁבוּ."⁵

More critical than any of the foregoing, is the negative attitude
of H. P. Smith, who tentatively combines אתה with the following
word in the form of the participle שָׁב, and, pending further light
upon the subject, leaves הרואה untranslated: "הרואה is obscure.
It is taken by Ewald as an address to Zadok, as if he were a *seer*,
which does not appear to be the fact. G^B reads ראו, which is sus-
picious from its recurrence at the beginning of verse 28. Well-

---

¹ *Handkommentar*, p. 212.
² In Kautzsch's *Heilige Schrift des A. T.*³, ad loc.
³ *Les Livres de Samuel*, p. 384.
⁴ But in Ez. 8, 6 the participle has an object. In 8, 15 17; 47, 6, on the other hand, the verb is perfect.
⁵ *Notes on the Text of Samuel*², p. 316. In the first edition of this book (p. 245) Driver had very pertinently observed: "The objection to this is that ראו used simi- larly occurs v. 28a; and the repetition of the same expression, in two contiguous verses, where no special stress rests upon it, is an inelegancy, of which the writer of these chapters of Samuel is not likely to have been guilty."

hausen supposes as insertion הכהן הראש which has been corrupted into the present text. It is impossible to decide with certainty."[1]

It is, I think, abundantly evident that no satisfactory interpretation of the text of this passage has yet been forthcoming, nor any suggestion for its emendation which is even moderately plausible. Yet we have only to assume that the sacred box was the organ of divination, and that Zadok and Abiathar carried it in the train of David on this occasion by virtue of their office as custodians and interpreters of the oracles of deity, and the passage becomes perfectly plain.

Observe, to begin with, that the clause הרואה אתה cannot be declarative: because (1) if it were declarative, הרואה would necessarily be a determinate participial noun, *the seer*. But there is no evidence that all Israel had a single seer, or that the court of David harbored a premier seer, "the seer" *par excellence*, or that an official seer habitually accompanied an Israelitish military expedition or band of emigrants. "Thou art the seer," without further qualification, would therefore be unintelligible. (2) Because such a declaration, addressed to Zadok, would be contrary to fact. Zadok was no sort of a seer, but occupied the distinct and well-defined office of priest. (3) Because a seer was the one person in the world who did claim the power to see and know whatever David might require concerning the activities of Absalom, without recourse to residence in Jerusalem. An assertion that Zadok actually was a seer would therefore go counter to the whole tenor of the following commission.

Jastrow (" רֹאֶה and חֹזֶה in the Old Testament," *Journal of Biblical Literature*, XXVIII, 1909, pp. 42 ff) does not sufficiently differentiate the several professions as they existed in earliest times. In our Old Testament texts they have been badly confused, and even in historical practice their activities may sometimes have overlapped. Nevertheless, the original and essential character of each can still be discerned. The כהן was the *custodian* of a shrine, and manipulator and *interpreter* of the *oracles* of deity. The ראה was a *clairvoyant*, a private practitioner, who by occult means actually *saw* things at a distance, whether of time or space. The חזה was an *observer* of the stars or other omens,

---

[1] *Commentary on Samuel*, p. 345.

an *astrologer* or *prognosticator;* his deliverance or *prognostication* was a חזון. The נביא was a *person possessed* by the (physical) *spirit* of a deity, which might become articulate through the vocal organs of the patient. Ahimelech was such a כהן, Samuel was such a ראה, Gad was David's official חזה, and Elijah was such a נביא. Only the כהן and the נביא were religious functionaries in the strict sense, consecrated to the service of an individual deity. The Hebrew could say נביא יהוה, כהן יהוה; but it could not say ראה יהוה, חזה יהוה. The etymology of the identically formed כהן (*diviner*), ראה (*seer*), חזה (*observer*), is transparent; that of נביא remains obscure. Not improbably the latter is a passive formation (Stade § 251) from plain Hebrew (that is, Canaanitish) בוא, signifying *one who has been entered*.

Consequently, we must accept the Masoretic vocalization of the initial ה of הרואה אתה. The sentence is interrogatory: *Art thou a seer?* or *Dost thou see?* — according as רואה is construed as a participial noun or as a participial verb. And since David neither pauses for a reply nor receives one, the question must be purely rhetorical. As such, it implies a negative answer, and is logically equivalent to one of the two assertions, *Thou art* (admittedly) *not a seer*, or *Thou* (admittedly) *dost not see*. But since the latter is not, in the in the actual context, a sensible alternative, we must abide by the former; the obvious burden of which is, that though a seer could, without being himself present in the flesh, do the things for which Zadok is ordered back to the city, Zadok, being nothing but a priest, can not.

Our author's narrative may accordingly be paraphrased as follows: " And among the rest came also Zadok and Abiathar carrying the sacred box, which they deposited upon the ground while waiting for the whole company of David's followers to be assembled on the farther side of the valley. And David, seeing them with the box, said to Zadok, one of the two priests, ' *Are you a clairvoyant?* Can you come with me and by means of this instrument of yours discover, as well as if you remain on the spot, all I shall want to know about Absalom's resources, his activities, and his designs against me? Return to the city, and let your colleague Abiathar go with you, and likewise the young men Ahimaaz and Jonathan. See, I will linger on this side the Jordan till I hear from you.' So Zadok and Abiathar took the sacred box back to Jerusalem and remained there."

That this interpretation is eminently plausible will not be questioned. But it is more than plausible; it is strictly necessary. For, in the first place, the words "Art thou a seer?" undeniably imply some pretensions in the premises on the part of the person addressed. We cannot imagine them being spoken to any layman — Joab for example — who might be charged with a similar commission in Jerusalem. Only in view of Zadok's office as dispenser of the divine oracles has the expression any pertinence at all. In short, "Art thou a seer?" is obviously addressed to Zadok *the diviner;* as, for that matter, the author himself seems to emphasize by the express (and otherwise superfluous) characterization of Zadok at this point as הכהן.

But, in the second place, Zadok *the diviner* necessarily carried with him *the instrument of priestly divination.* And we have no right whatever to dissociate from the matter in hand the one object which the author explicitly mentions in the context, namely the sacred box, and relegate it to the position of an irrelevant and purely symbolic fetich; while we draw from the depths of our imagination, or from the treasure house of scholastic tradition, some wholly fictitious organ of divination — Levitical breastplate with Urim and Thummim, hypothetical oracle-pouch, misbegotten "ephod," or what not — and proceed to bestow it, over the head of the author, in the respective bosoms or upon the respective persons of Zadok and Abiathar, whose hands are already encumbered with the sacred box. On the contrary, it is manifest that for our author and his prospective readers, the sacred box was itself the instrument of priestly divination.

Finally, there was no reason in the world why a purely symbolic fetich, and still less why a wonder-working palladium, should be left behind, simply because David considered the priests who brought it best fitted to do his business in Jerusalem. In fact, the desperate state of his fortunes should have rendered the possession of so precious an object especially welcome, and its retention imperative. An instrument of priestly divination, on the other hand, comes, as a matter of course, when the priests come; and must perforce return when the priests return. Therefore Zadok and Abiathar, being themselves ordered back to the city for duties which had no relation to the sacred box, "took the box back to Jerusalem and remained there."

For the rest, from the circumstance that two men, instead of one, are here seen carrying the sacred box, we may infer that this particular specimen was either of more than ordinary size, or else was provided with a special appliance — probably staves (1 Kings 8, 8) — for its more ceremonious conveyance. Presumably, then, this was not the regulation box which Abiathar carried alone during his wanderings with David in the days of outlawry. But it may well have been identical with the "box of Yahwe Militant" which David removed from Kirjath-jearim to Jerusalem early in his reign as king of all Israel. In that case, the fact that Zadok (although not the senior priest; cf. 1 Kings 2, 35) is so prominently associated with this box, would favor the conjecture that he was in reality the mysterious אחיו of 2 Sam. 6, 3 f, and consequently of Gibeonitish origin.[1]

XV

The last of the three passages which I adduce as special witnesses to the fact that the sacred box was the organ of priestly divination is **Judges 20, 27**.

Verses 27 and 28 of that chapter now read: וישאלו בני ישראל ביהוה ושם ארון ברית האלהים בימים ההם: ופינחס בן אלעזר בן אהרן עמד לפניו בימים ההם לאמר האוסף עוד לצאת למלחמה עם בני אם בנימן אחי אם אחדל ויאמר יהוה עלו כי מחר אתננו בידך.

Here the connection of the sacred box with the oracles of Yahwe appears on the surface of the traditional text. Whether it be an integral part of a very early narrative, or an integral part of a very late narrative, or (as is generally maintained) a palpable interpolation in an antecedent narrative of whatever date, the parenthetical sentence ושם ארון ברית האלהים בימים ההם — or whatever else may have been the original form of it — was obviously set down in this place

[1] See above, p. 62.

by a person who connected the sacred box in some way with the consultation of the oracles by the Israelitish people in the early days.

Nevertheless, we cannot leave the matter there; with the facile observation that, some sort of connection between the box and the oracles being manifestly indicated, our contention is, in so far forth, sustained. The question remains, as to just what that connection was, in the mind of the writer. Did he think of the sacred box as an instrument invariably employed by priests in the process of obtaining the divine responses? Or did he think of it as a unique Yahwistic shrine, at whose domicile for the time being the consultation of the oracles invariably took place? In other words, is the sacred box here mentioned an object such as Abiathar carried in the train of David? Or may it be only the fictional Sinaitic box of Jewish dogma?

Hitherto scholars have naturally interpreted the passage in the latter sense. And we must admit, that if it could be shown that the words in question were penned by a post-exilic Jew, living under the shadow of the Pentateuch, that interpretation would have something in its favor; in spite of the fact that nowhere in the Pentateuch is the imaginary box of the Sinaitic tables of the Law connected in any way with the supposed oracular function of the High Priest,[1] whereas in more than one passage of the historical books (with which such a Jew must have been more or less familiar) the oracles are consulted in places where there can be no thought of locating the Sinaitic box. On the other hand, if the words were penned by a pre-exilic writer who was actually acquainted with

[1] It is worth while recalling that the only other place in the traditional text of the Old Testament where the sacred box is explicitly mentioned in connection with the act of consulting the oracles is 1 Sam. 14, 18; and there the box is so evidently the immediate instrument of divination that, as we have seen, critics unanimously replace it with the "ephod." Perhaps one reason why they have never thought of doing the same thing in Judges 20, 27b is that it has never occurred to them that this statement could be anything but a bit of late Jewish theory, of a piece with the diaskeuastic mention of Phinehas which follows. Yet according to Jewish theory, the Sinaitic box was at Shiloh from the days of Joshua to the days of Eli: Josh. 18, 1; 19, 51; 21, 1 f; 22, 12; Judges 18, 31.

the historical institution of priestly divination among the ancient Israelites, the decision must be unhesitatingly in favor of the first alternative. For it is clear that the writer thinks of the presence of this sacred box as somehow essential to the consultation of the oracles; and it cannot be pretended that either the priest of Micah and the Danites, or Ahijah, or Ahimelech, or Abiathar consulted the oracles in the presence of a unique symbolic fetich answering to the " box of the Testimony " of the Pentateuch.

It is important, therefore, if the testimony of this passage is to be accepted in support of our contention, that the pre-exilic origin of its reference to the sacred box be established.

Unfortunately, in the present state of Old Testament studies, little would be gained by showing that verse 27b is not an interpolation, but a genuine parenthesis, and an authentic part of the paragraph (verses 26–28) in which it stands. For the pre-exilic date of that paragraph itself is generally denied, even by those who find much pre-exilic matter in the rest of the chapter. On the other hand, no less a critic than Wellhausen has gone so far as to attribute the entire story of the war with the Benjamites, Judges 19–21, to a Jewish book-worm of the latest post-exilic period. And although that extreme view has not commanded the assent of other scholars, it cannot be said to have been definitely disproved. Marks of very late date those chapters certainly exhibit in abundance; and so long as no convincing theory of their literary history is forthcoming, it is at least conceivable that the story as a whole may be no earlier than its demonstrably late parts.

Meanwhile, there is no more vexed question in the domain of Old Testament criticism than that of the composition and date of Judges 19–21.[1] In 1887 Kuenen spoke of that section of the book

[1] On the origin and date of Judges 19–21, see: Güdemann, *Monatsschrift für Geschichte und Wissenschaft des Judenthums*, 1869, pp. 357 ff (inaccessible to me); Graetz, *Geschichte der Juden*, I, pp. 351 ff; Wellhausen, in Bleek's *Einleitung*⁴, pp. 199 ff (= *Composition des Hexateuchs*², pp. 233 ff); Bertheau, *Das Buch der Richter und Ruth*², pp. 256 ff; Böhme, *Zeitschrift für die alttestamentliche Wissenschaft*, V, 1885, pp. 30 ff; Kuenen, *Onderzoek*², I, pp. 360 ff; Budde, *Richter und Samuel*, pp. 146 ff; *Kurzer Hand-Commentar*, pp. 125 ff; Moore, *International Critical Commentary*, pp.

as " in zijn geheel een nog niet volledig opgelost raadsel "; and twenty-two years later Boehmer could still write: " Die Komposition von Jdc 20 und 21 ist bekanntlich seit langem eine crux interpretum. Auch die gewiegtesten Kritiker und geübtesten Quellenscheider pflegen hier auf eine endgültige Lösung zu verzichten." Indeed, it is not too much to say that at the present time there is scarcely a single aspect of the subject on which critics are agreed — except perhaps as to the fact that in their existing form chapters 20 and 21 constitute a hodgepodge such as no human intellect at once free and rational is likely to have engendered. Some writers, following Kuenen, see in Judges 19–21, taken as a whole, a single original pre-exilic writing, edited with extensive extemporized elaborations (and perhaps some subtractions and substitutions) in post-exilic times. Others, following Bertheau, find traces of two or more independent and mutually discordant sources, combined by one or more redactors. But in neither case is there agreement as to the metes and bounds of the several elements; nor has either hypothesis resulted thus far in the recovery of a continuous, complete, and self-consistent narrative antecedent to the existing complex.

In the space at my disposal, I can do little more than present, in somewhat dogmatic fashion, the results of my own re-examination of this perplexing subject.[1] Scholars to whom the cardinal points in my analysis do not commend themselves, may simply disregard this part of the discussion entirely. The plurality of the sacred box and its intrinsic character as the instrument of priestly divination have, I think, been sufficiently demonstrated already. And I

---

402 ff; *Sacred Books of the O. T.*, English edition pp. 36 ff, 92 ff; Hebrew edition pp. 18 ff; Nowack, *Handkommentar*, pp. x f, xxviii, 156 ff; Lagrange, *Le Livre des Juges*, pp. 329 ff; Boehmer, *Zeitschrift für die alttestamentliche Wissenschaft*, XXIX, 1909, pp. 146 f; Bewer, *American Journal of Semitic Languages*, XXX, 1914, pp. 81 ff, 149 ff.

[1] It goes without saying, that I have obtained these results by standing on the shoulders of my predecessors, to several of whom, notably Kuenen and Lagrange, I am indebted for valuable observations and suggestions. Most of all, however, I owe to Moore, whose tentative analysis and invaluable commentary furnished the point of departure for my own investigation.

need hardly add, that if Judges 20, 27b is, after all, not of preexilic but of Jewish origin, it follows only that the passage has no bearing on our subject one way or the other. The matter will have been left exactly where it was at the end of the last section.

It is, in my judgment, quite certain that the present text of Judges 19-21 consists of three elements:

(1) An ancient narrative from the pen of the same author who composed the story of Micah and the Danites in Judges 17-18, and also, demonstrably, the early source in the Book of Samuel. His story of the war against the Benjamites has been preserved entire, in consecutive order, and (except at one point, where the figure 18,000 has been substituted for a smaller one) practically unaltered. There is no finer Hebrew anywhere in the Old Testament than that of this narrative. Its date may be fixed with certainty as not later than the tenth century B.C. For the only legitimate inference to be drawn from the language of Judges 18, 1a, and 19, 1a in the mouth of so unmistakable a Jerusalemite as this author, is that the two narratives were written, not only during the monarchy, but during the undivided monarchy — that is, *before the death of Solomon;* and it cannot be questioned that the entire reign of Solomon fell within the tenth century. On the other hand, 1 Kings 1-2 shows the author engaged in writing *after the accession of Solomon;* and while it does not necessarily follow that the narratives of Judges 17-21 formed part of the same work with 1 Kings 1-2, we may reasonably assume that they did. In which case they will have been composed in the reign of Solomon, and consequently in the tenth century B.C.[1] (1) was known to the author of Joshua 7-8, who based upon it his elaborate (and much later) romance of Joshua's war against the legendary city of " Ai." [2]

There is not the slightest reason for questioning the origin of Judges 18, 1a and 19, 1a. On the contrary, when mutually compared the two passages exhibit a perfection of style and a delicate control of the resources of Hebrew

[1] *A priori* we should expect the reign of Solomon to constitute the Periclean age of Israelitish literature; and there is good cause to believe that in fact it did. On 1 Sam. 27, 6b see H. P. Smith's commentary, *ad loc.*

[2] העי = *the Ruin;* and cf. Josh. 8, 28.

syntax such as no diaskeuast can be suspected of. In 18, 1a, when about to describe the independent activities of the Danites, the author of (1) begins by saying, בימים ההם אין מלך בישראל, *In those times there was no king in Israel;* whereas in 19, 1a, when he passes on to the story of the war against the Benjamites, he writes, ויהי בימים ההם ומלך אין בישראל ויהי איש לוי גר וג׳, *In those same times, when* (as we have already said) *there was no king in Israel, there was a Levite residing,* etc. For the rest, he mentions the lack of central authority, not to explain the occurrence of the crimes narrated — which, after all, might have been committed at any time — but to account for the action of the Israelites by clans. On the other hand, the author of 17, 6 and 21, 25, which are nothing but *midrash*, was deeply impressed with the lawlessness of those bad people, particularly that of Micah in establishing his own separate sanctuary and installing his own son as priest (17, 5), in direct contravention of the Mosaic Law. Accordingly, combining the language of 18, 1a with a reminiscence of Deut. 12, 8 f, he appended to 17, 5 the observation, *In those days there was no king in Israel; every man did that which was right in his own eyes,* and in 21, 25 dismissed the whole godless period with the same reflection.

The question of the historicity of (1) does not concern us, and must not be confused with that of literary date. It may, however, be pertinent to remark, that in the case of an author covering so wide a range of time and lacking antecedent literary sources, we have no right to expect uniform historicity, but only uniform good faith. The tradition which he incorporated necessarily grew less historical and more legendary as he travelled backward into the past; and in the story of the war against the Benjamites he is professedly writing of a by-gone age. The details of the narrative, such as the number of days the Levite made merry with his father-in-law, or the exact numbers of the survivors and the slain, will of course be imaginative. The number 600, for example, is a favorite one (see below). Nevertheless, we have no reason to doubt the historical character of the main facts. The theory of Nöldeke[1] that the story may be only an echo of David's wars with Ishbaal (2 Sam. 2 f) and the rebellion of Sheba the son of Bichri (2 Sam. 20), is untenable, if only because this very author has given us all we know of those affairs. Nor is it true that the episode is irreconcilable with the hegemony of Benjamin in the establishment of the Israelitish monarchy. On the contrary, the Benjamites are shown to be a proud and warlike brood, impatient of outside dictation or control, and man for man vastly superior to the rest of the Israelites; just the race to bring forth in due season the majestic figure of Saul and the dauntless chivalry of Jonathan. Of animus against the Benjamites the story betrays not a particle; rather the prevailing note is one of smothered tenderness and genuine regret. The defence of a scapegrace kinsman to the last ditch is anything but a vice in nomad society — or in modern society either, for that matter.

---

[1] See Budde, *Richter und Samuel,* pp. 154 f.

JUDGES 19–21

(2) A paraphrastic and epexegetical commentary, originally scribbled on the margins and between the lines of a manuscript of (1) by a Jewish scribe of no earlier date and far less literary ability than the Chronicler. This commentary, which shows acquaintance with both Gen. 19 and Josh. 7–8, never had any independent existence. It was transferred into the body of (1), with little judgment and quite mechanically, at the next copying of the manuscript; thus producing substantially the present complex of Judges 19–21. The location of the several sections of (2) in the text of (1) was determined largely by the accident of their endorsement between the lines or upon the right-hand, left-hand, upper, or lower margin of the original manuscript. There is no more wretched Hebrew anywhere in the Old Testament than that of this *midrash*.[1]

(3) A few additional glosses; some of which may be independent of (2), while others are clearly of a harmonistic nature, designed to smooth over inconcinnities caused by the introduction of (2) into (1).

To recover the authentic text of (1) the following spurious matter belonging to (2) and (3) must be rejected:[2]

In 19, 6, the obvious gloss וישתו.

In 19, 9, הנה חנות היום לין פה וייטב לבבך; *midrash* to the preceding הנה נא וג׳. Also והלכת לאהלך; *midrash* to לדרככם.

19, 12b–13; marginal *midrash* to verse 12a, based on verses 14–15a. Note גבעה without the article; which latter is indispensable, since גבעה is intrinsically nothing but an appellative; cf. p. 52 above. Moreover, הגבעה אשר לבנימן of verse 14 is necessarily the first mention of the city in the original narrative; cf. 20, 4 f.

---

[1] If it be asked, what use there was in attaching extensive paraphrases and exegesis to a simple and perfectly transparent text, I answer frankly that I cannot imagine any use. I only know that from time immemorial some commentators have always done that very thing, and presumably until the end of time some commentators always will. It may be an unfortunate way they have of showing their respect for the text and assuring themselves that they understand it; like Victor Hugo's old woman, who read to herself with loud voice "pour se donner sa parole d'honneur qu'elle lisait."

[2] Corruptions of a purely textual character are disregarded.

19, 16aβ–b; *midrash* to 16aa'.

(In 19, 18, ואת בית יהוה is a merely accidental corruption of ואל ביתי; cf. G and the commentaries.)

19, 24, entire; marginal *midrash* to verse 23, based on Gen. 19, 8. Note the grammar and diction of לא תעשו, להם, אותם, פילגשהו, דבר הנבלה.

19, 30a(M), entire. This verse must be studied in G^A, which with its congeners has preserved the full text of the expanded document (1) + (2), that is, of our Book of Judges: καὶ ἐγένετο πᾶς ὁ ὁρῶν ἔλεγεν· οὔτε ἐγενήθη οὔτε ὤφθη οὕτως ἀπὸ τῆς ἡμέρας ἀναβάσεως υἱῶν Ἰσραηλ ἐξ Αἰγύπτου ἕως τῆς ἡμέρας ταύτης. καὶ ἐνετείλατο τοῖς ἀνδράσιν οἷς ἐξαπέστειλεν λέγων· τάδε ἐρεῖτε πρὸς πάντα ἄνδρα Ἰσραηλ· εἰ γέγονεν κατὰ τὸ ῥῆμα τοῦτο ἀπὸ τῆς ἡμέρας ἀναβάσεως υἱῶν Ἰσραηλ ἐξ Αἰγύπτου ἕως τῆς ἡμέρας ταύτης· θέσθαι [sic] δὴ ἑαυτοῖς βουλὴν περὶ αὐτῆς καὶ λαλήσαται [sic].[1] 30a(M) is seen to be a marginal *midrash* which was intended to apply *after* the authentic section of (1) preserved in G^A, but which, nevertheless, was mechanically copied in *before* that section when (1) and (2) were combined.

In 20, 1, ותקהל העדה + למדן ועד באר שבע וארץ הגלעד; originally a continuous *midrash* to the rest of verse 1.

In 20, 2a, כל העם + בקהל עם האלהים, together with

20, 2b, entire; constituted originally a nominal sentence: *All the people in the assembly of the people of God were 400,000*, etc.; this continued the *midrash* to verse 1, as did also

20, 3a, entire.

In 20, 3b, בני ישראל; a harmonistic gloss, necessitated by the introduction of 3a.

In 20, 6, the glosses נחלת and זמה (with the following ו).

20, 9–11, entire; marginal *midrash* to verse 8.

20, 15–17, entire; marginal *midrash* to verse 14.

20, 18, entire; marginal *midrash* to verse 19, based on verse 26 and Judges 1, 1 f.

20, 20–23, entire; marginal *midrash* to verses 24–28.

---

[1] From the photographic reproduction of G^A.

JUDGES 19–21

In 20, 24, ביום השני; harmonistic gloss.

In 20, 25a, the harmonistic glosses ביום השנו and עוד. Also the numeral שמנת עשר אלף is certainly spurious, and will be derived from a supralinear correction (suggested perhaps by verse 44a) of an original which has disappeared; compare 1 Sam. 6, 19, where both the original שבעים איש and the supralinear substitute חמשים אלף איש have been preserved. The correction in this passage probably antedated the marginal *midrash*, verses 20–23, which no doubt intended to reproduce in verse 21 the figure it read in verse 25. Somewhere there has been confusion of שמנת עשר and שנים ועשרים. See further the commentary on the authentic text below.

20, 25b; gloss.

In 20, 26, the interlinear glosses ויצומו ביום ההוא וכל העם + ויבכו, and ושלמים. The first needs no discussion. On the second cf. 20, 23 and 21, 2, and contrast ויצומו ביום ההוא of 1 Sam. 7, 6 with the author's ויצמו עד הערב in 2 Sam. 1, 12. On ושלמים cf. 1 Sam. 13, 9; 2 Sam. 6, 17 f; 24, 25 (contrast verses 22 and 24); even 1 Kings 9, 25 is questionable, the usage elsewhere being זבח שלמים or עשה שלמים.

In 20, 27, the gloss ברית together with the article following it; see the commentary below.

20, 28, to בימים ההם; *midrash* to 27b; cf. the three contemporaneous generations of non-Aaronic Levites (which the situation seemed to call for) in 18, 30. The suffix in לפניו must refer to the preceding אלהים (!).

20, 30, from ביום השלישי; harmonistic.

20, 31, from הנתקו (cf. Josh. 8, 16, וינתקו מן העיר, where our commentator ignorantly construed the verb as Hophal because the active התיקנו of verse 6 was plainly Hiphil; and observe the asyndeton of the annotator), together with

20, 32–35, entire, and

20, 43, entire (note the asyndetic style); marginal *midrash* to verses 31a α + 36b to 42 + 44a. In verse 31b, כפעם בפעם is like

20, 36a; harmonistic.

20, 44b; gloss.

20, 45–46, entire; marginal *midrash* to verse 47.

In 20, 47, the gloss ארבעה חדשים; borrowed from 19, 2. The language of 21, 9 and 12b is incompatible with a four months' interval.

21, 2–4, entire; marginal *midrash* to verse 1.

21, 5, entire; marginal *midrash* to verse 8a.

In 21, 7, the gloss לנותרים; cf. verse 16.

21, 8b, entire; marginal *midrash* to verse 9.

21, 10, from העדה, together with

21, 11, entire; marginal *midrash* to וישלחו שם of verse 10 + verse 12. The worthy commentator forgot to supply the sequel to these sanguinary instructions.

In 21, 12, the glosses למשכב זכר and בנען בארץ אשר and שלה; cf. verse 11, and note the determinate המחנה.

In 21, 13, the gloss כל העדה.

In 21, 14, the gloss בעת ההיא.

21, 15–18, entire; marginal *midrash* to verses 6–7!

21, 19aβ–b; marginal *midrash* to 19aa.

21, 24, entire; marginal *midrash* to verse 23.

21, 25, entire; final comment on the whole document.

That we have been dealing with epexegetical matter which never had independent existence is beyond question; for whereas what is left for (1) yields, *without the slightest transposition or suppletion*, a complete, consecutive, organically articulated, and homogeneous narrative, the matter of (2) yields only a series of disjointed sections, each clearly suggested by, and bearing upon, a certain passage in the text of (1). It is equally evident that the commentary was not composed and appended in the act of transcribing or "editing" (1); but, on the contrary, was first endorsed upon the blank spaces of a manuscript of (1), and subsequently copied into the text. For, in the first place, it contains numerous paraphrases running parallel to the text of (1), for which the latter has no logical place. And secondly, instead of uniformly following the section of (1) to which it relates, the commentary sometimes follows that section, sometimes precedes it, sometimes is dovetailed into it, and more than once is, contrary to all rhyme and reason, entirely separated from it. In brief, the present text of Judges 19–21 is demonstrably not the product of a "compiler" or of an "editor," but of a half-educated annotator followed by a clodpated copyist.

The story of Micah and the Danites has been subjected to much the same treatment, apparently by the same hands. To recover the single antecedent document, the following interpolations must be rejected: 17, 2–4, entire. 17, 6, entire. In 17, 7, והוא גר שם. In 17, 10, וילך הלוי. 18, 1, from כי לא. In 18, 2, ממשפחתם; אנשים בני חיל; ויאמרו אלהם לכו חקרו את הארץ (replaces a clause of the original now missing); and וילינו שם. In 18, 3, ומה לך פה. In 18, 7, ויושבת לבטח כמשפט צידנים; and דבר בארץ יורש עצר. In 18, 9, לבא לרשת את הארץ. 18, 10, entire. 18, 12, from ביהודה (cf. page 54 above). In 18, 14, ליש; and ופסל ומסכה. In 18, 16, אשר מבני דן. 18, 17, from באו שמה (annotator's asyndeton). In 18, 18, ואלה באו בית מיכה; פסל; and ואת המסכה. In 18, 20, ואת הפסל. In 18, 28, והיא בעמק אשר לבית רחוב. 18, 29, from בשם דן. 18, 30–31, entire. Also, of course, as we are engaged in showing, throughout the narrative אפוד must be replaced by ארון. In 18, 27 the words הארון ואת התרפים must be restored after לקחו את. In 18, 16 read שש מאות האיש, but חגורים (without the article).

The displacements in 17, 2–4 are especially instructive. Let it be assumed that ותאמר אמו, at the beginning of verse 3b, and verse 4a are harmonistic glosses. The remainder of verses 2–4 may be divided into six successive sections, as follows:

1. Verse 2 as far as באזני . . . . . . which we may call א
2. הנה הכסף אתי אני לקחתיו . . . . " " " ג
3. Verses 2b and 3a . . . . " " " ה
4. From הקדש to מסכה in verse 3 . . " " " ב
5. ועתה אשיבנו לך . . . . " " " ד
6. Verse 4b . . . . " " " ו

It is apparent, that whereas the annotator wrote these sections passing alternately from the right-hand to the left-hand margin of the column,

    ב   א
    ד   ג
    ו   ה

the copyist entered first all the matter on the right, and then all that on the left.

With the excision of the spurious material I have indicated, and the correction of a few perfectly obvious textual errors which will be mentioned in the notes below, the original tenth-century narrative of the war against the Benjamites (beginning at the point where the present confusion seriously sets in) reads as follows:

JUDGES 19, 29 — 21, 23

(19, 29) ... ויבא אל ביתו ויקח את המאכלת ויחזק בפילנשו וינתחה לעצמיה לשנים עשר נתחים וישלחה בכל גבול ישראל (30) ויצו את האנשים אשר שלח לאמר כה תאמרו לכל איש ישראל אם נהיתה כדבר הזה למיום עלות בני ישראל מארץ מצרים עד היום הזה   שימו לכם עליה עצה ודברו

(20, 1) ויצאו כל בני ישראל כאיש אחד אל יהוה המצפה (2) ויתיצבו פנות כל שבטי ישראל (3) ויאמרו דברו איכה נהיתה הרעה הזאת (4) ויען האיש הלוי איש האשה הנרצחה ויאמר הגבעתה אשר לבנימן באתי אני ופילגשי ללון (5) ויקמו עלי בעלי הגבעה ויסבו עלי את הבית לילה   אותי דמו לחרג ואת פילגשי ענו ותמת (6) ואחז בפילגשי ואנתחה ואשלחה בכל שדה ישראל כי עשו נבלה בישראל (7) הנה כלכם בני ישראל הבו לכם דבר ועצה הלם (8) ויקם כל העם כאיש אחד לאמר לא נלך איש לאהלו ולא נסור איש לביתו

(12) וישלחו שבטי ישראל אנשים בכל שבטי בנימן לאמר מה הרעה הזאת אשר נהיתה בכם (13) ועתה תנו את האנשים בני בליעל אשר בגבעה ונמיתם ונבער הרעה מישראל   ולא אבו בנימן לשמע בקול אחיהם בני ישראל (14) ויאספו בני בנימן מן הערים הגבעתה לצאת למלחמה עם בני ישראל (19) ויקומו בני ישראל בבקר ויחנו על הגבעה (24) ויקרבו בני ישראל אל בני בנימן (25) ויצא בנימן לקראתם מן הגבעה וישחיתו בבני ישראל . . . . . . איש ארצה

(26) ויעלו כל בני ישראל ויבאו ביתאל וישבו שם לפני יהוה עד הערב ויעלו עלות לפני יהוה (27) וישאלו בני ישראל ביהוה ושם ארון אלהים בימים ההם (28) לאמר האוסף עוד לצאת למלחמה עם בני בנימן אחי אם אחדל   ויאמר יהוה עלה כי מחר אתננו בידך

(29) וישם ישראל ארבים אל הגבעה סביב (30) ויעלו בני ישראל אל בני בנימן (31) ויצאו בני בנימן לקראת העם (36b) ויתנו איש ישראל מקום לבנימן כי בטחו אל הארב אשר שמו על הגבעה (37) והארב החישו ויפשטו אל הגבעה וימשך הארב ויך את כל העיר לפי חרב (38) והמועד היה לאיש ישראל עם הארב מהרה להעלותם משאת העשן מן העיר (39) ויהפך איש ישראל במלחמה ובנימן החל להכות חללים באיש ישראל כשלשים איש כי אמרו אך נגוף נגף הוא לפנינו כמלחמה הראשנה (40) והמשאת החלה לעלות מן העיר עמוד עשן   ויפן בנימן אחריו והנה עלה כליל העיר השמימה (41) ואיש ישראל הפך   ויבהל איש בנימן כי ראה כי נגעה עליו הרעה (42) ויפן לפני איש ישראל אל דרך המדבר   והמלחמה

הדביקתהו ואשר מהעיר משחיתים אותו בתוך (44) ויפלו מבנימן שמנה עשר אלף
איש (47) ויפנו וינסו המדברה אל סלע רמון שש מאות איש וישבו בסלע רמון
(48) ואיש ישראל שבו אל בני בנימן ויכום לפי חרב מעיר מתם עד בהמה עד כל
הנמצא גם כל הערים הנמצאות שלחו באש

(21, 1) ואיש ישראל נשבע במצפה לאמר איש ממנו לא יתן בתו לבנימן לאשה
(6) וינחמו בני ישראל אל בנימן אחיהם ויאמרו נגדע היום שבט אחד מישראל
(7) (8) מה נעשה להם לנשים ואנחנו נשבענו ביהוה לבלתי תת להם מבנותינו לנשים
(9) ויאמרו מי אחד משבטי ישראל אשר לא עלה אל יהוה המצפה ויתפקד העם
והנה אין שם איש מיושבי יבש גלעד (10) וישלחו שם (12) וימצאו מיושבי
יבש גלעד ארבע מאות נערה בתולה אשר לא ידעה איש ויבאו אתהן אל המחנה
(13) וישלחו וידברו אל בני בנימן אשר בסלע רמון ויקראו להם שלום (14) וישב
בנימן ויתנו להם הנשים אשר היו מנשי יבש גלעד ולא מצאו להם כן (19) ויאמרו
הנה חג יהוה בשלה מימים ימימה (20) ויצוו את בני בנימן לאמר לכו וארבתם
בכרמים (21) וראיתם והנה אם יצאו בנות שלה לחול במחלות ויצאתם מן הכרמים
וחטפתם לכם איש אשתו מבנות שלה והלכתם ארץ בנימן (22) והיה כי יבאו
אבותן או אחיהן לריב אלינו ואמרנו אליהם חנו אותם כי לו לקחנו איש אשתו במלחמה
כי לו אתם נתתם להם כעת תאשמו (23) ויעשו כן בני בנימן וישאו נשים למספרם
מן המחללות אשר גזלו   וילכו וישובו אל נחלתם ויבנו את הערים וישבו בהן

JUDGES 19, 29 — 21, 23

... (19, 29) *And when he came to his house, he took a knife, and laid hold of his concubine, and cut her up, joint by joint, into twelve pieces, and sent them throughout all the borders of Israel. (30) And he commanded the men whom he sent out, saying, Thus shall ye say to all the men of Israel, Did ever a thing like this happen, from the time that the Israelites came up from the land of Egypt to this day? Take counsel about it, and speak!*

(20, 1) *And all the Israelites came out as one man to Yahwe at Mizpah. (2) And the principal men of all the Israelitish clans stood forth (3) and said, Relate, how did this crime happen? (4) And the Levite, the husbdnd of the murdered woman, answered and said, I came with my concubine to Gibeah which belongs to Benjamin, to pass the night; (5) and the citizens of Gibeah assailed me, and gathered about the house where I was, by night. Me they would have killed, and my concubine they ravished so that she died. (6) So I took my concubine,* and cut her in pieces, and sent the pieces throughout all the country of Israel; because they had wrought depravity in Israel. (7) Here all you Israelites are: give your word and counsel in the matter! (8) And all the people stood up as one man, saying, We will not go to our several habitations, nor will be disband to our several homes.

(12) And the Israelitish clans sent men throughout all the clans of Benjamin, saying, What is this crime which has been committed among you? (13) Now, therefore, give up those depraved fellows who are in Gibeah, and let us put them to death, and extirpate the evil from Israel. But the Benjamites refused to listen to the words of their brethren the Israelites.

(14) And the Benjamites gathered from their cities to Gibeah, to go to war with the Israelites. (19) And the Israelites set out in the morning and encamped against Gibeah. (24) And the Israelites drew near to attack the Benjamites. (25) But the Benjamites sallied from Gibeah to meet them, and struck down of the Israelites . . . (so and so many) . . . men.

(26) And all the Israelites went up and came to Bethel, and remained there before Yahwe until the evening, and offered burnt-offerings before Yahwe. (27) And the Israelites enquired of Yahwe — for there was a sacred box there in those days — (28) saying, Shall I again go out to battle with my Benjamite brethren, or shall I desist? And Yahwe answered, Go; for to-morrow I will give them into thine hand.

(29) And Israel put men in ambush against Gibeah, on all sides. (30) Then the Israelites marched against the Benjamites. (31) And the Benjamites sallied out to meet the army. (36b) But the men of Israel gave ground to Benjamin, relying upon the ambush which they had set against Gibeah. (37) Meanwhile, the ambush made haste and rushed upon Gibeah. And the ambush set to and slew without mercy all the inhabitants of the city. (38) Now it had been agreed between the men of Israel and the ambush, that immediately the latter sent up a signal-smoke from the city, (39) the men of Israel should turn about in the battle. And Benjamin had just begun to smite among the men of Israel, and had wounded about thirty men — for they said,

JUDGES 19-21

We have surely beaten them again, as in the former battle — (40) when the fire-signal began to rise from the city, a column of smoke. And the Benjamites looked back, and saw the whole city going up in flames heavenward. (41) At the same time the men of Israel turned suddenly about. And the men of Benjamin were in dismay, for they saw that disaster had overtaken them; (42) and they turned before the men of Israel in the direction of the Wilderness. But the battle drove hard upon them, while those who came from the city kept slaughtering them in the midst. (44) And there fell of Benjamin eighteen thousand men; (47) but there turned and escaped to the Wilderness, to the Cliff of Rimmon, six hundred men, who remained on the Cliff of Rimmon. (48) And the men of Israel came back to the (non-combatant) Benjamites, and slew without mercy both man and beast, to the last thing; also every town in existence they destroyed with fire.

(21, 1) Now the men of Israel had sworn at Mizpah, saying, No one of us shall give his daughter in marriage to a Benjamite. (6) And the Israelites were sorry for their Benjamite brethren, and said, One branch is cut off this day from Israel. (7) What shall we do for them in regard to wives; seeing that we have sworn by Yahwe not to give them any of our daughters as wives? (8) And they said, Is there any Israelitish clan that did not come up to Yahwe at Mizpah? (9) So the army was mustered, and lo, there was not a man there of the inhabitants of Jabesh Gilead. (10) And they sent thither, (12) and found among the inhabitants of Jabesh Gilead four hundred virgin girls, who had not known a man; and they brought them to the camp. (13) And they sent a message to the Benjamites who were at the Cliff of Rimmon, and proclaimed peace to them. (14) So the Benjamites returned, and they gave them the women that were of the women of Jabesh Gilead; but they had not enough for them. (19) And they bethought them of the festival of Yahwe held every year at Shiloh. (20) So they commanded the Benjamites, saying, Go, lie in wait in the vineyards, (21) and watch, and when the maidens of Shiloh come out to dance in the dances, come out from the vineyards, and snatch for yourselves every man a wife of the maidens of Shiloh, and make off to the land of Benjamin. (22) And if their fathers or brothers come to us to complain of you, we will say to them, *Forgive them; for what if they had each captured his wife in the war? only if ye yourselves had given* (wives) *to them, would ye now be guilty.* (23) *And the Benjamites did so, and carried away wives according to their number, of the dancers whom they had seized. And they went back again to their possession, and rebuilt their towns, and dwelt in them.*[1]

In connection with the few critical notes which follow, I cite from the older source of the Book of Samuel passages exhibiting noticeable affinity with our narrative in the matter of style or diction. Some of these parallels are not intrinsically very cogent, nor would even one or two of the more striking resemblances be sufficient to prove identity of authorship. But in the aggregate, and supplemented by such as might be adduced for chapters 17–18 and the omitted portion of chapter 19, they are, in my judgment, quite conclusive on that point.

By way of illustration as regards the omitted portion of chapter 19: With וישמח לקראתו of verse 3, cf. 1 Sam. 6, 13; 11, 9; 19, 5. With ויפצר בו of verse 7, cf. 1 Sam. 28, 23; 2 Sam. 13, 25 27 (where we must of course read פצר). With לכה נא ונסורה of verse 11, cf. 1 Sam. 9, 5 10; 14, 1 6; 20, 11. With תבא להם השמש אצל וג׳ of verse 14, cf. 2 Sam. 2, 32. With והנה איש זקן בא וג׳ of verse 16, cf. 1 Sam. 11, 5; 2 Sam. 1, 2; 3, 22; 16, 5; 18, 31; 1 Kings 1, 42. With אל אחי אל תרעו וג׳ of verse 23, cf. 2 Sam. 13, 12 25. With ויתעללו בה of verse 25, cf. 1 Sam. 31, 4. These parallels are just such as to argue identity of literary origin and to preclude any suggestion of slavish imitation on the part of the author of Judges 19–21.

19, 29. ויבא אל ביתו ויקח. Cf. 2 Sam. 20, 3.

וישלחה . . . וינתחה. Cf. 20, 6, and 1 Sam. 11, 7.

לשנים עשר נתחים. Stylistically, these words cannot be rejected unless we reject the preceding לעצמיה as well. But no Jewish interpolator of the former would have thought of interpolating the latter. The number of pieces of the body of the murdered woman which were dispatched " throughout all the borders of Israel " was determined, not by the number of " tribes " — of which, as we

---

[1] To avoid the semblance of difference where none exists, I have purposely adhered, so far as practicable, to the language of Moore's English translation in the *Sacred Books of the Old Testament*.

shall see, our author knows nothing, and which have no more to do with this matter than with the number of champions in 2 Sam. 2, 15 — but, as we are expressly told, by the number of " her bones "; evidently reckoning three joints to each limb.[1] With no instrument but a household " eating-knife " (מאכלת), that was the obvious dissection. Portable pieces of the trunk would not serve the purpose; while the head would of course not be bandied about, in the absence of any desire to add to the indignities heaped upon the wretched woman.

בכל גבול ישראל. Cf. 1 Sam. 11, 3 7; 27, 1; 2 Sam. 21, 5; 1 Kings 1, 3.

19, 30a. The text of this half-verse is restored after G^A; see page 102, above.

נהיתה כדבר הזה. Cf. 20, 3 12, and 1 Kings 1, 27.

למיום עלות וג׳. Cf. 1 Sam. 29, 3 6; 2 Sam. 13, 32; 19, 25.

19, 30b. For עצו of the Masoretic text, read עצה, with G; cf. 20, 7.

20, 1. ויצאו ... כאיש אחד. Cf. verse 8, and 1 Sam. 11, 7; 2 Sam. 19, 15. See further the note on לצאת למלחמה of verse 14, below.

20, 2. ויתיצבו. Cf. 2 Sam. 18, 13 30; 21, 5.

פנות כל שבטי ישראל. Cf. 1 Sam. 14, 38; and see the note on שבטי בנימן of verse 12, below.

20, 3. הרעה הזאת. Cf. verse 12, and 2 Sam. 13, 16.

20, 5. דמו לחרג. Cf. 2 Sam. 21, 5, and the commentaries on that passage.

20, 6. ואחז בפילגשי. Cf. 2 Sam. 4, 10; 6, 6; 20, 9; 1 Kings 1, 51; and observe the synonymous ויחזק ב in 1 Kings 1, 50 as in Judges 19, 29.

עשו נבלה בישראל. Cf. 19, 23, and 2 Sam. 13, 12. The word נבלה, essentially *rottenness*, *blight*, is cognate to the construct noun in the compound בליעל; the genitive in the latter being without doubt the designation of some spirit of evil (= Arabic *ghûl* ?).

20, 7. הנה כלכם בני ישראל. The construction of this troublesome sentence may be made plain by substituting העברים for בני ישראל. In the sentence הנה כלכם העברים, the last word cannot be predicate,

---

[1] Cf. Moore's commentary, p. 420, footnote; and 2 Sam. 4, 12.

if only because it is determinate; but it will be appositive to the suffix in בלכם (cf. Gesenius-Kautzsch § 131 n) rather than vocative. הבו לכם דבר וג׳. Cf. 2 Sam. 16, 20.

20, 8. לא נלך איש לאהלו וג׳. Cf. the balanced exclamation in 2 Sam. 20, 1. The latter is copied in 1 Kings 12, 16.

20, 12. שבטי בנימן. We must abide by the plural שבטי of the Masoretic text. The author does not employ the word שבט in the technical sense in which we understand it, but as a simple appellative, meaning *branch* (notice the verb נגדע, *chopped off*, in 21, 6) and quantitatively equivalent to משפחה. The same body of people which as a *clan* or group of kinsfolk constitutes a משפחה, as a *branch* or fraction of a larger whole constitutes a שבט. So the Danites are at once a שבט and a משפחה in Israel: Judges 18, 19. Judah is a משפחה: 17, 7; as well as Dan: 18, 11. Benjamin is one of the smallest of the שבטי ישראל, but Saul's משפחה is in turn the smallest of the שבטי בנימן: 1 Sam. 9, 21. In the latter passage the word משפחות is (like משפחת in Num. 4, 18; cf. 26, 57) an explanatory gloss, and a correct one. The single city of Jabesh Gilead is אחד משבטי ישראל: Judges 21, 8 f. And when Absalom asks a visitor to the capital, "Of what *city* art thou?" the man replies, "Thy servant is of such and such a *section* of Israel"—מאחד שבטי ישראל, 2 Sam. 15, 2; cf. 19, 10. It is evident that for our author שבט is quite as vague a term as משפחה, applicable not only to the major constituents of Israel, but to secondary fractions as well; and that he knows no more of a definite and fixed number of שבטים than he does of a definite and fixed number of משפחות. 2 Sam. 19, 44a is patently spurious; for verse 44b must originally have followed immediately upon verse 43.

20, 13. We must read וּנְבַעֵר הרעה instead of ונבערה רעה of the Masoretic text. רעה requires the article; whereas the cohortative particle is rather out of place with the verb, since it is not proposed that the Benjamites take part in the infliction of the penalty. For the language cf. 2 Sam. 4, 11.

ולא אבו ... לְ. Cf. 19, 10 25; 1 Sam. 22, 17; 26, 23; 31, 4; 2 Sam. 2, 21; 6, 10; 12, 17; 13, 14 16 25; and contrast 1 Sam. 15, 9.

בנימן. It is not necessary to follow the *Qrê* in prefixing בני. The latter is less likely to have been dropped by the tradition than omitted by the author; cf. ויתנו איש ישראל in verse 36, and הארב החישו ויפשטו in verse 37.

אחיהם בני ישראל. Cf. 18, 8 14; 19, 23; 20, 28; 21, 6; 2 Sam. 2, 26 f; 15, 20; 19, 13 42.

20, 14. הערים. Cf. 20, 48; 21, 23; 1 Sam. 31, 7; and contrast 1 Chron. 10, 7. The reading in the Samuel passage should not be altered to עריהם, with Budde, H. P. Smith, and Dhorme.

לצאת למלחמה. Cf. 20, 1 28; 1 Sam. 4, 1b; 11, 7; 13, 17 23; 18, 30; 24, 15; 28, 1; 2 Sam. 2, 12 f; 11, 1; 18, 2 f.

20, 25. וישחיתו. Cf. verse 42, and 1 Sam. 13, 17; 14, 15; 26, 9 15; 2 Sam. 11, 1; 20, 15 20.

As already observed above, the numeral שמנת עשר אלף of the existing text is certainly spurious, and must be rejected *in toto*. We cannot attempt to secure a more acceptable figure by dropping either שמנת or עשר; since neither שמנת אלף nor עשר אלף would be Hebrew. On the other hand, it will not do to drop the אלף and read שמנת עשר איש, as has been suggested.[1] For the logic of the story — we are not concerned with the historical event — demands a figure not only considerably lower than the number of the Benjamites finally slain, namely 18,000 (verse 44); but also one very much higher than the insignificant number of Israelites gladly sacrificed for strategic reasons at the beginning of the second day's battle, namely 30 (verse 39). Nor would our author have represented the whole Israelitish army as repairing to Bethel, crestfallen and bewildered, to implore Yahwe's guidance and the restoration of his favor, on account of the loss of eighteen, or even of forty men. Unlike the theocratic theorist of Josh. 7, 5 f, he doubtless knew that "battles are not won without losing men." To meet all the demands of the context, a loss of at least two or three thousand men must be assumed. If, therefore, it were worth while to fill up the lacuna in this passage with a query, I should suggest the reading כשלשת אלפים איש (cf. 1 Sam. 13, 2; 24, 3; 25, 2; 26,

---

[1] Bewer, *l. c.*, p. 157.

2 [1]). And that conjecture would be supported by the following consideration. Our narrative contained three different numerals, setting forth the number of men lost on one side or the other in the two days' fighting, namely those of verses 25, 39, and 44 respectively. Now in the story of the war against Ai (Josh. 7–8), which is unmistakably based upon this narrative, there can be little doubt that שנים עשר אלף of chap. 8, 25 represents the figure which the author of that story read at Judges 20, 44, while כשלשים וששה of Josh. 7, 5 just as certainly represents the figure which he read at Judges 20, 39. It is not improbable, therefore, that כשלשת אלפים of Josh. 7, 4, the number of the Israelites routed in the first day's battle with the men of Ai, represents the figure which he read at Judges 20, 25. For the rest, it is clear that in the case of the second figure our Judges text has preserved the original reading; since the particle כ is unnatural before the definite number שלשים וששה. But as regards the first, it is quite possible that שנים עשר rather than שמנה עשר was the authentic text of Judges 20, 44. We have no means of determining the question. Historically, the Benjamites are as likely to have had eighteen thousand men to lose as twelve thousand.

20, 27b. The precise reading to be adopted for this half-verse depends upon the origin which we are compelled to assign to it. If it be, like the following clause concerning Phinehas in verse 28a, a post-exilic interpolation — whether originating with the author of the marginal commentary or with some other Jewish annotator — the expression ארון ברית האלהים of the traditional text will be as much in place as it is in 1 Chron. 16, 6.[2] But if, on the other hand, we are obliged to accept the clause as a genuine parenthesis and an integral part of the early pre-exilic narrative, it will follow as a matter of course that the word ברית is the Deuteronomistic gloss which we have had repeated occasion to discard from early Old

---

[1] I purposely avoid mentioning Judges 15, 11; 16, 27.

[2] It is worth noting, however, that this would be the only other instance of an original ארון ברית האלהים in the Old Testament. Elsewhere the expression is distinctly the result of textual corruption.

Testament texts relating to the sacred box. And since, moreover, in that event the present text will have been shown to be corrupt, we shall not hesitate to reject also the article in ארון האלהים, as of a piece with the spurious ברית, if the context, interpreted in the light of what we know regarding the historical institution of the sacred box, so requires. For it should be borne in mind that all we are seeking to prove independently by means of this passage is the fact that the sacred box was the organ of priestly divination; and, as has already been pointed out,[1] if the reference to it in this verse is authentic, the box will necessarily be the instrument of divination, regardless of whether it happens to be called " the sacred box " or " a sacred box."

Now the clause verse 27b must be an integral part of the original pre-exilic record. For, to begin with, only on that assumption can we satisfactorily explain its present position in the text. If it had originated with the marginal annotator, we should certainly find it in verse 18, where that annotator mentioned for the first time — and before he reached his own paraphrase of verses 26 f (verse 23) — the resort of the Israelites to Bethel to consult the oracle of Yahwe. The same would be true if the clause in question were a subsequent interpolation, inserted by the copyist who introduced the marginal commentary into the body of the original narrative, or by any later diaskeuast; in that case too, we should find it after the word אלהים in verse 18. For the statement has absolutely no pertinence except at the very first mention of a journey to Bethel for the consultation of the oracle — whatever may have constituted such first mention at each stage in the history of the text. Similarly the insertion of the epexegetical note concerning Phinehas in verse 28 rather than in verse 18, while natural enough if 27b was already a part of the existing text, is otherwise quite inexplicable. So that verse 27b was either part of the original record, or else — a far-fetched alternative at best — it was inserted by some independent glossator antecedent to the author of our marginal *midrash* (who

---

[1] See pages 96 f.

presumably contributed both verse 18 and verse 28a α [1]). But if that extremely hypothetical glossator was an ancient Israelite living in pre-exilic times, he may, for the purposes of our argument, be treated as identical with the original writer. If, on the contrary, he was, like the author of the *midrash*, a post-exilic Jew, then we must imagine him not content with having the Israelites repair to Bethel to enquire of Yahwe (as the text alleged, and as they might conceivably have enquired at any other theoretically irregular sanctuary mentioned in the historical books — at Dan, for example), but actually going out of his way to create serious difficulty by gratuitously transporting to that hotbed of apostasy and schism the unique Sinaitic shrine which he, in common with his contemporaries, believed to have been domiciled at Shiloh throughout that period of Israelitish history.[2] For it was one thing for a post-exilic Jew to be forced to interpret an existing verse 27b in the sense of 28a α notwithstanding Jewish doctrine; and quite another for such a Jew to interpret 27a gratuitously in the direction of 27b, of which there was no more need than in Judges 1, 1 or 18, 5. It is, I think, sufficiently apparent that the difficulties in the way of assigning verse 27b to any source other than the original author are practically insuperable.

On the other hand, not only is this clause exactly where we should expect to find it if it originated with the author of our narrative, and the coupling of the sacred box with the ancient Israelitish sanctuary of Bethel[3] eminently appropriate in his case, but the clause actually cannot be discarded without leaving a noticeable hiatus in the record. For verse 27b does very much more than indicate the means whereby the consultation of the oracle took place. In fact, although it is for our purposes quite conclusive on that point, its form rather implies that the author's readers will take for granted the oracle was consulted by means of a sacred box. The question which verse 27b really answers, and which in the

---

[1] Compare once more the parallel to 20, 28a α in 18, 30b, where we of course read משה.

[2] Cf. p. 96, note.   [3] Cf. 1 Sam. 10, 3.

absence of that clause remains unanswered, has to do with the reason why the Israelites journeyed to Bethel for the purpose of consulting the oracle of Yahwe. For although they are represented as waiting reverently upon the deity until evening and propitiating him with burnt-offerings, it is clear that those proceedings were merely by way of ensuring a favorable response to their enquiry. It was not ultimately to worship Yahwe — which they might have done as well at Mizpah or elsewhere — but to seek his guidance, that they repaired in a body to the sanctuary at Bethel. Yet why to Bethel, rather than back to Mizpah? For that matter, why should they go anywhere at all; since neither Saul nor David in later times marched his armies to any particular spot to enquire of Yahwe? Incidentally, no doubt, because of the pre-eminence of Bethel among the sanctuaries of Israel and its accessibility in the existing situation. But more especially because neither in the camp of the army nor at Mizpah was there an oracle of Yahwe, whereas at Bethel *there was a sacred box in those days*. The sanctuary at Bethel, that is, was not an open-air high place, like that of Mizpah, the "beacon-hill" at which they had originally assembled; but a היכל, like that of Shiloh, with a resident priesthood guarding the cherished instrument of the oracles of Yahwe. The author was not obliged to tell his readers that Yahwe was habitually consulted by means of the sacred box; but there might well be some among them who would need to be reminded that a hastily-gathered volunteer force in those primitive times did not, like the well-organized royal armies of Saul and David (and doubtless also of Solomon), include an army chaplain; while probably most would need to be told that the famous sanctuary at Bethel was already in those early days in possession of a full-fledged priestly establishment. If there is one thing, however, which we may be sure the author had no intention of implying, it is that there had ceased to be a sacred box at Bethel at the time of writing. His readers presumably knew as well as he that such was not the case.

We must accordingly hold verse 27b to be part of the original narrative of the war against the Benjamites. And if so, the setting demands that not merely the word ברית, but likewise the article which follows it, be discarded.¹ For this sacred box was obviously not an appurtenance of the Israelitish army; and our author knows nothing of any Sacred Box κατ' ἐξοχήν. The authentic text was therefore: ושם ארון אלהים בימים ההם. Compare ושם אבן גדולה, 1 Sam. 6, 14; ושם מערה, 1 Sam. 24, 4; and especially ושם איש מעבדי שאול, 1 Sam. 21, 8. For the phrase בימים ההם, cf. Judges 18, 1; 19, 1; 1 Sam. 28, 1; 2 Sam. 16, 23.

It remains to point out that nothing should give us less concern than the fact that this clause, if held to be authentic, is obtrusively parenthetical.² For no modern writer could employ the real parenthesis — as distinguished from the ordinary circumstantial or explanatory clause of Hebrew syntax — with more perfect ease and naturalness than does this ancient Israelite.³ Note the parenthetical clause כי אמרו וג׳, actually separating protasis and apodosis in the balanced sentence ובנימן החל . . . והמשאת החלה וג׳ in verses 39 f of this chapter.⁴ Further compare 1 Sam. 14, 18b⁵; 2 Sam. 4, 2b–3⁶; 14, 26⁷;

---

[1] The existing readings are probably to be explained as follows. A supralinear gloss ״ ברית (cf. the error in 19, 18) over the authentic ארון אלהים produced ארון ברית האלהים, preserved in M and in the text of Jerome. This was corrupted, either in the Hebrew or in the Greek, into the more natural ἡ κιβωτὸς διαθήκης κυρίου of G^A and congeners. A similar explanation will apply to the reading of the Peshīṭa; whereas G^B, κιβωτὸς διαθήκης κυρίου τοῦ θεοῦ, merely combines G and M.

[2] The transposition advocated by Geddes (*The Holy Bible translated from Corrected Texts of the Originals*, vol. II, 1797, p. 42), namely, verse 26 + 27b + 28aα + 27a + 28aβ, is already to be found in G^B. We may be quite certain, however, that the reading of G^B was as innocent of objective basis as that of Geddes. G^A and congeners support the Masoretic text.

[3] It is the misfortune of this great man that his writings have come down to us within the bounds of an ecclesiastical canon of Holy Scripture; otherwise students of the humanities would hardly continue to ignore a prose which, for combined simplicity and distinction, has remained unmatched in the literature of the world, and which the progressive sophistication of mankind has long since rendered forever unapproachable.

[4] Cf. Gesenius-Kautzsch § 164 b.

[5] As restored; see p. 16.

[6] The authentic text is continued in verse 5; verse 4, like 6 and 7 (to משכבו), is interpolated.

[7] The authentic parenthesis is כי כבד עליו וגלחו, separating the apodosis verse 26b from the protasis ובגלחו את ראשו. Only the clause ויהי מקץ וג׳ (!) is inter-

21, 2b[1]; and especially (a case as striking as it is unquestionable) 14, 13: *And the woman said, Why then dost thou design this injury to the nation — whoever argues with the king on this subject is impertinent*[2] *— not to bring back thine exiled son?*

20, 28. אחדל. Cf. 1 Sam. 23, 13.

עֲלֵה is of course the correct reading. The Masoretic עלי follows the *midrash* of verse 23. Both question and answer doubtless made use of stereotyped forms, which were couched in the singular number. Compare 1 Sam. 14, 37; 30, 8; 2 Sam. 2, 1; 5, 19.[3] The response of Judges 18, 6 is not direct.

20, 29. ארבים. Cf. verses 36 ff, and 1 Sam. 22, 8 13.

20, 37. החישו. Cf. 1 Sam. 20, 38.

ויפשטו. Cf. 1 Sam. 23, 27; 27, 8 10; 30, 1 14.

וימשך. The essential meaning of משך is *to take hold*, as in Arabic. It then comes to signify *to take hold for the purpose of pulling*, and hence *to pull;* cf. Gen. 37, 28; Ex. 12, 21; Jer. 38, 13. In this passage it is used figuratively, in the sense of *to take hold of a task*

polated. אבן המלך, *the standard weight*, has no more to do with the king of Babylon than has דרך המלך, *the public road*, in Num. 20, 17. For the rest, seven or eight pounds of hair (as much as would be contained in a good-sized cushion) is, what it was meant to be, a marvelous quantity of hair; but it is not enough to be fantastic. On the whole passage, cf. the present writer's article, "The Interpretation of קרנים מידו לו, Hab. 3, 4," *American Journal of Semitic Languages*, XXI, 1905, pp. 167 ff.

[1] The resuming clause at the beginning of verse 3 shows that we are dealing with a genuine parenthesis; only the final ויהודה is interpolated. With the expression והנבעונים לא מבני ישראל המה, cf. Judges 19, 12a.

[2] That the clause is parenthetical and the above general sense of it, is beyond question. The exact text is not so certain. Probably we should read הַמְדַבֵּר בַּמֶּלֶךְ; cf. Num. 12, 1 8; 21, 5 7. As Budde points out (*Kurzer Hand-Commentar*, p. 266), the Masoretic pointing intends, not the Hithpael participle, but the Piel infinitive with מן. But the current interpretation is, in any event, quite impossible. No peasant woman would tell a king that he was next thing to a criminal, because he kept a murderer in exile; nor, if she did, would this be the Hebrew for it. In fact, the only connection with the woman's own case is delicately supplied by the initial ו of ולמה — if the king so readily pardons her fratricide son, why not his own? The sentence beginning with וחשב in verse 14 is a bit of scribal exegesis, which hits the nail on the wrong end.

[3] The forms were carried over into divination by means of prophecy; cf. 1 Kings 22, 6 12 15.

with energy and dispatch — to "*pitch in.*" "And the ambush pitched in and killed all the inhabitants of the city" reproduces exactly the force of the Hebrew.

ויך ... לפי חרב. Cf. 18, 17; 20, 48; 1 Sam. 22, 19; 2 Sam. 15, 14.

20, 38. המועד. Cf. 1 Sam. 9, 24; 20, 35; 2 Sam. 20, 5.

For the meaningless letters הרב of the Masoretic text, we must obviously read מְהֵרָה; which modifies the following temporal clause, like the Greek εὐθύς in similar case. The word occurs 1 Sam. 20, 38; 2 Sam. 17, 16 18 21.[1]

להעלותם וג׳. Cf. 2 Sam. 18, 29.

20, 39. Point וְיַהֲפֹךְ, and interpret as jussive. Compare the use of this word in 1 Sam. 25, 12.

החל. Cf. 1 Sam. 22, 15. The word is correlated with החלה in verse 40. On the parenthesis כי אמרו וג׳, separating protasis and apodosis, see the note on 20, 27b.

בשלשים איש. Cf. 1 Sam. 9, 22.

20, 41. ויבהל. Cf. 1 Sam. 28, 21; 2 Sam. 4, 1.

20, 42. Read מהעיר, ויפן, and בַּתָּוֶךְ (cf. Josh. 8, 22), for the corrupt מהערים, ויפנו, and בתוכו of the Masoretic text. For a similar use of פנה see verse 47 and chap. 18, 21 26.

הדביקתהו. Cf. 18, 22; 1 Sam. 14, 22; 31, 2; 2 Sam. 1, 6.[2]

20, 44. שמנה עשר אלף. See the note on verse 25, above.

20, 47. The author of course wrote uniformly either סלע רמין or סלע הרמון, we cannot be quite sure which. I conform the reading in verse 47a to that of the authentic 47b and chap. 21, 13 rather than to that of the spurious verse 45. סלע רמון is also intrinsically more plausible, since רמון in this connection is more likely to be a proper name than the appellative for "pomegranate."

---

[1] In 2 Kings 1, 11 the vocalization must not be altered to מְהֵרָה (as Brown-Driver-Briggs). 1 Sam. 23, 27 is not at all in the same case; one does not say "at once!" to a king, though one may urge him to "hasten."

[2] 2 Sam. 1, 6 ff belongs to the same document with 1 Sam. 31, 4; cf. 2 Sam. 4, 10. Having just given the reader his own account of the actual manner of Saul's death in 1 Sam. 31, the author did not think it necessary, when reproducing the luckless Amalekite's bragging narration in 2 Sam. 1, to point out that the fellow was lying.

שש מאות איש. Cf. 18, 11 16; 1 Sam. 13, 15; 14, 2; 23, 13; 25, 13; 27, 2; 30, 9; 2 Sam. 15, 18. For the style of verse 47a, cf. Judges 18, 11.

20, 48. ואיש ישראל שבו = οἱ δὲ Ἰσραηλῖται ἐπέστρεψαν. Cf. 1 Sam. 26, 25; 2 Sam. 2, 30; 20, 22.

מתם. We must of course vocalize and interpret as in Deut. 2, 34; 3, 6.

הנמצאות, כל הנמצא. Cf. 1 Sam. 13, 15 f; 21, 4.

21, 6. אחיו of the Masoretic text is hardly possible here; read אֲחִיהֶם.

21, 7. לבלתי תת. Cf. 2 Sam. 14, 7 13.

21, 9. ויתפקד. Cf. 1 Sam. 13, 15; 14, 17; 2 Sam. 18, 1. There was no commander-in-chief in this case; so the army *musters itself*.

21, 12. נערה בתולה. Cf. 1 Kings 1, 2. The expression לא ידעה איש, it may be noted, is found elsewhere only Gen. 19, 8 and Judges 11, 39.

אותם of the Masoretic text is ungrammatical in a writing of this date; we must read אֶתְהֶן.

21, 13. ויקראו להם שלום. Cf. 1 Kings 2, 13.

21, 14. הָיוּ, literally *had been*, has been corrupted to חִיּוּ, *had saved alive*, under the influence of the *midrash* of verses 10 f. Cf. 18, 27; 2 Sam. 8, 7.

21, 19. ויאמרו, *and they thought*, is followed in verse 20 by ויצוו, *and they commanded*; just as ויאמרו, *and they said to themselves*, in verse 6, is followed by ויאמרו, *and they said*, in verse 8. In 2 Sam. 5, 6 the order is reversed: ויאמר לדוד לאמר ... לאמר ונ׳ = *and he said to David ... thinking, David cannot come up here*; cf. 1 Sam. 9, 24: כי למועד שמור לך לאמר ונ׳ = *for it was purposely saved for thee, thinking*, etc. See further the footnote on 1 Sam. 4, 7, page 12.

שלה. The author certainly employed this spelling, both here and in verse 21, as in 1 Sam. 4.

21, 20. ויצוו. For the sake of legibility I have added a ו; though יצו was possibly the original for the third person plural.

21, 21. אם יצאו ... במחלות. Cf. 1 Sam. 18, 6; 21, 12; 29, 5.

21, 22. Read אבותן, אחיהן, חנו, לו לקחו, and לו אתם, for אבותם, אחיהם, חנונו, לא לקחנו, and לא אתם, respectively, of the Masoretic text. The readings חנו and לקחו are supported by some of the best manuscripts of the Septuagint, as well as by the Peshîta and Jerome. The clause לו לקחו וג׳ must be interpreted in the light of Gen. 50, 15: לו ישטמנו יוסף וג׳, *What if Joseph were to turn hostile to us for all the injury we did him?*

כעת. For another instance of this word introducing an apodosis after a protasis with לו, see Judges 13, 23. The reading כעת can hardly be the result of corruption in both passages, as supposed by Moore. In 13, 23 כעת (analogous to כַּיּוֹם) is not *a minute ago*, but *at this time* — "If Yahwe intended to slay us, he would not *now* be promising us a son."

תאשמו. Cf. 2 Sam. 14, 13.

21, 23. וישאו is here employed exactly as in 1 Sam. 4, 4 and 2 Sam. 6, 3, in the sense of *carried away*, not *married* (wives).

למספרם. Cf. 1 Sam. 6, 4; 27, 7; 2 Sam. 2, 11 15.

וישבו בהן. Cf. 18, 28; 20, 47; 1 Sam. 23, 25; 24, 1; 31, 7; 2 Sam. 2, 3; 5, 9; 15, 29. The form בהם, with reference to a feminine antecedent, is possible in Biblical Hebrew; but we may be sure our author wrote more correctly בהן, as in 1 Sam. 31, 7; with which contrast 1 Chron. 10, 7.

XVI

We have completed our survey of the Old Testament passages which bear witness to the fact that the historical sacred box of the ancient Hebrews was a manifold object regularly employed as the instrument of priestly divination. And with that fact established, we may return to the passage from which our investigation set out, namely 1 Sam. 14, 18.

It has now been shown that the first of the two objections urged by modern critics against the authenticity of the Masoretic reading ארון האלהים in this passage, namely that the box of 1 Sam. 4 ff was at the time in question lodged in the house of Abinadab at Kirjath-jearim, and could not therefore have been in the camp of

Saul near Gibeah of Benjamin, is entirely irrelevant; since the box of 1 Sam. 14, 18 was obviously another box. Similarly the second objection, that the instrument demanded by the context is not the sacred box but the "ephod," is seen to be without foundation; since, whether or not a problematical "ephod" was ever employed in divination, there can no longer be any question that the sacred box actually was so employed. There remains, therefore, no ground whatever for refusing to accept as the original and authentic text of 1 Sam. 14, 18 the reading which results from the application of sound principles of textual criticism to the existing data, namely:
ויאמר שאול לאחיה הגישה ארון האלהים כי הוא נשׂא ארון האלהים ביום ההוא לפני ישראל.[1]

But if ארון האלהים was part of the original text in 1 Sam. 14, 18, the reading τὸ ἐφούδ which replaces it in the Septuagint furnishes objective and conclusive evidence that אפוד was deliberately substituted for an original ארון in at least one passage in one early Hebrew manuscript. I say deliberately, because, as has been pointed out, האפוד could never replace ארון האלהים by accident. And since we cannot, by any amount of contortion, escape the conclusion that the reading אפוד, wherever it stands for a solid object, has been methodically substituted for some more troublesome word,[2] we may reasonably infer that, as demonstrably in 1 Sam. 14, 18, so everywhere else in the Old Testament that troublesome word was ארון.

In point of fact, however, it is more than a reasonable inference that אפוד has displaced an original ארון in every passage in the Old Testament where it stands for the so-called solid "ephod." Leaving aside for the moment Hosea 3, 4, which demands separate treatment, the solid "ephod" is found in the story of Gideon, Judges 8, 27; in the story of Micah and the Danites, Judges 17-18; and in 1 Sam. 2, 28; 14, 3; 21, 10; 22, 18; 23, 6 9; 30, 7. Now, quite apart from the fact that the "ephod" of these passages ostensibly represents the very instrument of priestly divination which our investigation has shown the sacred box to be, purely

---

[1] See pages 13 ff.   [2] Cf. pages 9 f.

literary considerations make it evident that if the genuine reading in 1 Sam. 14, 18a is הגישה ארון האלהים, that of 30, 7a (where, in the same source, David addresses Abiathar under precisely the same circumstances as Saul does Ahijah in 14, 18) must be, not הגישה נא לי האפוד, but הגישה נא לי הארון[1]; and equally evident, consequently, that both in 30, 7b and in 23, 6 9 the original reading was likewise, not אפוד, but ארון. All of which is demonstrated independently by the testimony of 1 Kings 2, 26[2]; and confirmed, at least as to 23, 9, by the Septuagint reading presently to be mentioned. But if the original text of 23, 6 was not אפוד ירד בידו, but ארון אלהים ירד בידו (the instrument of the priestly office, which Abiathar carried with him in his flight from Nob, being not an "ephod" but a sacred box[3]), then there can be little doubt that the mysterious object belonging to the sanctuary at Nob which the Masoretic text of 1 Sam. 21, 10 calls האפוד was originally הארון.

Again, if the genuine text of 1 Sam. 14, 18b is נשא ארון האלהים, it is evident that the original expression in verse 3 of the same chapter (where the same person is being described in the same relation) was likewise, not נשא אפוד, but נשא ארון. But if נשא ארון was the conventional description of the priestly office in 14, 3, we may be certain that the same conventional description was employed originally also in 22, 18; where שמנים וחמשה איש נשא ארון signified, of course, not that the sanctuary at Nob possessed eighty-five separate sacred boxes, but merely that the family of Ahimelech comprised eighty-five persons consecrated to the office of priest and competent to employ that instrument[4] — although there may

---

[1] Unless it is to be maintained that אפוד and ארון were only different names for the same thing. But the one thing no one has yet thought to make of the "ephod" is a box.

[2] See pages 67 ff, above.

[3] In the sentence אפוד ירד בידו, the last word is idiomatic Hebrew for *with him*. It no more follows from this passage that the object in question was "easily carried in the hand" (Foote, *l. c.*, p. 41) than it follows from the statement וינשו כל העם איש שורו בידו of 1 Sam. 14, 34 that an ox was easily carried in the hand. Cf. also 2 Sam. 8, 10.

[4] Foote's rendering of the existing text, "eighty-five men bearing an ephod" (*l. c.*, p. 10), is incorrect. The text says "eighty-five ephod-bearers" — a very different

well have been more than one box at the disposal of so great a company.¹ And finally, if according to 1 Sam. 14, 3 and 22, 18 the priest was essentially a נשא ארון or *box-bearer*, then indubitably the original text of 1 Sam. 2, 28 declared that the family of Eli was chosen, not לשאת אפוד לפני, but לשאת ארון לפני — a fact strikingly confirmed by the existing text of Deut. 10, 8, according to which the Levites were set apart לשאת את ארון (ברית) יהוה לעמד לפני יהוה וג'; cf. Deut. 31, 9 25.

This actually disposes, by a process as objective as the nature of the case permits, of every mention of the solid "ephod" in the Book of Samuel. And with this result achieved, we need not hesitate to make the same disposition of the two remaining instances of the solid "ephod," which we find in Judges 8, 27 and chapters 17 f. In Judges 8, 27 we will accordingly read ויעש אתו גדעון לארון, incidentally solving at one stroke all the difficulties which have attended the interpretation of that passage; and similarly in chapters 17 f we will read את הארון, or ארון ואת התרפים, or ארון ותרפים, as the case may require.²

---

thing. The classical Hebrew for "eighty-five men bearing an ephod" would be שמנים וחמשה איש נשאים אפוד; cf., for example, Judges 18, 16, and contrast the scribal jargon of verse 17b.

¹ The word בד in 1 Sam. 22, 18 must be rejected as a scribal gloss (with Budde, Nowack, Dhorme, and Driver²). It was lacking in the prototype of G. Besides, its retention entails the interpretation of נשא in the sense of *to wear*, which that verb can never have. The statement of Nowack (*Handkommentar*, p. 115) that "נשא wird sonst nur vom Tragen eines Kleidungsstückes gebraucht, spec. in Bezug auf אפוד בד pflegt man חגר zu sagen," is an amazingly bad argument in a good cause. Or can " nur " be a misprint for " nicht " ?

² The question whether the text of the diaskeuastic passage 18, 17aβ was ever הארון — that is, whether the annotator wrote prior to the alteration of ארון to אפוד in Judges 17 f — is apparently to be answered in the affirmative; since the alteration was introduced systematically and no doubt simultaneously into the canonical books of Judges and Samuel.

Just why the word אפוד should have been selected to cover the obnoxious ארון, is a speculative question which need not trouble us, since it has been demonstrated that that word was in fact so selected. Doubtless, however, two factors combined to indicate the choice: one was the circumstance that the ephod was a prominent item in the ceremonial equipment of the High Priest; the other, and probably the more decisive, was the fact that the alteration of ארון to אפוד involved a minimum of textual change.

Hosea 3, 4 presents a different problem. The reading to be adopted there depends upon the question whether verses 4 and 5 of that chapter are part of the authentic prophecy of Hosea, or merely a late scribal amplification of the preceding paragraph. If the verses are genuine, we should certainly read in Hosea 3, 4, as in Judges 17, 5 and 18, 14, ארון ותרפים; whereas if they are spurious, the locution will be taken bodily from Judges 17–18, and may very well have been borrowed after the alteration of ארון to אפוד was carried out in the Book of Judges. My own judgment is that verses 4 f are unmistakably spurious, and the phrase in question reminiscent of Judges 17–18; the interpolator having concerned himself only with the fact that the two objects figured jointly and prominently in the history of the illegitimate cultus of North Israel. Hosea would hardly have delivered such a prophecy to the public prostitute[1] whom he is addressing in verse 3. If verses 4 f were genuine, we should certainly find them immediately after verse 1; cf. 1, 2bβ 4b 6b 9b. Nor can we suppose the prophet to have occupied himself with the Jewish millennium and "David their king"; while it is impossible to detach the protasis of verse 4 from the apodosis of verse 5, assigning the one to Hosea and the other to an interpolator.

XVII

Merely by way of confirming the conclusion at which we have arrived, we may recall at this point one or two phenomena which have already been mentioned incidentally in the foregoing pages.

It was observed at the outset that whereas the real ephod is *worn* about the waist (חגר: 1 Sam. 2, 18; 2 Sam. 6, 14; cf. Lev. 8, 7), the spurious "ephod" is not worn but *carried* (נשא: 1 Sam. 2, 28; 14, 3; 14, 18 [G]; 22, 18). Now נשא, it is hardly necessary to say, is just the word we should expect to find surviving in the context if the object originally referred to in those passages was the

---

[1] That the abandoned woman of Hos. 3 is identical with the wife of chapter 1, is a fiction as baseless as it appears to be dear to the heart of Biblical theologians. The only reason why the wife of Hosea *and her legitimate children* are called אשת זנונים וילדי זנונים is explicitly set forth in 1, 2.

sacred box; cf. Deut. 10, 8; 31, 9 25; Josh. 3, 3, etc.; 1 Sam. 4, 4; 2 Sam. 6, 4; 15, 24; 1 Kings 2, 26; 8, 3.

Similarly in Judges 8, 27 we are told that Gideon *deposited* the "ephod" in his native city of Ophra: ויצג אותו בעירו בעפרה. And here again, הציג is precisely the word we should expect to find employed in that sentence if the object in question was in reality the sacred box; cf. 1 Sam. 5, 2: ויקחו פלשתים את ארון האלהים ויבאו אתו בית דגון ויציגו אתו אצל דגון ;2 Sam. 6, 17 (= 1 Chron. 16, 1): ויצגו את ;2 Sam. 15, 24: ויבאו את ארון יהוה ויצגו אתו במקומו בתוך האהל ונ' ארון האלהים עד תם כל העם לעבור מן העיר.[1] In view of the fact that these citations actually embrace one-fourth of all the occurrences of יצג in the Old Testament, the phraseology of Judges 8, 27 is especially significant.

Finally in 1 Sam. 23, 9, for the clause הגישה האפוד of the Masoretic text, which is reflected in all the later versions, the Septuagint has προσάγαγε τὸ ἐφοὺδ κυρίου.[2] As the combination ἐφοὺδ κυρίου is meaningless, and occurs nowhere else in the Old Testament, κυρίου can hardly be the result of a slip or of conjecture and interpolation in the Greek, but must represent the actual text of the Hebrew prototype of G. But neither could יהוה in the underlying Hebrew be the result of accident or of conjecture and interpolation; since, as already observed, Judaism knows nothing of an אפוד יהוה, any more than it knows of a מעיל יהוה. The presence of an אפוד יהוה in this passage can be satisfactorily explained only upon the assumption that the genitive יהוה itself was authentic, whatever may have been the fact regarding the preceding אפוד. But again, יהוה is just the genitive we are least surprised to find in this sentence if the object designated by the preceding construct noun was originally the

---

[1] See page 65. The word הציג invariably means *to deposit on the ground*, either literally or figuratively; and is never employed in the sense of *to set up* — an idol or anything else.

[2] According to Holmes and Parsons, this is the reading of all the manuscripts except a few cursives. I have been at pains to verify the reading in the photographs of A and B. Among recent commentators on the Book of Samuel, Budde and Dhorme alone seem to have noticed this pregnant Septuagint reading; and they barely mention it, apparently as a mere curiosity.

sacred box. Note the language in 1 Sam. 14, 18a and the alternation of ארון האלהים and ארון יהוה in 2 Sam. 6. It cannot be doubted that the authentic text of 1 Sam. 23, 9 was ארון יהוה. This was replaced in the ancestor of M by האפוד, just as in 14, 18 an original ארון האלהים was replaced in the ancestor of G by האפוד; whereas in this instance the ancestor of G carelessly substituted אפוד for ארון, and left the genitive יהוה standing, a persistent witness to the true reading of the original text.

It remains to notice the important fact that, with the single exception of 1 Sam. 2, 28 (where the alteration apparently took place, as the grammarians say, by attraction, in the wake of 14, 3, etc.), the solid "ephod" appears only in contexts where the Jewish doctrine of a single Sinaitic box of Yahwe could not tolerate the mention of the historical sacred box, for the reason that by no amount of sophistry could the one be identified with the other. So in Judges 8, 27 the reader was explicitly told that the box was *made by Gideon* out of the gold captured from the Midianites; and a good Deuteronomistic editor, who of course refrained from invoking the favorite ברית, had accordingly not hesitated to assert that "all Israel went a whoring after it," in spite of the fact that Gideon's avowed object was to substitute an oracle of Yahwe for his personal rule (verse 23). Obviously there was no way of identifying that sacred box with the one made under the direction of Moses at the foot of Mount Sinai. Again in Judges 17, 5 the reader was expressly told that the box of the ensuing narrative was *made by Micah* for his private sanctuary; and in 18, 27 that box was finally located at the notoriously illegitimate sanctuary of Dan, to constitute the forerunner and the occasion of full half the sin "wherewith Jeroboam the son of Nebat made Israel to sin." Manifestly it was impossible to identify that sacred box with the Mosaic "box of the Covenant" which was supposed to have rested finally in the cella of Solomon's temple at Jerusalem. Similarly in 1 Sam. 14, 3 18; 21, 10; 22, 18; 23, 6 9; 30, 7, it is evident that the sacred box could in no conceivable way be identified with the (supposedly Sinaitic) box of Yahwe Militant, which in 1 Sam. 7, 1 had been lodged in the house of Abinadab at Kirjath-jearim, and which remained there until removed to Jerusalem by David in 2 Sam. 6. All this in addition to the circumstance that, directly or indirectly, every one of these refractory passages betrayed the fact that it had to do with an ordinary and plural instrument of divination, rather than with a unique receptacle for the two tables of stone inscribed with the Sinaitic Law.

Happily, in one manuscript (from which our Masoretic text of Samuel is descended) the transformation of the sacred box into the " ephod " was neglected in 1 Sam. 14, 18; with the consequence that later on, when perhaps the recollection of what the " ephod " represented had passed away, the difficulty was awkwardly met by the purposed mutilation of the second half of that verse. It was of course only the eventually mutilated half-verse 18b, *for he carried the sacred box before Israel that day*, which clearly affirmed that the box was present in the camp of Saul, and which was therefore utterly irreconcilable with Jewish doctrine. With 18b corrupted beyond recognition, 18a of itself could be speciously interpreted as merely expressing Saul's desire that the box of Yahwe might be brought to him from Kirjath-jearim.

In other passages where we might expect it, the substitution of אפוד for ארון was never attempted in any manuscript. 1 Kings 2, 26 could, at a pinch, be understood to refer to the box of 2 Sam. 15, 24–29 and the Solomonic temple (cf. G) — as it has been since, by both Jewish and Christian scholars; while the sacred box of Judges 20, 27 had been identified with the " box of the Covenant " through the addition of the *midrash* concerning the High Priesthood of Phinehas in verse 28a, as well as by the insertion of the Deuteronomistic ברית.[1]

---

[1] The remaining passages of the older literature, in which the (not too obtrusively oracular) sacred box has been retained, offered of course no difficulty. Not merely were they easily reconciled with the theory of a single Sinaitic box; they were largely responsible for it, their several boxes having been identified seriatim with the " box of the Covenant," by means of the Deuteronomistic gloss ברית; cf. Num. 10, 33; 14, 44; Josh. 3, 3, etc.; 1 Sam. 4, 3 ff; 2 Sam. 15, 24; 1 Kings 3, 15; 6, 19; 8, 1 6; Jer. 3, 16. Even Deut. 10, 8; 31, 9 25 26 should probably be included in this category.

XVIII

It must not be supposed, however, that 1 Sam. 14, 18b furnishes the only instance of a device other than the substitution of אפוד for ridding the text of an embarrassing ארון. In Judges 18, 27 the Masoretic text, which is reproduced in all the ancient versions, now reads: והמה לקחו את אשר עשה מיכה ואת הכהן וג׳. It is apparent that the words הארון ואת התרפים have been struck out bodily before אשר. Jerome's paraphrase expressed very well his sense of the deliberate avoidance involved: *Sexcenti autem viri tulerunt sacerdotem et quae supra diximus.* In 1 Sam. 21, 10 the words אחרי האפוד of the Masoretic text have no counterpart in G^B, and were undoubtedly lacking in both the Alexandrian version and its Hebrew prototype. That is, instead of being replaced by אחרי האפוד, the troublesome phrase אחרי הארון had been eliminated entirely in some earlier manuscript. Similarly in 1 Sam. 30, 7 the clause ויגש אביתר את (האפוד) אל דוד, which is lacking in G^B (reminding one of the mutilated second half of 14, 18 in M), had obviously been struck out of the ancestor of G. In all these cases the excision doubtless took place before the alteration of ארון to אפוד had been effected.

More interesting than any of these cases of evident amputation is the corrupt, though universally attested, text of 1 Sam. 15, 23. Here Samuel is rebuking Saul for his failure to "devote" completely the Amalekites and all their substance, as commanded by Yahwe. In reply to Saul's plea that his pious followers had but saved out some of the sheep and oxen for a sacrifice to Yahwe in Gilgal, Samuel retorts, *Does Yahwe delight in burnt-offerings and sacrifices, as in listening to the voice of Yahwe? Behold, obedience is better than sacrifice, and hearkening than the fat of rams.* Then follow the words: כי חטאת קסם מרי ואון ותרפים הפצר. This sentence has been copied, translated, and expounded; but from the days of the Alexandrian interpreters to the present moment, no one has succeeded in reading any sense into it. The interpretation of our own Authorized Version is as good and as bad as any: *For rebellion is as the sin of witchcraft, and stubbornness is as iniquity and idolatry —*

which puts the cart before the horse in both clauses, mistranslates more than one word, and then yields only a nerveless and remote banality. Yet the interpretation is very easy, if only we will read ארון for און, and will not insist on making Samuel talk like a rabbi. What he is represented as saying is: *For a sin against the oracle is rebellion, and box and teraphim are not to be gainsaid* (literally, *are obligation*)! On חטאת קסם cf. Gesenius-Kautzsch § 128 *h;* and for a similar use of the infinitive absolute in the predicate, cf. Isa. 32, 17: והיה ׃ ׃ ׃ עברת הצדקה השקט, *and the product of righteousness shall be tranquilization*. Of course the original expression was the same here as in Judges 17 f; and an אפוד, we may be sure, would never have been altered to און.[1] For the rest, whether the traditional reading און was derived from an original ארן by the change of ר to ו, or from an original ארון by the dropping of the ר, is a point we need not undertake to decide. Nor need we concern ourselves with the question whether the above apothegm originated with the author of the story of Saul's war against the Amalekites, or was an old and current saying which he quoted. It is enough for our purposes that neither text nor interpretation admits of any question whatsoever.

XIX

For the reader whose patience has been equal to the inordinate demands made upon it, the results of our study may be summed up in few words.

Our idea of the Israelitish *ephod* must be formed exclusively on the basis of the two passages 1 Sam. 2, 18 and 2 Sam. 6, 14 (= 1 Chron. 15, 27), supplemented by the descriptions of its more ornate but essentially identical successor, the ephod of the Jewish High Priest, contained in the Priest Code of the Pentateuch and in later

---

[1] Wellhausen long ago suggested that און ותרפים in this passage was equivalent to (not substituted for, as Foote reports, *l. c.*, p. 40) the phrase אפוד ותרפים of Judges 17 f and Hos. 3, 4; but he persisted in construing הפצר as subject instead of predicate, and made no attempt to account for the continued use of תרפים though (as he supposed) אפוד was abandoned for און. See Bleek-Wellhausen, *Einleitung*[4], p. 216; *Bücher Samuelis*, p. 100.

Jewish writings. The ephod, then, was nothing but the primitive loincloth, transformed, like the Arabian *izār*, into a ceremonial apron, and worn by all persons, old or young, priest or lay, when engaged in solemn religious exercises in the immediate presence of the deity. So in the reign of David; and so still when the story of Samuel was written, some time in the seventh century. This ceremonial garment survived into the post-exilic period; but in the ritual of the Second Temple and the corresponding Priestly legislation of the Pentateuch its use was limited to the High Priest, possibly because in the Jewish system the latter was the only person allowed to enter the divine presence. Neither in the practice of pre-exilic times nor in the Aaronic theory of Judaism had the ephod any direct relation to the oracles of Yahwe or to the oracular function of the priesthood; although it is probable enough that the pre-exilic priest — and perhaps ordinarily the lay enquirer — actually assumed the ephod during the consultation of the oracle. Judaism itself — as distinguished from its theoretical reconstruction of the Mosaic age — never in fact had any such thing as an oracle of Yahwe.

Our description of the *box of Yahwe*, on the other hand, must take account not only of those passages in the older literature where the mention of it has been preserved intact, but also of all those more significant passages in which the box has been replaced by the solid "ephod," and likewise of 1 Sam. 15, 23, where an original ארון has been altered to און.

The box of Yahwe was thus a plural object, employed by the Israelitish priests as their professional organ of divination. It was of course a box — there can no longer be any question as to that. Nor, as an instrument of divination, was it peculiar to the religion of Israel and the oracles of Yahwe.[1] On the contrary, the existence of the antecedent appellative ארון אלהים, *a sacred box*, implies that it was a common Palestinian institution, as familiar to the non-

---

[1] A parallel, perhaps more curious than relevant, is the olive wood oracle-box at Praeneste, described by Cicero, *De divinatione*, II, 41; cf. Bouché Leclercq, *Histoire de la Divination*, IV, p. 149.

Israelitish inhabitants of Canaan as was, for example, the functionary called איש אלהים, or the establishment called בית אלהים. The expression ארון אלהים was pretty certainly of Palestinian origin. Whether the thing itself was known to the Israelites under another name before their settlement in Canaan, we have no means of saying. The earliest historical sacred boxes of which we have record date from the period of the Judges.

Practically the box served as a repository for the sacred lots and as the receptacle from which those lots were drawn. In theory, it was of course much more; since a smaller and more pliable object would have served the purpose of a mere receptacle quite as well. There can in fact be little doubt that the sacred box was conceived of as a miniature temple, which actually housed the spirit of the divinity at the moment when the disposition of the sacred lots was being effected — a sort of shrine or refuge within which the numen could work its mysterious spell upon the lots while shielded from the scrutiny of the human eye. And when once a box had been so tenanted, it was naturally sacred for ever after.

Ordinarily the sacred box was not too large to be carried by a single person; cf. 1 Sam. 14, 18; 23, 9; 30, 7; 1 Kings 2, 26; and perhaps we should add Judges 18, 20. Not merely when being conveyed from one place to another, but also, and more particularly, during the formal act of consultation, the box was carried by the priest; cf. Deut. 10, 8; 1 Sam. 2, 28; 14, 18; 1 Kings 2, 26. We may suppose that it was supported by means of a strap passing over the shoulders and around the neck, somewhat after the fashion of a modern barrel organ.[1]

Before the sacred box thus borne by the priest, the lay enquirer took his stand and himself put the question, invoking the deity with full, sonorous title, יהוה אלהי ישראל; cf. 1 Sam. 14, 41 [2]; 23, 10. In the case of the box especially dedicated to *Yahwe Militant*,

---

[1] It is barely possible that this may be the ultimate origin of the twin כתפות or shoulder straps which supported the חשן of the Jewish High Priest in later times.

[2] אל before יהוה אלהי ישראל is clearly impossible, regardless of the testimony of the Septuagint text.

the invocation was of course יהוה צבאות אלהי ישראל; cf. 2 Sam. 6, 18; Isa. 37, 16. The questions were invariably such as could be answered with a simple yes or no, or else they called for the selection of one of two equally distinct alternatives; cf. 1 Sam. 14, 37 41; 23, 10 ff; 30, 8; 2 Sam. 5, 19. Even such a response as that of 2 Sam. 2, 1b will have been secured by the same method. Through some sort of aperture (cf. 1 Sam. 6, 19) especially provided for the purpose, the priest introduced his hand into the box, and, after an appreciable length of time (cf. 1 Sam. 14, 19) spent either in manipulating its contents or in reciting some formula, drew out the lots; which he proceeded to interpret to the enquirer in a single sentence, conforming the language of the answer to that of the question.

From the fact that on occasion no categorical answer was forthcoming (cf. 1 Sam. 14, 37; 28, 6), it is evident that the lots cannot have consisted of two single objects of opposite value. Nor, since the lots were not cast out of the box but drawn, is it likely that astralagi were employed. On the other hand, that the lots consisted of a considerable number of small objects (perhaps pebbles of variegated aspect) is suggested by the technical phrase מלא את יד פ׳ = *to invest with the priesthood;* which, since the most important function of the priest was divination, will probably refer to his induction into office by " filling his hand " with the sacred lots. However that may be, we can be sure that the manipulation and interpretation of the sacred lots was not so simple a matter as to be learned by any bystander through casual observation of one or two performances.

The prevalent assumption, that while we do not know the exact nature or number of the sacred lots, we do know their names, will not bear examination. It is, to say the least, extremely problematical whether any such correlative and antithetical terms as *Urim* and *Thummim* existed in pre-exilic Hebrew usage. אורים alone is evidenced by 1 Sam. 28, 6; where the context unmistakably indicates the comprehensive meaning *priestly oracles*, and precludes a reference to one of two complementary elements. P's own use of the word in the ostensibly ancient phrase משפט האורים (Num. 27, 21) also demands this interpretation. And in this sense it was still employed by Ben Sira in a passage which, unfortunately, has not been preserved in the original Hebrew

(33, 3b). The good Hebrew word אורים — whose traditional vocalization is unexceptionable — will then be in some way cognate to תורה.¹

For the correlated and assonant but etymologically questionable תֻּמִּים,² on the other hand, there is no respectable pre-exilic testimony whatever. In 1 Sam. 14, 41 the simple idiomatic הבה תָמִים (= *vouchsafe a true answer*) of the Masoretic text is — against all modern authorities — to be preferred to the patently inflated Greek reading; cf. 2 Sam. 20, 18; Judges 9, 16 19; Amos 5, 8. The plus of the Septuagint represents, not a better text, but a late interpolation based on the Pentateuchal law. The slovenly καὶ ἐὰν τάδε εἴπῃ = ואם כה יאמר (cf. the interpolated 2 Sam. 15, 26) alone makes this certain.³ Ezra 2, 63 (= Neh. 7, 65) is of course based upon our Pentateuch. So that it is more than likely that the אורים and תמים of Ex. 28, 30 and Lev. 8, 8 rest upon nothing but P's combination of 1 Sam. 28, 6 (and the otherwise current אורים) with 1 Sam. 14, 41. Nor is the mystifying passage Deut. 33, 8 by any means conclusive against this view. For Deut. 33 is, at least in its present form, demonstrably post-exilic; and the verse in question (which is addressed, not to Yahwe, but to Levi) unmistakably limits the custody and manipulation of the tribal "Thummim" and "Urim" to *a single person* (איש חסידך = אישך החסיד); who, since Moses is the speaker, must be Aaron! — with confused reminiscence of Num. 16, Ex. 17, 7, and Num. 20, 1-13.

In connection with this whole question the significant fact should not be overlooked, that although, as we have seen,⁴ "Urim and Thummim" were entirely unknown after the Exile, and P could not assume the slightest familiarity with them on the part of his readers, he nevertheless made no attempt whatever to describe them, not even indicating the material of which they were made; and this in spite of his pedantic and meticulous circumstantiality regarding all the other accoutrements of "Aaron."⁵ Apparently אורים and

¹ Hardly, however, through Babylonian *ūrtu* and *tērtu;* as Muss-Arnolt, *American Journal of Semitic Languages*, XVI, 1900, pp. 218, 222.

² We should expect תְּמִימִים for the plural of a concrete object.

³ The Lucianic καὶ εἰ τάδε εἴποις is much more likely to be an amelioration of the text of G^B than is the latter to be a corruption of the former. Compare also the manifest inflation of the parallel invocation of 1 Sam. 23, 10 f; where all of verse 10 from שמע, besides the first four words of verse 11 and the second יהוה אלהי ישראל, must be rejected.

⁴ Page 9.

⁵ The fact that while minute directions are given for the fabrication of every other part of the High Priest's equipment, none whatever are given for the Urim and Thummim, and that it is nowhere stated that the latter were manufactured by the artificers of Moses, was noticed by the rabbis of the Middle Ages; in particular by Moses ben Naḥman, who buttressed with it the rabbinical theory that Urim and Thummim were nothing but inscriptions or engravings of the ineffable Name. See the Targum Yerushalmi and the rabbinical commentaries on Ex. 28, 30, and Buxtorf the younger's *Historia Urim et Thummim*, Basel, 1659, pp. 282, 284.

תמים were purely fictitious labels which he concocted on the basis of passages dealing with divination in the older literature, and which answered to nothing objective even in his own imagination. The vocalization תֻּמִּים is of course chargeable to the synagogue.

The question naturally suggests itself whether the term תרפים, which is coupled with the priestly organ of divination in Judges 17 f and 1 Sam. 15, 23, may not after all represent collectively the lots employed in connection with the sacred box. Such a view would find support in 2 Kings 23, 24; Ez. 21, 26; Zech. 10, 2; nor would it be contradicted by Gen. 31, 19 34 35. But it would involve the assumption that at least in 1 Sam. 19, 13 16 תרפים has been substituted for some other word. Cf. in this connection Moore's *Commentary on Judges*, p. 382. Nothing is at times more difficult than to penetrate the fog in which Judaism has enveloped its heathen antecedents.

At least during the so-called period of the Judges and well into the reign of Solomon, an oracular box of Yahwe such as we have described existed wherever there was a sanctuary of Yahwe in the custody of a consecrated priesthood. In fact, it constituted the central and most venerated object in every such sanctuary (cf. Judges 8, 27; 1 Sam. 4, 13 18; 1 King 6, 19) and the indispensable concomitant of every such priesthood (cf. Judges 17, 5; 1 Sam. 22, 18).

For the period of the Judges, there is credible record of the existence of a sacred box of extraordinary magnificence [1] in a sanctuary at the Ephraimite town of Ophrah, whose establishment tradition ascribed to Gideon (Judges 8, 27). And reaching back into the same period there was a sacred box — as we should expect — at the important Israelitish sanctuary of Dan (Judges 18, 27 ff), and another at the equally important Israelitish sanctuary of Bethel (Judges 20, 27). At the ancient sanctuary of Shiloh (Judges 21, 19 ff) there was a box, apparently more remarkable for its size than for its intrinsic value, especially dedicated to *Yahwe Militant*

---

[1] At this point it is legitimate enough to query whether the 1700 shekels of gold represented as having gone into the manufacture of that box should not be taken with a grain of salt. But the essential fact of the existence of this exceptionally valuable and celebrated box is confirmed by the appended comment of the Deuteronomistic editor. For instances of gold or gold-plated deity-boxes among neighboring peoples in antiquity, see Bähr, *Symbolik des mosaischen Kultus*, I, pp. 483 f, and the references there given.

(1 Sam. 4, 3 f), under which title the national deity was worshipped there (cf. 1 Sam. 1, 3). And a little later, in the reign of Saul, we meet a casual reference to "the box" of the sanctuary at Nob (1 Sam. 21, 10) which clearly implies that a like object was to be found at the time in every similar establishment.

Not only at great public sanctuaries, such as Ophrah, Dan, Bethel, Shiloh, and Nob, but even in the chapels of well-to-do private citizens who could afford the luxury of a domestic chaplain, the sacred box was apparently to be found. Such at least, according to tradition, had been the original home of the sacred box of Dan (Judges 17 f).

The box of Yahwe was consulted by all sorts of people under all sorts of circumstances (Judges 8, 23; 17, 5 13; 1 Sam. 22, 13; cf. Jer. 3, 16). But of course its counsels were most highly prized in connection with military enterprises (Judges 18, 5 f; 20, 27; 1 Sam. 14, 18 36 f; 23, 10 ff; 30, 8; 2 Sam. 2, 1; 5, 19). Accordingly we find a sacred box with its attendant priest regularly accompanying the royal forces on their military expeditions, both in the reign of Saul (1 Sam. 14, 18b, as restored) and in the reign of David (2 Sam. 11, 11; 15, 24). And early in his career, while leading the life of an outlaw chief, David had eagerly welcomed the accession of a fugitive priest with a box of Yahwe (1 Sam. 22, 23; 23, 6), which he never thereafter omitted to consult.[1]

The box which figures most prominently in the history of Israel is the above-mentioned Shilonite *box of Yahwe Militant*. Its story is too familiar to need rehearsal. The first mention of it occurs in connection with its removal from Shiloh to be carried into battle (1 Sam. 4), at an early stage in the contest between Israelites and Philistines for the control of Canaan; while the last — after its capture by the Philistines, return to Israelitish territory, long residence at Kirjath-jearim, removal to Jerusalem, and lodgment in the sanctuary of David — relates to its final installation in the דביר or sanctum of Solomon's temple which had been especially prepared for its reception (1 Kings 8).

---

[1] The consultations of 1 Sam. 23, 2-4 are spurious.

From the point of view adopted in this essay the question of the ultimate fate of this individual sacred box loses much of its importance. It is not likely that the box was of sufficient intrinsic value to tempt the cupidity of any one of the successive (direct or indirect) spoilers of the Solomonic temple, whether Shishak (1 Kings 14, 26), Hazael (2 Kings 12, 18), Tiglathpileser (2 Kings 16, 8), Sennacherib (2 Kings 18, 15 f), or Nebuchadnezzar (2 Kings 25, 13 ff). Nor, since it was far from being the unique national fetich it has been supposed, would even Joash of Israel (2 Kings 14, 14) have had any interest in removing it. If it survived the ravages of four hundred years — which, for a plain wooden box at least fifty years old at the outset, housed in a damp stone building not seldom out of repair, is rather doubtful — it will have perished in the flames when the temple of Solomon was finally destroyed.[1] But more probably it fell into decay before 586 B.C., and was not replaced.

For long before the disappearance of the last vestige of Israelitish independence in 586 B.C., the institution of priestly divination by means of the box of Yahwe had given place, in official circles, to the more direct and comprehensive method of ascertaining the divine will through the instrumentality of *inspired human speech* — the institution of prophecy; which, though originating on the lowest plane of animistic superstition, and affording great scope for quackery and pathological aberration, nevertheless held within itself the germs of umlimited religious progress and the highest moral elevation. In 1 Sam. 28, 6 consultation of Yahwe by means of prophecy is carried back to the reign of Saul, though only as an alternative to the priestly oracles; with what justification, however, we have no means of determining. But there can be no question that by the middle of the ninth century the new institution had entirely supplanted priestly divination at the court of the kings of Israel (1 Kings 22, 5 ff), and that by the time of Isaiah it had thoroughly established itself in the kingdom of Judah as well.

---

[1] Jeremiah (2 Macc. 2, 4 ff) would have been the last person in the world to concern himself with its salvation; compare page 75, above.

Nevertheless, the old practice continued to be followed in out of the way places and among the lower orders of the people down to the very end of the pre-exilic period (Jer. 3, 16);[1] while the language of sacerdotal circles never ceased to identify the priestly office and prerogative with the ancient right to *bear the box of Yahwe* (1 Sam. 2, 28; Deut. 10, 8; cf. Deut. 31, 9 25 26). Nor did the imaginative writers of the period, when treating of the early days of Israel's history, hesitate to project backwards into the days of Moses and Joshua just such an individual *box of Yahwe* as had accompanied the armies of Saul and David in later times. For so we must interpret the rôle of the imaginary *box of Yahwe* in Num. 10, 33 35 36; 14, 44, and in the pre-exilic stratum of Joshua 3–8.[2]

Not until some time after the temple of Solomon had been swept away — hardly much before 500 B.C. — did it occur to anyone to question the original purpose of the Solomonic box. This transition from the box of historical fact and historical imagination to the box of Jewish dogma was effected by means of two correlated sets of interpolations, the one in Deut. 10, 1–5, the other in 1 Kings 8, 9 21.[3] The original stories of the Sinaitic tables of stone had nothing to say about a box — naturally enough, for public laws are not put under a bushel. And the original story of the box of the Solomonic temple had nothing to say about two Sinaitic tables of stone. By means of these two sets of interpolations, a box was wrapped about the Sinaitic tables of stone in Deut. 10, and the Sinaitic tables of stone were thrust into the box of the Solomonic temple in 1 Kings 8. It should be noticed, however,

---

[1] Possibly we should infer from the mention of תרפים in 2 Kings 23, 24 that Josiah destroyed a few surviving sacred boxes, which were still used for divination, in the immediate vicinity of Jerusalem.

Whether the two priests (cf. *Journal of Biblical Literature*, XXXI, 1912, p. 22) of the Judean temple at Elephantine practiced divination in the name of Yahwe, we cannot say. The papyri furnish no evidence of it. On the passage in the Temple Papyrus supposed by Sachau to contain the report of such an oracle, see Excursus II, below.

[2] The formulae of Num. 10, 35 f, if historical, will reflect the usage of later times. They make the impression, however, of having been composed *ad hoc*, and by an annotator at that.

[3] Cf. page 5, note 1.

that nothing was further from the mind of the Deuteronomistic glossators than to efface the traces of the oracular institution of the early days. On the contrary, they were concerned merely with *differentiating* the box of the legitimate Solomonic sanctuary at Jerusalem from the other boxes of Yahwe mentioned in the ancient literature. With that object in view, the above-mentioned interpolations were supplemented by the methodical insertion of the distinguishing genitive ברית in a whole series of passages connecting the box of 1 Kings 8, on the one hand, with that which accompanied the Israelites away from Sinai in Num. 10, 33, on the other. The box of Yahwe Militant was easily followed back to the days of Eli; beyond which it was identified, first with that of the sanctuary at Bethel, which had been venerated by all Israel during the war against the Benjamites (Judges 20, 27), and then with the box of Josh. 3–8, Deut. 31, and Num. 10 and 14. Simultaneously with these emendations of the existing texts, certain more extensive expansions of the story of Joshua employed for the first time the genuinely Deuteronomistic expression ארון הברית (Josh. 3, 6, etc.).

It was in this state of the text that the Priestly document of the Pentateuch was composed; in which the now thoroughly established unique Sinaitic "box of the Covenant" was made to figure as the "box of the Testimony." Unlike the Deuteronomists, P would not recognize that another kind of "box of Yahwe" had ever existed, but replaced the oracle-box of the older days with the inoffensive חשן of the High Priest, to which were attached the incorporeal entities he called אורים and תמים. What disposition P would have made of the patently non-Mosaic sacred boxes of the older historical writings if he had continued his narrative beyond the days of Joshua, we cannot say. The Chronicler simply ignores them, as he ignores everything else that is inconvenient. And so long as the Pentateuch alone furnished the Scripture reading of the synagogue, they could continue to be ignored. But with the general circulation of the Prophetic Canon, those disconcerting witnesses to the plural and divinatory character of the historical box of Yahwe, and to the factitious character of the High Priestly חשן, had to be silenced. They were very effectively silenced; in one passage by the alteration of ארון to אן, in others by the mutilation of the traditional text, but for the most part by the systematic substitution of אפוד for ארון.

EXCURSUS I

THE DIVINE NAME YAHWE ṢEBAOTH

IN spite of all that has been written on the subject of the divine name *Yahwe Ṣebaoth*, there continues to be much uncertainty and not a little positive misapprehension both as regards the historical connotation of the phrase and as regards its original and essential form.[1]

On the subject of the purport of the qualifying word צבאות much cosmological nonsense has been uttered. But the customary rejoinder, that the plural of צבא occurs otherwise in the Old Testament only of armies of men, is too superficial and not quite to the point. The grammatical number is not of itself conclusive; and those who hold that צבאות refers to *the armies* of Israel are only a little less misguided than those who hold that it refers to *the armies* of heaven.

The fact is, the most serious obstacle in the way of the correct understanding of the expression has been the prevalent and misleading German rendering, *Jahveh der Heerscharen*. This is an equivalent, not of Hebrew יהוה צבאות, but of Hebrew יהוה הצבאות, and naturally raises the question, "What hosts?" — about which factitious question the discussions of the subject have hitherto turned.

The pertinent and decisive facts are, first, צבאות is *indeterminate;* and second, the word is an *adjectival genitive*. To serve the purpose of an adjectival genitive, the noun must be employed in its generic form; which, in the case of a word not intrinsically generic, is

---

[1] For the literature of the subject, and a comprehensive presentation of the Old Testament data and the contending opinions of modern scholars, see the article by Kautzsch, *Protestantische Realencyklopädie*,[3] XXI, pp. 621 ff. A full tabular survey of the occurrences of the name — more ambitious than critical — is given by Löhr, *Untersuchungen zum Buch Amos* (Beihefte zur *ZATW*, IV), pp. 38 ff.

necessarily the plural. So the Hebrew says זרע אדם, *human progeny;* but it must say זרע אנשׁים, *male progeny,* because אישׁ is not intrinsically generic, but singular. צבא is *a single army* or *military expedition*[1]; שׂר הצבא is *the commander of the army, the commander-in-chief;* and *a commander-in-chief* is accordingly שׂר צבא (2 Sam. 2, 8; 19, 14; 1 Kings 16, 16). But *a military commander* (one of a number) is שׂר צבאות; cf. שׂרי צבאות, *military commanders,* Deut. 20, 9[2]; שׁני שׂרי צבאות ישׂראל, (the) *two Israelitish military commanders,* 1 Kings 2, 5.[3] יהוה צבאות is therefore, not *Yahwe of the Armies,* whether Israelitish or celestial, but the plainest sort of Hebrew for *the military Yahwe = Yahwe on the War-Path, Yahwe Militant.* צבאות is seen to be no definition, but just such an epithet as would be Yahwe "the Victorious."

A few citations may serve to demonstrate the fitness of this interpretation. Josh. 6, 16 f: "And Joshua said unto the people, Shout! for Yahwe hath given you the city. And the city shall be devoted (חרם), it and all that is therein, unto *Yahwe Militant* [with G]." 1 Sam. 15, 2 f; "Thus saith *Yahwe Militant*, I am mindful of what Amalek did to Israel, how he arrayed himself against him in the way, when he came up from Egypt. Now go and smite Amalek, and *devote* him and all that is his. And thou shalt not spare him; but shalt slay man and woman, child and suckling, ox and sheep, camel and ass." Isa. 13, 4: "A sound of a multitude in the mountains, like as a great people! a sound of a tumult of kingdoms, nations gathered together! *Yahwe Militant* mustering an army for

---

[1] It is possible that two originally distinct nouns, ṣaba' and ṣab'a(t), have coalesced in the Hebrew צבא.

[2] This is manifestly not a case where Gesenius-Kautzsch § 124 *q* (cf. König, *Lehrgebäude,* II, pp. 438 f; III, pp. 215 f) can apply. Moreover, the instances properly adduced under that rubric — where we have a clear case of the attraction of the genitive into the number of the construct — are symptomatic of degenerate Hebrew.

[3] So, in spite of 1 Kings 2, 32. The emphasis is on the word "Israelitish"; which common nationality should have protected both Abner the Benjamite and Amasa the Judahite. Had David intended *the two commanders-in-chief of the Israelitish army,* he would have said שׁני שׂרי צבא ישׂראל. In 1 Kings 1, 25 שׂרי הצבא must be corrected to שׂר הצבא; cf. the Lucianic Greek and verse 19. The usage of the Chronicler may be disregarded.

battle!" Jer. 46, 10: "It shall be a day of vengeance for *Yahwe Militant*, that he may avenge him of his enemies. And the sword shall devour and be satiated, and be made drunk with their blood. For there is to be *a sacrifice to Yahwe Militant* in the north country by the river Euphrates." Ps. 24, 8 10: "And who is the king of glory? *Yahwe strong and mighty, Yahwe mighty in battle.* . . . And who is the king of glory? *Yahwe Militant*, he is the king of glory." Of course, *Yahwe Militant* may turn against his own people on occasion; Isa. 6, 9 ff, etc.

With this construction of the name, one must travel far to reach the stars. Doubtless its original connotation was not always present to the consciousness of the Jews of later times, and it came to be identified, in a vague way, with the conception of God as *the Irresistible* ($\pi\alpha\nu\tau o\kappa\rho\acute{\alpha}\tau\omega\rho$). But to maintain that, even in later times, the Deity was called יהוה צבאות with conscious reference to his control of the "armies" of the heavenly bodies, the angels, the world of demons, or the forces of the universe, is much the same as if one should assert that a modern industrial magnate, who happens to be named John Smith, is called so with reference to the transcontinental lines of railway which he "forges."

On the other hand, the theory continues to be entertained among Old Testament scholars, that the original form of the name was (1) יהוה אלהי הצבאות, and that this was subsequently shortened, first to (2) יהוה אלהי צבאות, and then to (3) יהוה צבאות. This theory turns the whole body of the Old Testament evidence upside down and inside out.

The form (3) is frequently employed by the prophet Isaiah; whereas neither (1) nor (2) occurs anywhere in the Book of Isaiah.[1] (3) is used constantly by the prophet Jeremiah [2]; (1) never occurs in the Book of Jeremiah; and in the five passages where (2) occurs (5, 14; 15, 16; 35, 17; 38, 17; 44, 7), the Septuagint shows that the אלהי of the Masoretic text is interpolated in every case — as

---

[1] In the "Second Isaiah" even (3) occurs only by interpolation: 44, 6; 45, 13; 47, 4; 48, 2; 51, 15; 54, 5.

[2] On the testimony of the Septuagint, see below.

indeed is sufficiently attested by the absence (in classical Hebrew) of the article before צבאות, required to put the word אלהים into formal apposition with the determinate proper name יהוה. In good Hebrew, יהוה אלהי צבאות can only be *Yahwe is a military deity*. (3) occurs constantly in Haggai, Zechariah (including chapters 9–14), and Malachi; as well as twice in Zephaniah, once in Habakkuk, once in an anonymous prophecy in Micah, and twice (though only through the editorial insertion of צבאות after יהוה of the original prophecy) in Nahum. But in none of these do we ever find either (1) or (2).

The erroneous theory above-mentioned is based principally on what are assumed to be among the earliest occurrences of the name, in the writings of Amos and Hosea. But the fact is that neither (1), (2), nor (3) is to be found in the authentic utterances of either prophet. (1) occurs in Amos 3, 13; 6, 14; Hosea 12, 6; (2) in Amos 4, 13; 5, 14 15 16 27; 6, 8; (3), remarkably enough, occurs nowhere in Amos or Hosea,[1] although Amos 9, 5 exhibits the impossible form יהוה הצבאות = *the Yahwe of the armies* (Yahwe not characterized, but defined!), where, however, the Septuagint has (1). But Amos 3, 13 f is interpolated entire. The same is true of Amos 4, 12b–13; 5, 13–15; and 5, 25–27. In Amos 5, 16 אלהי צבאות אדני (after יהוה) obviously represents successive interpolations, first of אדני, and then of אלהי צבאות. In Amos 6 it needs no argument or Septuagint evidence to show that נאם יהוה אלהי (ה)צבאות is interpolated after נשבע יהוה בנפשו in verse 8, and before the belated גוי in verse 14. That at least verses 5 and 6 of Amos 9 are interpolated, is universally admitted. Finally, that Hosea 12, 6, ויהוה אלהי הצבאות יהוה זכרו, and pretty much the whole chapter, was written by a pompous but muddled scribe, tolerably familiar with our Genesis-Kings, should require no demonstration.

Besides the passages disposed of, there are only four occurrences of (2) and none at all of (1) in the Old Testament. In 2 Sam. 5, 10

---

[1] It is perhaps not without significance, that in the authentic prophecies which have come down to us, the title יהוה צבאות is first employed by Isaiah (cf. chapter 6!), and thereafter only by prophets who exercised their office under the shadow of the Jerusalem sanctuary. Cf. p. 38 above.

אלהי is lacking in B and most manuscripts of the Septuagint, as well as in the parallel text of 1 Chron. 11, 9; while in 1 Kings 19, 10, and again in the identical verse 14, אלהי is not in the Septuagint. Finally, the line Ps. 89, 9a is obviously overweighted; but, admitting that אלהי is original, the psalm itself can hardly be older than the scribal interpolations above-mentioned.

The manifestly hybrid forms, יהוה אלהים צבאות of Ps. 59, 6; 80, 5 20; 84, 9, where a supralinear surrogate for יהוה has been mechanically dropped into the line, and אלהים צבאות of Ps. 80, 8 15, where the same surrogate has replaced יהוה, need not detain us.

It is apparent that there is no respectable evidence whatever for the historical and legitimate existence of any form of the name but יהוה צבאות. The rest, יהוה אלהי הצבאות, יהוה אלהי צבאות, and יהוה הצבאות — which latter is really no worse than the other two — are the tardy product of slovenly scribes, with little concern for the exact purport or the original construction of the historic name.

Nevertheless, it is not likely that the illegitimate forms were deliberately coined. Rather they were blundered into. And there can be little doubt that they owe their origin to the use of אלהי צבאות as an oral surrogate of יהוה צבאות. For when אדני was used at all in this connection in the early synagogue, it must have replaced the entire name,[1] since אדני צבאות was not, as yet, a construable expression. This substitutionary אלהי being occasionally written into the text, resulted in the conflate form יהוה אלהי צבאות, pronounced אדני אלהי צבאות. And spontaneous grammatical adjustment — which, it should be noted, appears only in cases where the entire name is of scribal contribution — produced in turn the form יהוה אלהי הצבאות,[2] for which אדני יהוה הצבאות of Amos 9, 5 *was merely a different spelling*.[3] It is not too much to say that the very existence

---

[1] As האדון necessarily did in Isa. 1, 24; 3, 1; 10, 16 (cf. G); 10, 33; 19, 4 (cf. G). So the אדני of אדני יהוה צבאות in Isaiah, Jeremiah, and Ps. 69, 7 is doubtless to be explained; and likewise the ultimate disappearance of צבאות (the surviving יהוה doing duty for *Adonai*) in the Hebrew text of Josh. 6, 17, where Theodotion apparently still found it, though Origen did not. See further pages 31, 38, 147, and note 3 in the chart at the end of this treatise. [2] Amos 3, 13 (cf. G); 6, 14; Hosea 12, 6.

[3] So the Chronicler reproduces אדני יהוה of 2 Sam. 7, 18 f with יהוה אלהים, 1 Chron. 17, 16 f. Both alike were pronounced *Adonai Elohim*.

of the text last quoted proves the correctness of our hypothesis. For only אלהי can have been uttered before the determinate הצבאות. But if אלהי was read when יהוה was written, we need look no further for the origin of יהוה אלהי צבאות.

A few words in conclusion regarding the Greek renderings. In the great majority of instances where the Hebrew of Jeremiah has יהוה צבאות, the Septuagint has only κύριος. Nevertheless, we must not conclude that צבאות was lacking in the translator's Hebrew manuscript. On the contrary, we may be certain that κύριος, like *Adonai*, was employed to represent the composite יהוה צבאות as well as the simple יהוה. Compare in this respect the Septuagint of 1 Sam. 4, 4, where the presence of צבאות in the Hebrew text at all times does not admit of question. Moreover, the insistent use of the name יהוה צבאות in Haggai, Zechariah, and Malachi can be explained only as deliberate imitation of the two great pre-exilic prophets, Isaiah and Jeremiah.

The fact is, we have reason to believe that in the Book of Isaiah, too, the Septuagint translator rendered the combined יהוה צבאות by κύριος alone; and that σαβαωθ, which generally, but not invariably, follows it in the present text, has been methodically introduced from the Hebrew at some later time. The same will be true in 1 Samuel. Κύριε ελωε σαβαωθ of 1 Sam. 1, 11 is illuminating; and well-nigh conclusive as to the secondary character of σαβαωθ wherever it occurs in the Septuagint. For, as we have already seen, except when they made *Adonai* do duty for the entire name, the Palestinian Jews employed *Elohê Ṣebaoth* as the oral surrogate of יהוה צבאות. And κύριε ελωε σαβαωθ is manifestly not a Septuagint rendering of יהוה אלהי צבאות (which never stood in the Hebrew text of 1 Sam. 1, 11, and would not have been so rendered into Greek if it had stood there), but a conflate text, containing the original Septuagint rendering of the composite name, namely κύριε, and a distinctive Hebrew *Qrê* of the same introduced into the Greek text at a later time. Another suggestive passage is Isa. 44, 6, where the same *Qrê*, this time rendered θεὸς σαβαωθ, has been inserted by a later hand, obviously because the original Septuagint had not even κύριος at this point; that is, it still lacked the interpolated יהוה צבאות of the Masoretic text.

For the rest, it seems certain that κύριος παντοκράτωρ of the Minor Prophets — and some passages in the present text of Jeremiah, 2 Samuel, and 1 Kings — is a genuine Septuagint rendering. But (κύριος) τῶν δυνάμεων, to judge from the available evidence, originated with Theodotion, and later found its way into a few passages of the Septuagint which had retained the simple κύριος. Aquila, we may be sure, rendered the name uniformly by κύριος στρατιῶν. Symmachus apparently followed Theodotion. The whole subject of the Greek renderings of יהוה צבאות will bear more systematic investigation along the line I have indicated.

EXCURSUS II

ON A TROUBLESOME PASSAGE IN THE ELEPHANTINE TEMPLE PAPYRUS [1]

Owing to the damaged condition of the papyrus or the presence of words unfamiliar to modern scholars, the Aramaic manuscripts discovered at Elphantine contain not a few passages which are difficult of interpretation and some that will always remain obscure. But there is one passage which has hitherto baffled all efforts to extract from it a satisfactory meaning, although it occurs in the text which has commanded the most widespread interest and the most careful study, and notwithstanding the fact that it has been preserved in perfect condition and contains not a single word which is incomprehensible to Aramaic scholars. I refer to lines 16 and 17 of the letter to Bagoas, Sachau Papyrus 1, a fragmentary duplicate of which is contained in Papyrus 2, lines 15 f.

Lines 1 to 3 of this document, it will be recalled, consist of the usual superscription and conventional greetings. These are followed by a straightforward account of the destruction of the temple of Yahwe at Elephantine by the Egyptian priests, in alliance with certain Persian officers, three years before the date of writing (lines 4 to 12). Lines 13 and 14 add a retrospective statement, to the effect that the temple destroyed was in existence before the Persian conquest, and was especially spared by Cambyses when all the Egyptian sanctuaries were overthrown. The next line, 15, turns to the events following the outrage upon the temple, describing the distress of the Jewish colony; their mourning, fasting, and prayer; and their strenuous but unavailing efforts to obtain redress and permission to rebuild the temple. This section continues to the

---

[1] Read at the meeting of the *Society of Biblical Literature and Exegesis* in New York, December 27, 1915.

middle of line 22, where the document passes on, naturally and logically, to the final paragraph, imploring the aid of Bagoas and promising such rewards as the petitioners are able to bestow.

Now it is in the midst of the section describing the distress of the petitioners and their efforts to secure relief (lines 15 to 22), after the account of the outrage, and before the statement of the present appeal, that the troublesome passage occurs. To give the connection, I quote the preceding line 15, about the interpretation of which there is no difficulty: וכזי כזנה עביד אנחנה עם נשין ובנין שקקן לבשן הוין וציםין ומצלין ליהו מרא שמיא, *And at the time this happened, we together with our wives and our children wore sackcloth and fasted and prayed to Yahu the Lord of Heaven* . . . The text of the papyrus then proceeds:

(16) זי החוין בוידרנג זך כלביא הנפקו כבלא מן רגלוהי וכל נכסין זי קנה אבדו
וכל גברין (17) זי בעו באיש לאגורא זך כל קטילו וחזין בהום.

In his first edition of this text Sachau rendered lines 15–17 as follows: (15) *Und nachdem sie also getan hatten* [reading erroneously עבדו], *trugen wir samt unsern Frauen und Kindern Trauerkleider, fasteten und beteten zu Jâhû, dem Herrn des Himmels,* (16) *der uns (alsdann? später?) Kenntnis gegeben hat von jenem Waidrang* כלביא (?). *Sie haben* (man hat) *die Fusskette von seinen Füssen entfernt, und alle Schätze, die er erworben hatte, sind zu Grunde gegangen. Und alle Menschen* (17) *welche jenem Tempel Böses gewünscht hatten, alle sind getötet, und wir haben es zu unserer Genugtuung mit angesehen.*[1] He inclined to the opinion that there was a serious omission after line 15 in our papyrus; for lines 16 f, which tell of a judicial punishment, should have been preceded by at least some such statement as " and Yahu sent deliverance, and we gave him thanks " — *that he had*, etc. (line 16). And in any case, the vindication seemed of strangely little consequence, in view of the severe punishment visited upon the culprits; since the temple remained in ruins.[2]

The objections to this faltering interpretation were pointed out more strongly and convincingly by Sachau himself in his second

---

[1] *Drei aramäische Papyrus Urkunden aus Elephantine*, 1908, p. 10.
[2] *Ibid.*, pp. 31 f.

publication, where he discarded entirely the view that the passage describes an actual occurrence. " Eine solche Darstellung," he there asserts, " ist absolut zusammenhangslos." Between the words מרא שמיא at the end of line 15 and זי החוין at the beginning of line 16, we should have been told how the sudden change in the situation had been brought about; how it came to pass that so crushing a punishment fell upon the conspirators, concerning whose unchecked misdeeds the letter has been complaining up to this very point. The transition would be of unexampled abruptness; and would, moreover, involve a distinct change of style from the otherwise calm and orderly progress of the whole composition. Then too, as the rest of the document clearly shows, this supposed punishment was quite useless, bringing no relief whatever to the afflicted Jews. As a possible way out of the difficulty, he had thought the troublesome passage might be construed as a quotation from some other letter or from some literary text familiar to both the writers and Bagoas. But a little reflection compelled him to abandon that tack. Only one possibility remained: to interpret the passage as setting forth the content of an oracle.[1] He accordingly adopted the following translation: (15) *Nachdem man also verfahren hatte* [still reading עבדו], *trugen wir samt unseren Frauen und unseren Kindern Trauerkleider, fasteten und beteten zu Jaho, dem Herrn des Himmels,* (16) *welcher uns mit Bezug auf den genannten hündischen* (?) *Waidereng kund tat* (was folgt): " *Man wird die Kette von seinen Füssen entfernt haben, und man wird alle Schätze, die er erworben, vernichtet haben, und alle Männer,* (17) *welche versucht haben werden, dem genannten Tempel Böses anzutun, werden insgesamt getötet worden sein, und wir werden auf ihren Untergang herabgeschaut haben.*" [2]

The fact is, however, that all Sachau has said about the lack of proper transition and setting for the passage if interpreted as history, holds in equal measure when it is interpreted as prophecy. The matter-of-fact recital of line 15 is calmly continued after line 17, without the slightest hint that the history has been interrupted to

---

[1] *Aramäische Papyrus und Ostraka aus einer jüdischen Militär-Kolonie zu Elephantine*, 1911, p. 16. [2] *Ibid.*, p. 21.

cast a glance into the future and rehearse the content of an oracle regarding it. Nor is there any mention of the agency through which the oracle was secured, to say nothing of any move on the part of the colony to obtain it. Furthermore, an oracle promising vengeance and deliverance would be clearly out of place at this point in the letter. Far from heightening the impression of distress which the petitioners aim to produce, it would seriously counteract that impression. If it were intended for the encouragement of Bagoas, it should have been inserted after the story was finished, in connection with the appeal beginning in line 22. With such assurance of divine aid, moreover, the colonists might be expected to await patiently the day of their vindication, without hastening to invoke the aid of the High Priest or of Bagoas.

The desperate interpretation of Sachau's definitive edition has been quite summarily and unanimously rejected by other scholars, who cling to the opinion that the words of our passage describe a past event. So Nöldeke asks, "Warum sollen sie nicht geschehenes aussagen?" and rejects unhesitatingly the hypothesis of an oracle.[1] Lidzbarski renders, *Der Herr des Himmels gewährte uns ein Schauspiel der Lust an jenem Widarnag, die Hunde zerrten ihm die Fesseln von den Füssen, und alle Güter, die er erworben hatte, gingen verloren.* He thinks Widarnag was executed, his body remained exposed, and dogs tore off the chains wherewith he had been bound.[2] Similarly Eduard Meyer: *Die Hunde haben die Fesseln von seinen Füssen gerissen* [on the corpse of Widarnag, which had been thrown to them], *und alle Schätze, die er erworben hatte, sind zugrunde gegangen, und alle Leute, die jenem Tempel Böses gewünscht hatten, sind getötet worden, und wir haben unsere Lust an ihnen geschaut.* Meyer adds confidently, "An ein Orakel, wie Sachau vermutet, ist gewiss nicht zu denken."[3] Lagrange stands by his own variation of the historical interpretation: Widarnag was presumably buried alive, head downward, and the dogs allowed to gnaw at his protruding feet.

[1] *Literarisches Zentralblatt*, 1911, col. 1505.
[2] *Ephemeris*, III, 1912, p. 240 (= *Deutsche Literaturzeitung*, 1911, col. 2967).
[3] *Der Papyrusfund von Elephantine*, 1912, p. 83.

He realizes that dogs are not accustomed to bite through iron, and so renders כבלא *muscle* instead of *chain*; for which he confesses he has no warrant except that a wholly different word was used in Assyria to designate both *ligature* and *tendon*.[1] That the passage is historical is maintained also in the most recent discussion of the subject, by Van Hoonacker, who translates: *Nous avons jeûné et addressé nos prières a Jahô, le dieu du ciel, qui nous a donné en spectacle ce Widarnag. Les chiens ont arraché les cordons de ses pieds et tous les hommes qui avait tramé du mal contre ce temple, tous ont été tués et nous les avons eus en spectacle.* Van Hoonacker recognizes that no regularly constituted tribunal would have put to death a multitude of persons for merely " wishing evil to the temple "; he concludes that a Judeo-Aramaean mob massacred all such persons before Arsames could return to Egypt and restore peace in his turbulent satrapy.[2]

In spite of this consensus of learned opinion, Sachau's objections to the historical interpretation are well-founded; nor have they been disposed of by his opponents. The view that the letter recounts the substance of an oracle is unsatisfactory, but it is not intrinsically absurd, as Eduard Meyer implies; whereas the interpretation to which the latter adheres is really absurd. A satrap who had slain scores of persons for merely " wishing harm to the temple of Yahu," and had thrown the body of a Persian commandant to the dogs for carrying out their evil designs, certainly required no pressure from Palestine to induce him to permit the restoration of the violated sanctuary. The cruel punishment assumed might conceivably have been inflicted upon anybody in those days; but it is inconceivable that it should have overtaken Widarnag and his accomplices and yet have left room for complaint on the part of

---

[1] *Revue Biblique*, V, 1908, pp. 326, 335, 342; IX, 1912, p. 129.

[2] *Une communauté Judéo-Araméenne à Élephantine*, 1915, pp. 42, 45 f. Since the desire of their hearts could only be suspected, the victims must have been numerous. Compare further: Peters, *Die jüdische Gemeinde von Elephantine und ihr Tempel*, 1910, p. 55; Staerk, *Alte und neue aramäische Texte*, 1912, pp. 26 f; Steuernagel, *Zeitschrift des Deutschen Palästina-Vereins*, XXXV, 1912, p. 89; S. A. Cook, *American Journal of Theology*, XIX, 1915, p. 361.

the Judean colony, or that the story of so overwhelming a revenge should have been recited by the petitioners in quite so casual a manner. The fact is, that Sachau's revised rendering, although actually incorrect, is nevertheless on the right scent grammatically. The verbs החוין, הנפקו, אבדו, קטילו, חוין are not historical perfects, but *perfects of imprecation*.[1]

Both Sachau and his critics have made the mistake of construing מצלין at the end of line 15 absolutely, in the sense of *offering prayer*, instead of in the sense of *beseeching*, which the context actually demands. For that matter, even in line 26 of this papyrus צלה is employed only as in Ezra 6, 10, not as in Dan. 6, 11. Prayer as a formal and independent religious exercise must not be credited to the Judeans of Elephantine; who, we shall do well to bear constantly in mind, were not Jews in the strict sense of the term. Note the absence of מצלין after the words שקקן לבשן וציםן in line 20. Nor, on the other hand, can זי at the beginning of line 16 be rendered as a relative pronoun without considerable straining of syntactical usage. It of course does not introduce an attributive clause identifying or describing Yahu: *we prayed to* (that same) *Yahu who*, or *we prayed to Yahu, who is the one that;* nor does it point forward to a following predicate: *who showed us . . . he did so and so.* As a matter of fact, the current interpretations construe the word as a loosely annexed relative, introducing a new sentence, much as if it were the Greek ὅς or ὃς καί of a Pauline epistle. But the papyrus would certainly have employed הו or the simple verb with ו for that purpose. זי must therefore of necessity be construed as a conjunction, introducing the object of מצלין.[2]

Our passage should accordingly be rendered: (15) *And at the time this happened, we together with our wives and our children wore sackcloth and fasted and prayed to Yahu the Lord of Heaven,* (16) *that*

---

[1] Cf. Wright-DeGoeje, *Arabic Grammar*, II, § 1, (f); Caspari-Müller, *Arabische Grammatik*, § 367, 6; Nöldeke, *Syrische Grammatik*, § 260.

[2] Cf. Sachau Papyrus 56, col. 2, line 8; Dan. 2, 16; Nöldeke § 358 A. In Dan. 6, 11 f מצלא and בעה are used as synonyms.

he show us that our Widarnag with his anklets wrenched from his feet (despoiled of his rank) *and bereft of all his possessions, and that all the men* (17) *who sought evil against that temple be slain and we be privileged to look upon their dead bodies.* The imprecatory psalms had ancient models.

A few additional notes are called for.

Line 15. עביד. Sachau, in both his editions, and Ungnad (*Aramäische Papyrus aus Elephantine*, 1911, pp. 3, 7) read עבדו in Papyrus 1, and contrast the reading with עביד of Papyrus 2, line 14. But Papyrus 1 also exhibits עביד quite distinctly, as has been observed by Lagrange.

יהו. On the correct pronunciation of this word, see the writer's remarks, *Journal of Biblical Literature*, XXXI, 1912, p. 22.[1] Van Hoonacker, *l. c.*, pp. 67 ff, argues at great length that *Yahô* (as he and others persist in pronouncing יהו of the papyri) was the actual and original name of the divinity; and that *Yahweh* (= יהוה of the Old Testament and the Mesha Stone) was a secondary and purely artificial form, developed under the influence of the dogmatic theory of Ex. 3, 14, and employed only for literary purposes. The discussion betrays a lack of familiarity with the ancient data, with the modern literature of the subject, and with the first principles of phonetics. We may therefore content ourselves with enquiring whether the Hebrew verb יִשְׁתַּחֲוֶה is likewise a "purely artificial form" of יִשְׁתַּחוּ; whether the Masoretic tradition is wrong in accenting the latter on the penult; and what dogmatic theory was operative in the "development" in the case of this word. For the rest, Ex. 3, 14 has no theory of the divine name except that in its exact form it must not be pronounced; see *Journal of Biblical*

---

[1] I seize this opportunity to correct a culpable misstatement in the article above referred to. In the note on the phrase על אחרן of Sachau Papyrus 11, line 4, I wrote, "We have here the phrase which has hitherto baffled the efforts and ingenuity of the commentators on the Aramaic text of Dan. 4, 5." The word אחרין in the latter passage had, however, been correctly interpreted by Torrey, in his "Notes on the Aramaic Part of Daniel," *Transactions of the Connecticut Academy of Arts and Sciences*, XV, 1909, p. 267.

Literature, XXIV, 1905, pp. 140 ff. And as for the noisy testimony of Assyriology, it is worth as much, when the question is one of exact vocalization rather than of general identity, as is that of mediaeval Latin on the Arabic name *Ibn Rushd*.

Line 16. החוין בוידרנג. החוי is not *to tell*, but *to show* = Hebrew הראה. In Dan. 2, 6 9, החוי is used, as here, with the accusative suffix of the person to whom the object is exhibited. So also frequently in the Talmud.[1] The construction and idiomatic value of the expression החוי ב׳ is the same as that of Hebrew הראה ב׳ in אלהים יראני בשררי, *God will let me exult* (literally *gloat*) *over mine enemies*, Ps. 59, 11; הראני בכל שנאי, *he* (Chemosh) *caused me to exult over all mine enemies*, Mesha Stone, line 4. In Ps. 79, 10 we have the same idea differently phrased: יודע בגוים לעינינו נקמת דם עבדיך השפוך, *Let the avenging of the spilt blood of thy servants be made manifest upon the heathen before our eyes.*

כלביא. We must read כַּלְבָּיָא, *a person of canine extraction*, not כַּלְבַּיָּא, *the dogs*. That the word is an adjective in apposition to וידרנג, and not a plural substantive, subject of הנפקו, is sufficiently attested by the presence of זך; which can hardly attach to the proper name, and must therefore attach to this epithet. And it is conclusively demonstrated by the parallel use of לְחִיָא (passive participle, emphatic of לְחֵא, *annihilated, accursed*) in Papyrus 1, line 7: וידרנג זך לחיא; the construction of which does not admit of question, if only because the phrase appears in the form וידרנג לחיא זך in Papyrus 3, line 6. כלביא is the regular Aramaic form for an adjectival derivative, and supplies exactly what is required after וידרנג זך. The only question is as to its precise connotation. Those who construe the word as an adjective take it to mean *dog-like, canine,* "*hündisch*" (Sachau), equivalent to "contemptible dog." To this Lidzbarski, who interprets the word as a substantive subject of הנפקו, replies by asking whether one can imagine a modern Arab calling an offensive person *kalbi*.[2] He means, of course, that

---

[1] Epstein, *Zeitschrift für die alttestamentliche Wissenschaft*, XXXII, 1912, p. 128.
[2] *Ephemeris*, III, 1912, p. 240, note 2.

the Arab would say *kalb*, and be done with it. But that depends. The Arab would hardly use the epithet *kalb* in such a context as this. He uses *kalb* as a term of contempt — of an alien or infidel, for example.¹ But when in his impotent rage he wishes to level against a highly-placed malefactor, a governor or other official — behind his back, of course — an epithet indicative of irremediable moral depravity, he employs, not *kalb*, but *ibn el kalb*.² The distinction between the two terms is a very real one, and familiar to every Arabic-speaking person. It happens that in the English of vulgar vituperation the same distinction obtains. A "dog" is a contemptible person. But when it is desired to impute utter and incurable depravity, with a suggestion of congenital distemper, the enemy's canine ancestry is followed up one generation. Now the exact Aramaic equivalent of Arabic *ibn el kalb* is כלביא. Nor is there any other. The Aramaic בר כלבא, it need hardly be observed, is not available for this purpose; since בר כלבא would merely be Aramaic for *a dog* (as such), just as בר אנשא is Aramaic for *a man* (as such). The word "cur" which I have employed in the translation does not represent the original exactly.

כבלא, literally *the band*. The reading כבלוהי, *his bands*, of Papyrus 2 is perhaps preferable, but not strictly necessary. The reference is not to *fetters* used for constraint, but to ornamental *anklets* connected by a dangling chain, and indicative of exalted rank.³ In Syriac the same word is used of "*annuli* seu *ornamenta crurum*," the Arabic *khalâkhîl* (Brun, *Dictionarium Syriaco-Latinum*). The Mishna, *Sabbath* vi. 4, mentions כבלים among the accoutrements which may not be worn abroad on the Sabbath; and the Gemara on the passage (*b. Sabbath* 63b) defines כבלים as *anklets joined together by means of a chain* (שלשלת).⁴ The matter is made perfectly plain by a story which the Gemara goes on to relate, of a Jewish

---

¹ Cf. 1 Sam. 17, 43; 2 Sam. 3, 8.
² Cf. the use of Hebrew בן בליעל in 1 Sam. 25, 17.
³ Cf. W. Max Müller, "Die Fussspange als Adelszeichen bei den Semiten," *Orientalistische Literaturzeitung*, XII, 1909, col. 381 f.
⁴ Cf. Epstein, *l. c.*, p. 128.

family in Jerusalem, the members of which habitually took such long strides in walking that the girls ran the risk of spoiling their virginity. To guard against this, they were made to wear anklets (כבלים) fastened together with a chain.[1]

Line 17. כל. Papyrus 2 more correctly, כלא.

וחזין בהום, *and that we look upon them;* the active form corresponding to the causative החזין בוידרנג; cf. וארא בה ובבתה, *but I exulted over him and over his house*, Mesha Stone, line 7.

---

[1] Krauss, *Talmudische Archäologie*, I, pp. 205, 665, misinterprets this statement.

INDEX

INDEX OF SCRIPTURE PASSAGES

C = Chart at the end of the volume.

CHAPTER	GENESIS	PAGE
2, 11		34
10, 19		58
19		101
19, 8		102, 121
28, 12		29
28, 22		29, 32
31, 8		82
31, 19 34 f		136
31, 30 32		11
37, 28		119
38, 14 21		57
42, 9		88
48, 16		60
50, 15		122
50, 26		5

CHAPTER	EXODUS	PAGE
1, 5		13
3, 14		38, 155
3, 15		74
4, 21		84
7, 23		89
10, 6		89
10, 24		65
12, 21		119
13, 19		5
17, 7		135
23, 11		63
23, 13		74
23, 19		32
25, 10		61
25, 10 ff		5, 26
25, 37		35
28		8
28, 6		18
28, 6–12		23
28, 30		8, 135
28, 36		25
29, 5		8, 23

CHAPTER		PAGE
31, 7		C
31, 18		5
34, 26		32
34, 29		26
37, 1		61
37, 1 ff		5, 26
39		8
39, 2–7		23

CHAPTER	LEVITICUS	PAGE
8, 7		8, 23, 126
8, 8		8, 135

CHAPTER	NUMBERS	PAGE
1, 50		80
3, 31		80
4, 18		112
10, 33		129, 140, C
10, 33–36		33, 139
10, 35 f		139
11, 5		65
12, 1 8		119
14, 44		25, 33, 129, 139, 140
16		135
20, 1–13		135
20, 17		119
21, 5 7		119
22, 1		83
26, 57		112
27, 21		134

CHAPTER	DEUTERONOMY	PAGE
2, 34		121
3, 6		121
10		26
10, 1–5		5, 34, 139
10, 8		80, 125, 127, 129, 133, 139
10, 10		5
12, 8 f		100

15, 2 f	63	18, 16	50, 51, 52
19, 5	63	18, 28	53, 57
20, 9	143	19, 51	96
28, 9	60	21, 1 f	96
28, 10	60	22, 12	96
28, 56	65	23, 7	74
31, 9 25	125, 127, 129	24, 11	58
31, 9 25 f	139, 140		
31, 26	5, C		
33, 1	31		
33, 8	135		

JUDGES

1, 1	116
1, 1 f	102
1, 2	41
6, 37	65
7, 18 20	60
8, 23	128, 137
8, 23–27	9
8, 27	10, 11, 27, 65, 123, 125, 127, 128, 136, C
9, 2 ff	58
9, 16 19	135
9, 46 f	58
9, 49	58
11, 39	121
13, 5	29
13, 5 7	32
13, 6	30
13, 8	30
13, 23	122
15, 1	74
15, 11	114
15, 13	61
16, 7 11	67
16, 17	32
16, 27	114
17–18	11, 27, 99, 105, 123, 125, 126, 131, 136, 137
17–21	99
17, 2–4	10, 105
17, 5	12, 29, 100, 126, 128, 136
17, 5 13	137
17, 6	100, 105
17, 7	105, 112
17, 10	105
18	10
18, 1	99, 100, 105, 118
18, 2	105
18, 3	105
18, 5	12, 116
18, 5 f	41, 137

JOSHUA

3–8	33, 139, 140
3, 3	127, 129, C
3, 6	140
3, 11	C
3, 13	C
3, 14	C
3, 17	C
4, 5	C
4, 13	83
4, 19	83
5, 10	83
6, 16 f	143
6, 17	146
6, 24	32
7–8	99, 101
7, 4	114
7, 5	114
7, 5 f	113
8, 4	84
8, 6	103
8, 16	103
8, 22	120
8, 25	114
8, 28	99
9, 13	61
9, 17	54, 57, 61
9, 22–27	62
14, 6	31
15, 8	50, 51
15, 9	52
15, 9 f	53, 54
15, 11	53
15, 29	53
15, 60	53
18, 1	96
18, 14 f	53, 54

18, 5 24	12	20, 3	102, 111
18, 6	119	20, 3 12	111
18, 7	105	20, 4 f	101
18, 8 14	113	20, 5	111
18, 9	105	20, 6	102, 110, 111
18, 10	105	20, 7	111
18, 11	112, 121	20, 8	102, 111, 112
18, 11 16	121	20, 9–11	102
18, 12	54, 57, 105	20, 12	111, 112
18, 14	105, 126	20, 13	112–113
18, 16	105	20, 14	102, 113
18, 17	105, 120, 125, C	20, 15–17	102
18, 18	105	20, 18	102, 115, 116
18, 19	112	20, 19	102
18, 20	105, 133	20, 20–23	102, 103
18, 21 26	120	20, 21	103
18, 22	120	20, 23	103, 115, 119
18, 24	11	20, 24	103
18, 27	105, 121, 128, 130	20, 24–28	102
18, 27 ff	136	20, 25	103, 113–114
18, 28	105, 122	20, 26	102, 103
18, 29	105	20, 26 f	115
18, 30	103, 116	20, 26–28	97, 118
18, 30 f	105	20, 27	34, 95–97, 103, 114–119, 129, 136, 137, 140, C
18, 31	96		
19–21	97–122	20, 27 f	95
19, 1	99, 100, 118	20, 28	41, 103, 113, 114, 115, 116, 119, 129
19, 2	104		
19, 3	110	20, 29	119
19, 6	101	20, 30	103
19, 7	110	20, 31	103
19, 9	101	20, 31 36 etc.	103
19, 10 25	112	20, 32–35	103
19, 11	110	20, 36	103, 113
19, 12	119	20, 36 ff	119
19, 12 f	101	20, 37	113, 119–120
19, 14	101, 110	20, 38	120
19, 14 f	101	20, 39	113, 114, 120
19, 16	102, 110	20, 39 f	118
19, 18	102, 118	20, 40	120
19, 23	102, 110, 111, 113	20, 41	120
19, 24	102	20, 42	113, 120
19, 25	110	20, 43	103
19, 29	110–111	20, 44	103, 113, 114, 120
19, 29–21, 23	106–110	20, 45	120
19, 30	102, 111	20, 45 f	104
20, 1	102, 111	20, 47	104, 120–121, 122
20, 1 28	113	20, 48	113, 120, 121
20, 2	102, 111	21, 1	104

Reference	Page(s)
21, 2	103
21, 2–4	104
21, 5	104
21, 6	112, 113, 121
21, 6 f.	104
21, 6–8	121
21, 7	104, 121
21, 8	104
21, 8 f.	112
21, 9	104, 121
21, 9 12	104
21, 10	104
21, 10 f.	121
21, 11	104
21, 12	104, 121
21, 13	104, 120, 121
21, 14	104, 121
21, 15	41
21, 15–18	104
21, 16	104
21, 19	104, 121
21, 19 ff.	136
21, 20	121
21, 21	121
21, 22	122
21, 23	104, 113, 122
21, 24	104
21, 25	100, 104

1 Samuel

Reference	Page(s)
1–6	35
1, 3	137
1, 3 11	38
1, 7 24	32
1, 9	32
1, 11	147
1, 12	64
1, 17	35
2, 2	35
2, 18	8, 22, 126, 131
2, 25	35
2, 27	30, 35
2, 27–36	15
2, 28	11, 14, 70, 90, 123, 126, 128, 133, 139
2, 30	35
3, 3	34–36
3, 13	35, 42
3, 17	35
4–6	28, 40
4–7	5, 122
4, 1	113
4, 3	36
4, 3 f.	34, 36–40, 137
4, 3 ff.	78, 79, 129
4, 4	38, 61, 62, 122, 127, 147, C
4, 4 11 etc.	33, 35
4, 7	12, 35
4, 8	12, 35
4, 11	36
4, 13 18	136
4, 17	36
4, 19–22	15
5, 1 2 10	33, 35
5, 2	65, 127
5, 7	35
5, 7 8 10 11	35
5, 11	35
6, 3 5	35
6, 4	122
6, 5	35
6, 7	61
6, 13	110
6, 14	118
6, 19	103, 134
6, 20	35
6, 21	54, 57
7, 1	20, 21, 22, 23, 52, 54, 57, 68, 128
7, 2	15, 20, 21, 23
7, 6	103
9, 5 10	110
9, 6	30
9, 7 8 10	30
9, 9	87, 89
9, 9 11 18 19	85
9, 21	112
9, 22	120
9, 24	120, 121
10, 3	116
10, 9	64
10, 13	65
11, 3 7	111
11, 5	110
11, 7	110, 111, 113
11, 9	110
13, 2	113
13, 9	103
13, 10	66

INDEX

13, 15 f	121	22, 15	120
13, 17 23	113	22, 17	112
14, 1 6	110	22, 18	11, 14, 90, 123, 124, 125, 126, 128, 136
14, 2	14, 121		
14, 2 5 16	52	22, 19	120
14, 3	11, 14-15, 18, 20, 21, 70, 123, 124, 125, 126, 128	22, 20 ff	68, 69
		22, 23	137
14, 9	82	23, 2-4	137
14, 15	113	23, 6	20, 124, 137, C
14, 17	121	23, 6 9	14, 18, 27, 68, 71, 72, 123, 124, 128
14, 18	13-23, 25, 26, 27, 33, 34, 40, 67, 70, 71, 72, 80, 96, 118, 122-124, 126, 128, 129, 130, 133, 137, C		
		23, 9	12, 19, 20, 22, 70, 124, 127-128, 133, C
14, 18 f	78, 79	23, 9 ff	41
14, 19	19, 20, 134	23, 10	61, 133
14, 22	120	23, 10 f	135
14, 34	124	23, 10 ff	134, 137
14, 36	12	23, 11 f	58
14, 36 f	137	23, 13	119, 121
14, 37	12, 119	23, 25	122
14, 37 40 ff	41	23, 27	119, 120
14, 37 41	134	24, 1	122
14, 37-42	19	24, 3	113
14, 38	111	24, 4	118
14, 41	61, 70, 133, 135	24, 15	113
14, 49	61	25, 2	113
15, 2 f	143	25, 12	120
15, 9	112	25, 13	121
15, 23	130-131, 132, 136, C	25, 14	66
17, 43	157	25, 17	157
17, 52	58	25, 41	66
18, 6	121	26, 2	113
18, 30	113	26, 9 15	113
19, 5	110	26, 23	112
19, 13 16	136	26, 25	121
20, 11	110	27, 2	121
20, 35	120	27, 6	99
20, 38	119, 120	27, 7	122
21, 4	121	27, 8 10	119
21, 8	118	28, 1	113, 118
21, 10	9, 10, 11, 12, 14, 17, 27, 123, 124, 128, 130, 137	28, 6	134, 135, 138
		28, 21	120
21, 12	121	28, 23	110
22-30	68	29, 3 6	111
22, 8 13	119	29, 5	121
22, 9 20	15	30, 1 14	119
22, 13	137	30, 7	12, 14, 18, 19, 20, 22, 27, 68, 71, 72, 123, 124, 128, 130, 133
22, 13 15	12		

30, 8	41, 119, 134, 137	5, 20–24	41
30, 9	121	5, 22	50
31, 2	120	5, 25	41, 52, 57, 58
31, 4	110, 112, 120	6	5, 22, 23, 28, 40–67, 69, 128, 129
31, 7	113, 122	6, 1	40, 41, 43, 53
		6, 1 ff	20

2 Samuel

1, 2	110	6, 2	31, 34, 38, 40, 41–42, 43, 53, 54, 58–61, C
1, 6	59, 120	6, 2 ff	21
1, 6 ff	120	6, 2 3 etc.	33
1, 12	103	6, 2 10 etc.	64
2–3	100	6, 3	23, 41, 52, 57, 61, 68, 122
2, 1	41, 119, 134, 137	6, 3 f	62, 95
2, 3	122	6, 4	41, 62, 127
2, 8	143	6, 5	41, 42
2, 11 15	122	6, 6	41, 62–63, 111
2, 12 f	113	6, 7	62, 63, 64
2, 15	111	6, 8	41, 42
2, 18	67	6, 9	41
2, 21	112	6, 10	64, 112
2, 26 f	113	6, 12	69
2, 29	83	6, 13	41
2, 30	121	6, 14	8, 22, 64, 126, 131, C
2, 32	110	6, 15	42
3, 2–5	42	6, 16	64
3, 8	157	6, 17	42, 65, 127
3, 22	110	6, 17 f	103
4, 1	120	6, 18	31, 42, 61, 65, 134
4, 2 f	54, 118	6, 19	42, 65
4, 4	42	6, 20	43, 66
4, 4 5 6 7	118	6, 21	14, 42, 43
4, 7	83	6, 22	67
4, 8	25	6, 23	42
4, 10	111, 120	7	42, 82
4, 11	112	7, 2 ff	25
4, 12	111	7, 4	31
5–6	40	7, 8	82
5, 6	121	7, 8 26	31
5, 9	46, 122	7, 18 f	31, 146
5, 10	31	8	42
5, 13–16	42	8, 7	121
5, 17	41, 46, 52, 59	8, 10	124
5, 17 f	41, 50	8, 17	15
5, 17 18 19 25	64	9, 2	64
5, 17–6, 22	43–46	10, 7	78
5, 18	49, 50, 52	10, 12	78
5, 18 22	50	11, 1	77, 113
5, 19	52, 119, 134, 137	11, 11	5, 19, 25, 26, 27, 34, 77–80, 137
5, 20	41	12, 14	39

12, 17	112	19, 44	112
12, 20	32	20	100
12, 28	60	20, 1	112
13, 12	111	20, 3	64, 110
13, 12 25	110	20, 5	120
13, 13	67	20, 9	111
13, 14 16 25	112	20, 15 20	113
13, 16	111	20, 18	135
13, 25 27	110	20, 22	121
13, 32	111	21, 1	62
14, 7 13	121	21, 1–5	54
14, 11	74	21, 2 f	119
14, 13	119, 122	21, 2 6	54
14, 17	29	21, 5	111
14, 26	118	21, 16	61
14, 27	42	23, 13–17	50
15, 2	112	24, 11	85
15, 14	120	24, 22 24	103
15, 18	121	24, 25	103
15, 20	113		
15, 24	65, 80–81, 127, 129, 137, C	1 KINGS	
15, 24–29	5, 33, 34, 69, 70, 80–95, 129	1–2	99
15, 25 f	81–82	1, 2	121
15, 26	135	1, 3	111
15, 27	84–94	1, 19	143
15, 27 f	81–82	1, 25	143
15, 28	82–83, 85	1, 27	111
15, 29	68, 122	1, 42	110
15, 35 f	82	1, 50	111
16, 5	110	1, 51	111
16, 20	112	2, 5	143
16, 23	118	2, 13	121
17, 15–22	82	2, 26	5, 20, 27, 34, 67–72, 124, 127, 129, 133, C
17, 16 18 21	120		
17, 29	69	2, 27	15
18, 1	121	2, 28	32
18, 2 f	113	2, 32	143
18, 13 30	111	2, 35	95
18, 18	42	3, 15	129, C
18, 29	120	6, 19	129, 136
18, 31	110	6, 23 ff	37
19	83	7, 49	35
19, 10	112	8	140
19, 13 42	113	8, 1 6	129
19, 14	143	8, 3	127
19, 15	111	8, 6	37
19, 19	82	8, 8	95
19, 25	111	8, 9	75
19, 43	112	8, 9 21	5, 34, 139

168 INDEX

8, 21	C
8, 43	60
9, 15	46, 49
9, 24	46
9, 25	103
11, 27	46
11, 29 f	61
12, 16	112
12, 22	30, 31
13, 1	30
13, 4 5 etc.	30
14, 26	138
15, 2	42
16, 16	143
17, 18	30
17, 24	29, 30
18, 30	32
19, 10	32, 146
19, 14	146
20, 12 16	77
20, 28	30
22, 5 ff	138
22, 6 12 15	119
22, 19	38

2 Kings

1, 9 11 13	30
1, 10	30
1, 11	120
1, 12	30
4, 7	30
4, 9	30
4, 16 40	30
4, 21 22 etc.	30
4, 29	66
5, 8 20	30
5, 14 f	30
6, 6 9 10 15	30
6, 32	84
7, 2 17 ff	30
8, 2 4 etc.	30
9, 33	63
10, 15	43
12, 10 f	6, C
12, 18	138
12, 21	46
13, 19	30
14, 14	138
16, 8	138

16, 12	65
17, 6 18 etc.	75
18, 15 f	138
19, 15	38, 39
23, 16 f	30
23, 24	136, 139
25, 4 f	83
25, 13 ff	138

Isaiah

1, 24	146
3, 1	146
4, 1	60
6	145
6, 1	38
6, 3 5	38
6, 9 ff	144
10, 16	146
10, 33	146
13, 4	143
17, 5	50
19, 4	146
22, 13	66
26, 13	74
28, 6	38
32, 17	131
37, 16	38, 39, 134
40, 22	38
43, 7	60
44, 6	144, 147
45, 13	144
47, 4	144
48, 1	60, 74
48, 2	144
49, 1	74
51, 15	144
54, 5	144
62, 6 f	74
63, 19	60

Jeremiah

2	76
2, 4–3, 5	76
2, 11 15 etc.	76
3, 3 7 etc.	76
3, 6	72, 76
3, 6 ff	76
3, 7	76
3, 14–16	73

INDEX

3, 16	34, 72–76, 129, 137, 139	5, 13–16	145
3, 17 ff	76	5, 19	29
3, 22–25	76	5, 25–27	145
5, 14	144	6, 8	145
7, 2 3 etc.	38	6, 10	74
7, 10 11 etc.	60	6, 14	145, 146
7, 30	59	9, 5	145, 146
14, 9	60	9, 5 f	145
15, 16	60, 144	9, 12	59, 60
17, 4	63		
17, 25	38	**HABAKKUK**	
25, 29	59, 60	3, 4	119
26, 20	57		
32, 34	59, 60	**ZECHARIAH**	
34, 15	59, 60		
35, 4	30	7, 3	38
35, 17	144	10, 2	136
38, 13	119		
38, 17	144	**PSALMS**	
44, 7	144	10, 3	39
46, 10	144	20, 8	74
47, 3	89	24, 8 10	144
		38, 1	74
EZEKIEL		59, 6	146
8, 3	89	59, 11	156
8, 6	91	69, 7	146
8, 15 17	91	70, 1	74
9, 2	89	72, 10	66
21, 26	136	79, 10	156
27, 15	66	80, 2	39
47, 6	91	80, 5 20	146
		80, 8 15	146
		84, 9	146
HOSEA		89, 9	146
1	126	90, 1	31
1, 2	126	99, 1	39
1, 2 4 6 9	126	132, 8	C
2, 19	74	141, 6 f	63
3	126		
3, 1	66	**PROVERBS**	
3, 4	123, 126, 131	20, 8	38
3, 4 f	126		
12, 6	145, 146	**SONG OF SONGS**	
		2, 5	65
AMOS			
3, 13	145, 146	**RUTH**	
3, 13 f	145		
4, 12 f	145	2, 4	66
5, 8	135	2, 16	64

Daniel

2, 6 9	156
2, 16	154
4, 5	155
6, 11 f	154
9, 18 f	60

Ezra

2, 63	9, 135
3, 2	31
6, 10	154

Nehemiah

3, 19	47
3, 20	47
3, 24 f	47
7, 65	9, 135
12, 24 36	31

1 Chronicles

5, 34	15
6, 37 f	15
8, 31	61
9, 37	61
10, 7	113, 122
11, 9	31, 146
11, 15	50
12, 22	31
13–14	40
13, 3	C
13, 6	31, 53, C
13, 9	63
14, 9 13	50
14, 13	41
14, 16	58
15	70
15, 2	80
15, 11	69
15, 27	131, C
16, 1	65, 127
16, 2	31
16, 6	114, C
17, 3	31
17, 7 24	31
17, 16 f	31, 146
18, 16	15
23, 14	31

2 Chronicles

4, 4	89
6, 11	C
6, 33	60
6, 41	C
7, 14	60
8, 14	31
11, 2	31
15, 1	31
20, 29	31
24, 8	C
24, 8 10 f	6
24, 10	31
25, 7	30, 31
25, 9	31
26, 9	47
30, 16	31
32, 5	47
34, 9	31
34, 32	31
35, 3	C
35, 22	31

Sirach

33, 3	134
45, 8–10	8
45, 10 f	9

2 Maccabees

2, 4 ff	138

Luke

24, 13	55

I PRE–EXILIC, HISTORICAL USAGE

1 ארון *a box* (ordinary or sacred, according to the context).

2 הארון *the box* (determinate form of 1).

3 ארון אלהים *a sacred box* (of a box consecrated to any deity).

4 ארון האלהים *the sacred box* (determinate form of 3).

5 ארון יהוה *the box of Yahwe* (of any box consecrated to Yahwe).

6 ארון אלהי ישראל *the box of the god of Israel* (= 5; in the mouth of foreigners only).

7 ארון יהוה צבאות *the box of Yahwe Militant* (the name of a particular box of Yahwe, originally attached to the sanctuary of Shiloh, where Yahwe was worshipped under that title; captured by the Philistines, and later removed to Jerusalem by David).

II POST–DEUTERONOMIC, DOCTRINAL FICTIONS

8 ארון הברית *the box of the Covenant* (Deuteronomistic).

9 ארון העדות *the box of the Testimony* (Priestly).

NOTES

1 I have not included in my table (as does Seyring, *ZATW*, XI, p. 115) ארון האלהים אשר נקרא שם (שם) יהוה צבאות (ישב הכרבים) עליו of 2 Sam. 6, 2, and הארון אשר שם ברית יהוה of 1 Kings 8, 21; 2 Chron. 6, 11; for the reason that only ארון האלהים in the one case, and הארון in the other, are actual designations of the box, the remainder in each case being a descriptive phrase identifying it. A similar reason accounts for the omission of הארון לעדות of Ex. 31, 7. On the other hand, Seyring's assumed forms 1 (ארון יהוה אלהי צבאות ישב הכרבים) and 12 (ארון ברית יהוה האלהים) could arise only through additional scribal glossing; and, as a matter of fact, they did not arise.

2 The forms in I were the only ones in use in pre-exilic times. But it is not to be inferred that none of them were employed by later writers; only Nos. 3, 6, and 7 ceased to be available, while 1 was restricted to the ordinary box.

ארון IN THE OLD TESTAMENT

III FORMS AND READINGS ORIGINATING IN EDITORIAL AND SCRIBAL EMENDATIONS

A. Deuteronomistic

(2) 10 הארון הברית (Josh. 3[14]).

(2) 11 הארון ברית יהוה (Josh. 3[17]).

(3) 12 ארון ברית האלהים (Jud. 20[27]).

(4) 12 ארון ברית האלהים (1 Sam. 4[4], 2 Sam. 15[24]).

(5) 13 ארון ברית יהוה (Num. 10[33], et al.).

(5) 14 ארון יהוה אלהיכם (Josh 4[5]).

(14) 15 ארון ברית יהוה אלהיכם (Deut. 31[26], Josh. 3[3]).

(7) 16 ארון ברית יהוה צבאות (1 Sam. 4[4]).

B. Jewish

(1) α אפוד (Jud. 8[27], et al.).   ⎫
(1) β און (1 Sam. 15[23]).   ⎪
(2) γ האפוד (Jud. 18[17], et al.). ⎪ Substituted
                                    ⎪ for the
(3) α אפוד (1 Sam. 23[6]).   ⎬ manifold
                                    ⎪ sacred box
(4) γ האפוד (1 Sam. 14[18] G).   ⎪ where it
                                    ⎪ was found
                                    ⎪ impossible
                                    ⎪ to identify it
                                    ⎪ with the box
(5) δ אפוד יהוה (1 Sam. 23[9] G). ⎪ of Nos. 8
                                    ⎪ and 9.
(5) γ האפוד (1 Sam. 23[9] M).   ⎭

(5) 17 ארון יהוה אדון כל הארץ (Josh. 3[13]).

(5) 18 ארון אדני יהוה (1 Kings 2[26]).

(13) 19 ארון ברית אדני (1 Kings 3[15]).

(16) 20 ארון ברית יהוה צבאות ישב הכרבים (1 Sam. 4[4]).

(8) 21 ארון הברית אדון כל הארץ (Josh. 3[11]).

NOTES

1 The captions A and B indicate the influences under which the two sets of emendations were made. In a general way the one influence antedated the other, but they are not to be identified with two mutually exclusive periods of time.

2 Numbers in parentheses indicate the forms emended or replaced.

3 The resultant forms 10, 11, and 21 are ungrammatical; while the strict sense yielded by 12 is *the box of the solemn covenant* rather than *the box of the covenant of God*.

4 No. 14 may have been employed by Deuteronomistic editors in sections of their own composition. But all the other forms in III are distinctly the result of the *alteration of existing texts;* though it is possible that No. 13 has been *reproduced* by Deuteronomistic editors in one or two cases. The question, as regards both 13 and 14, cannot be fully determined without a more satisfactory literary analysis of Deuteronomy and Joshua than exists at present. The above table may prove of some assistance in that direction.

IV USAGE OF THE CHRONICLER

Reflecting the mixed state of contemporary texts and dominated by the fictional Jewish conception of the times

(1) אָרוֹן *a box* (only II 24^8, of the contribution-box placed in the temple under Joash, 2 Kings 12^{10}).

(2) הָאָרוֹן *the box* (3 times of the above, and 16 times of *the Box* κατ' ἐξοχήν).

(3 is of course impossible in the mouth of the Chronicler except as the equivalent of ארון יהוה, and in fact does not occur.)

(4) אֲרוֹן הָאֱלֹהִים *the Box of (the) God* (of which there had been only one; 12 times).

(12) אֲרוֹן בְּרִית הָאֱלֹהִים *the Box of the Covenant of (the) God* (only I 16^6).

(5) אֲרוֹן יְהוָה *the Box of THE LORD* (3 times; to the Chronicler יהוה was the ideogram for אדני).

22 אֲרוֹן אֱלֹהֵינוּ *the Box of our God* (only I 13^3; in the mouth of David).

(13) אֲרוֹן בְּרִית יְהוָה (= ארון ברית אדני; 11 times).

(17, 18, and 19 are impossible from the pen of the Chronicler; see note 3 below.)

23 אֲרוֹן יְהוָה אֱלֹהֵי יִשְׂרָאֵל (= ארון אדני אלהי ישראל; once in the mouth of David, and once in narration).

24 אֲרוֹן הַקֹּדֶשׁ *the Holy Box* (only II 35^3, where the Chronicler is romancing independently).

25 אֲרוֹן עֻזֶּךָ *the Box of Thy strength* (poetical; only II 6^{41} = Ps. 132^8).

NOTES

1 Numbers in parentheses indicate the forms reproduced.

2 The Chronicler does not reproduce any sections of the earlier histories which contain the solid " ephod." The word אֵפוֹד occurs only I 15, 27, of David's linen ephod, 2 Sam. 6, 14.

3 ארון האלהים יהוה יושב הכרובים אשר נקרא שם (I 13, 6), the Chronicler's shuffling paraphrase of 2 Sam. 6, 2, shows clearly enough that he found his source troublesome. For him there had been but one Sacred Box, concerning which he represented David as saying, לא דרשנהו בימי שאול (verse 3). He concluded by disregarding the final עליו and construing the words which follow האלהים as an independent nominal sentence: אשר נקרא שֵׁם שֵׁם יהוה צבאות ישב הכרבים, *what was uttered there was the name Yahwe*, etc. Transposing subject and predicate, he omitted the initial שֵׁם, perhaps because it implied that the Tetragrammaton itself was sacrilegiously employed at Kirjath-jearim, and so produced the innocuous statement, *it was* יהוה יושב הכרובים *who was invoked there*. The omission of צבאות may be accounted for by assuming that the Chronicler's oral surrogate for the composite יהוה צבאות, as well as for the simple Tetragrammaton, was *Adonai* (cf. the LXX of Jeremiah, *passim*, and 1 Sam. 4, 4); and *Adonai* he invariably *wrote* יהוה; see page 31.

www.ingramcontent.com/pod-product-compliance
Lightning Source LLC
Chambersburg PA
CBHW051101160426
43193CB00010B/1267